foto fever

START TO — COLLECT

Published by :

Snoeck Publishers
Sint Kwintensberg 83
9000 Gent
BELGIUM
Tel : + 32 9 430 55 07
www.snoeckpublishers.be

FOTOFEVER SAS
5 rue de Charonne
75011 Paris
FRANCE
+33 1 43 59 46 06
fotofever.com

Design : Caroline Alida Van Poucke

Printed in the European Union

ISBN 9789461615770
Legal deposit D/2019/0012/87

© Julia Amarger, Secret n°12,
série Ceci est un secret, 2015
Lauréate 2019 du fotofever prize
with dahinden

fotofever vous accueille pour sa 8ème édition au Carrousel du Louvre avec un programme inspirant pour un public international. Cette année plus que jamais les femmes sont à l'honneur au cœur de la ville lumière!

Plus de 200 artistes, 100 galeristes et éditeurs et 20 nationalités sont réunis pour cette saison inédite. Une fois encore, fotofever confirme son engagement auprès des artistes vivants et offre aux collectionneurs, aux professionnels des arts et au public la possibilité d'acquérir des œuvres parmi une sélection inattendue, accessible et exigeante.

Pour le 180e anniversaire de l'invention de la photographie, fotofever dévoile l'audace et la créativité de la scène française.

Découvrez également les lauréats 2019 du fotofever prize with dahinden, une sélection de solo shows de jeunes galeries dans la Ruche et un espace édition en partenariat avec la librairie parisienne La Comète.

Et ne manquez pas notre programme Start to Collect avec l'Appartement du Collectionneur, une sélection d'œuvres à moins de 1000€, des visites guidées et des talks avec des collectionneurs inspirants.

Cette année, avec une équipe exclusivement féminine, nous sommes déterminées à faire progresser la représentation des femmes en commençant par notre propre programmation: de 30% en 2018 à plus de 40% en 2019, nous nous engageons à atteindre l'égalité en 2020!

Que la fièvre de la photographie soit avec vous!

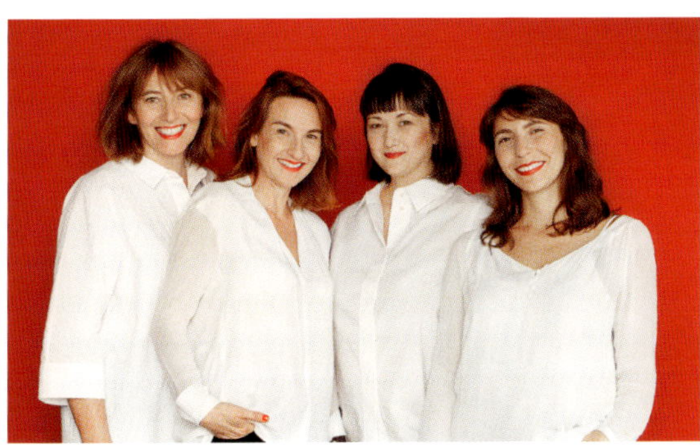

Cécile Schall (fondatrice et directrice), Laura Kosmenzoff (directrice VIP), Yuki Baumgarten (directrice artistique), Christelle Roubaud (directrice marketing). © Laura Bonnefous

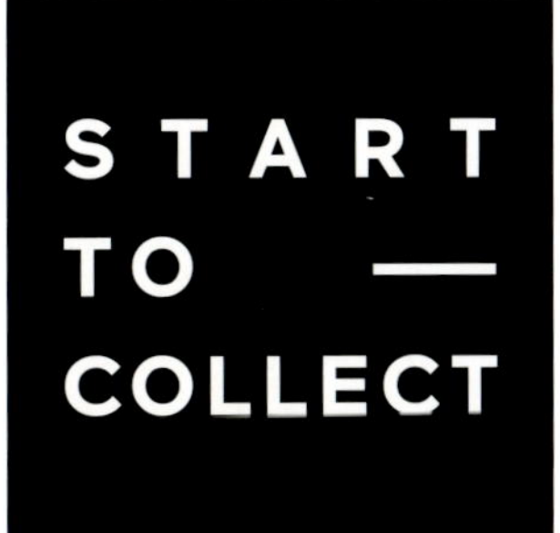

fotofever welcomes you for its 8th edition at the Carrousel du Louvre with an inspiring program for an international audience. This year more than ever Women Artists are honored in the heart of the city of light!

More than 200 artists, 100 galleries and publishers from 20 countries are gathered for this new edition. And once again, fotofever confirms its commitment towards living artists and offers collectors, art professionals and the public the opportunity to acquire works from a novel, accessible yet exacting selection.

For the 180th anniversary of the invention of photography, fotofever unveils the boldness and creativity of the French scene.

Also discover the 2019 winners of the fotofever prize with dahinden, a selection of solo shows by young galleries in the Hive, a publishers' section and a pop up bookstore in partnership with the Parisian bookseller La Comète.

Don't miss our Start to Collect program with the Collector's Apartment, a selection of artworks below €1,000, guided tours and talks with inspiring collectors.

Starting this year, with an all-female team, we are determined to increase the representation of women artists through our program: from 30% in 2018 to more than 40% in 2019, we are committed to achieving equality in 2020!

May the fever of photography be with you!

fotofever prize

with dahinden

Faire découvrir le talent de jeunes artistes au cœur du marché de l'art à Paris et dans la capitale mondiale de la photographie à Arles : c'est ce que propose le fotofever prize with dahinden !
En partenariat avec le laboratoire professionnel Dahinden, fotofever accompagne ses 3 lauréats de la production à la promotion de leurs travaux photographiques, exposés à fotofever paris au cœur de l'Appartement du Collectionneur.
Créé en 1968, Dahinden est devenu en 50 ans le partenaire incontournable des photographes et des grandes marques.

Introducing young talents *to the art market, both in Paris and in the world capital of photography Arles: this is what is offered by the fotofever prize with dahinden!*
In partnership with the professional photo lab Dahinden, fotofever accompanies its 3 winners, from production to promotion of their works, exhibited at fotofever paris in the heart of the Collector's Apartment. Created in 1968, Dahinden has become the indispensable partner for photographers and major luxury brands.

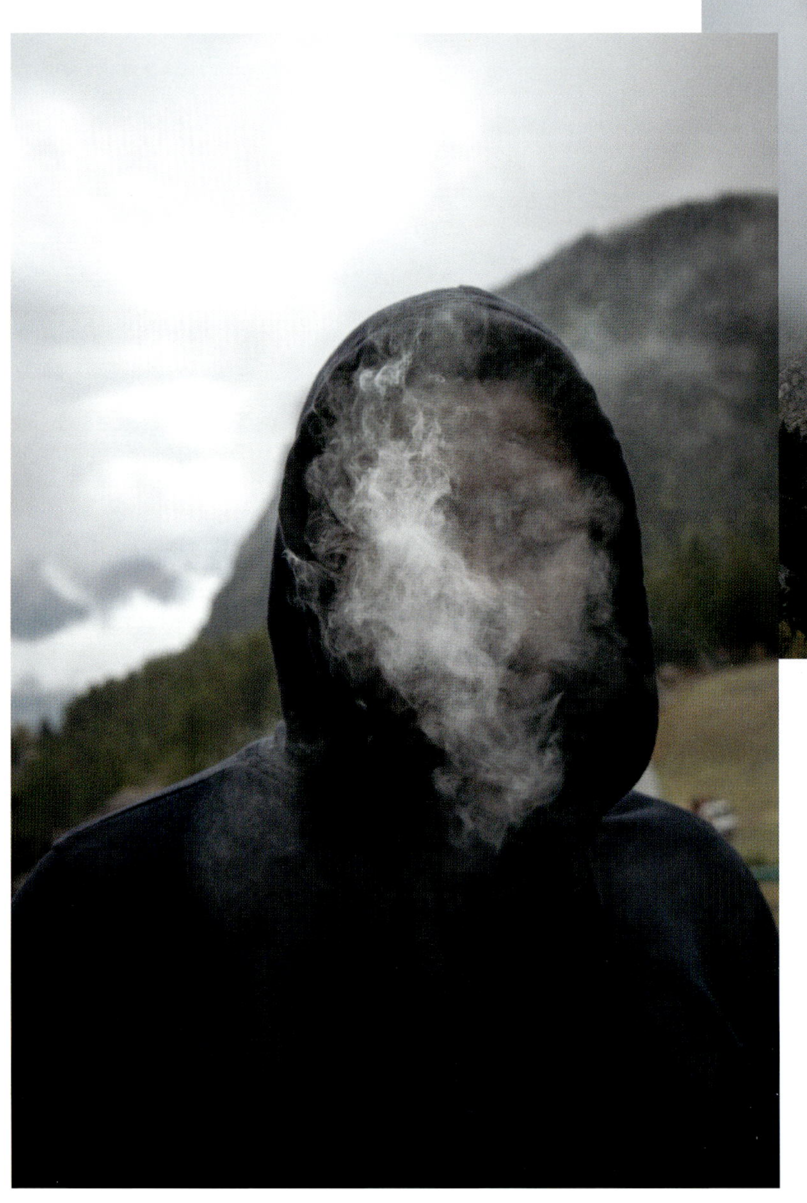

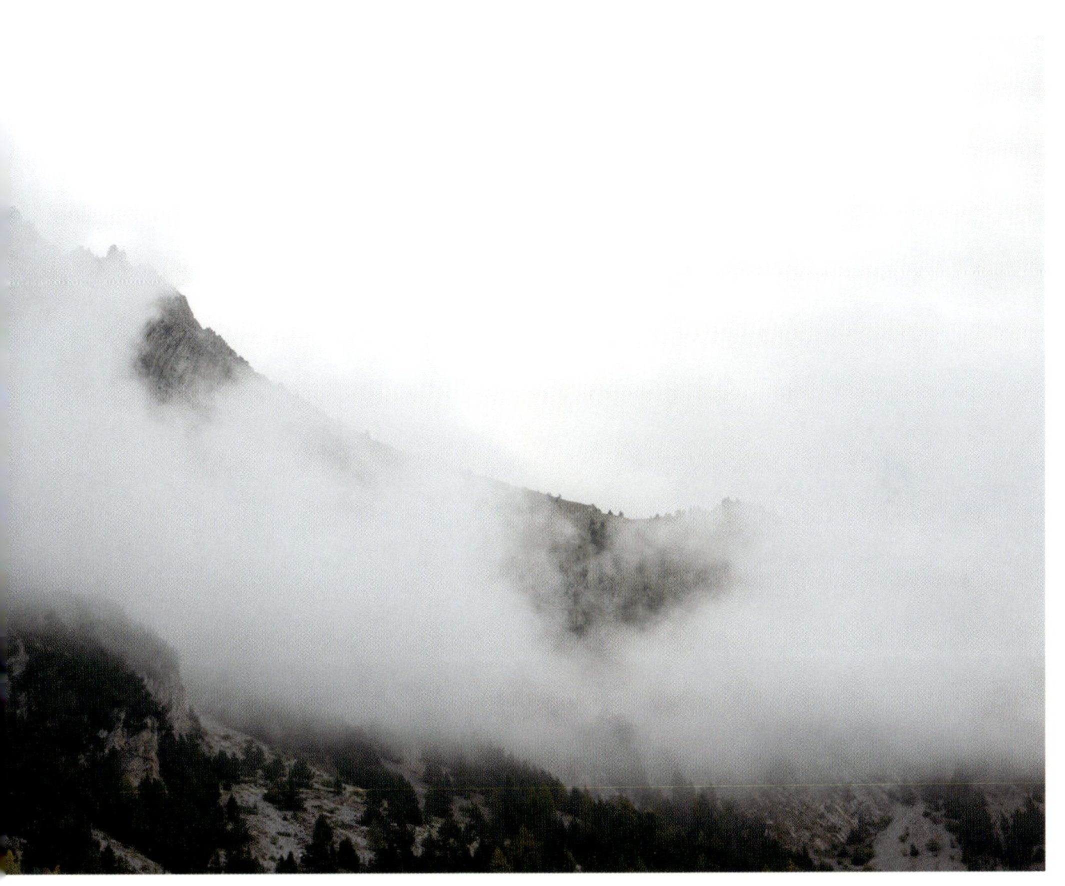

Rose Lecat
Les pensées d'Ibrahim, 2018

fotofever prize

with dahinden

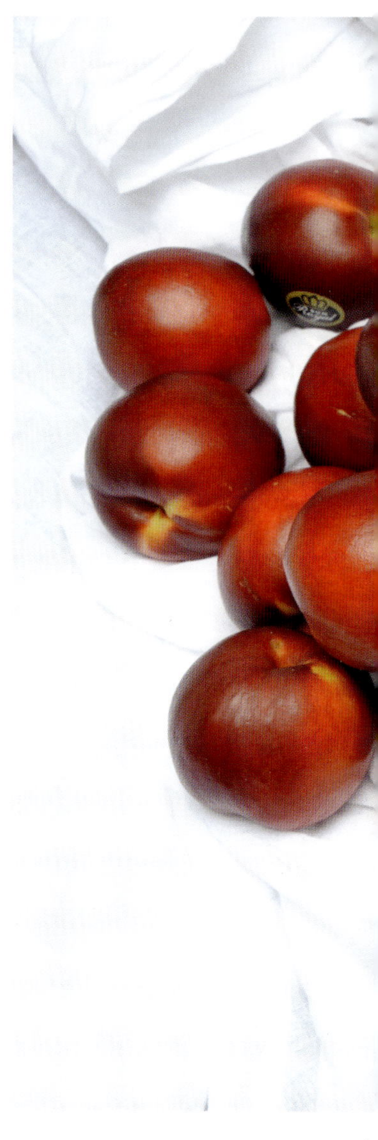

Alain Polo Nzuzi
Nature morte, fruits délicieux, 2016

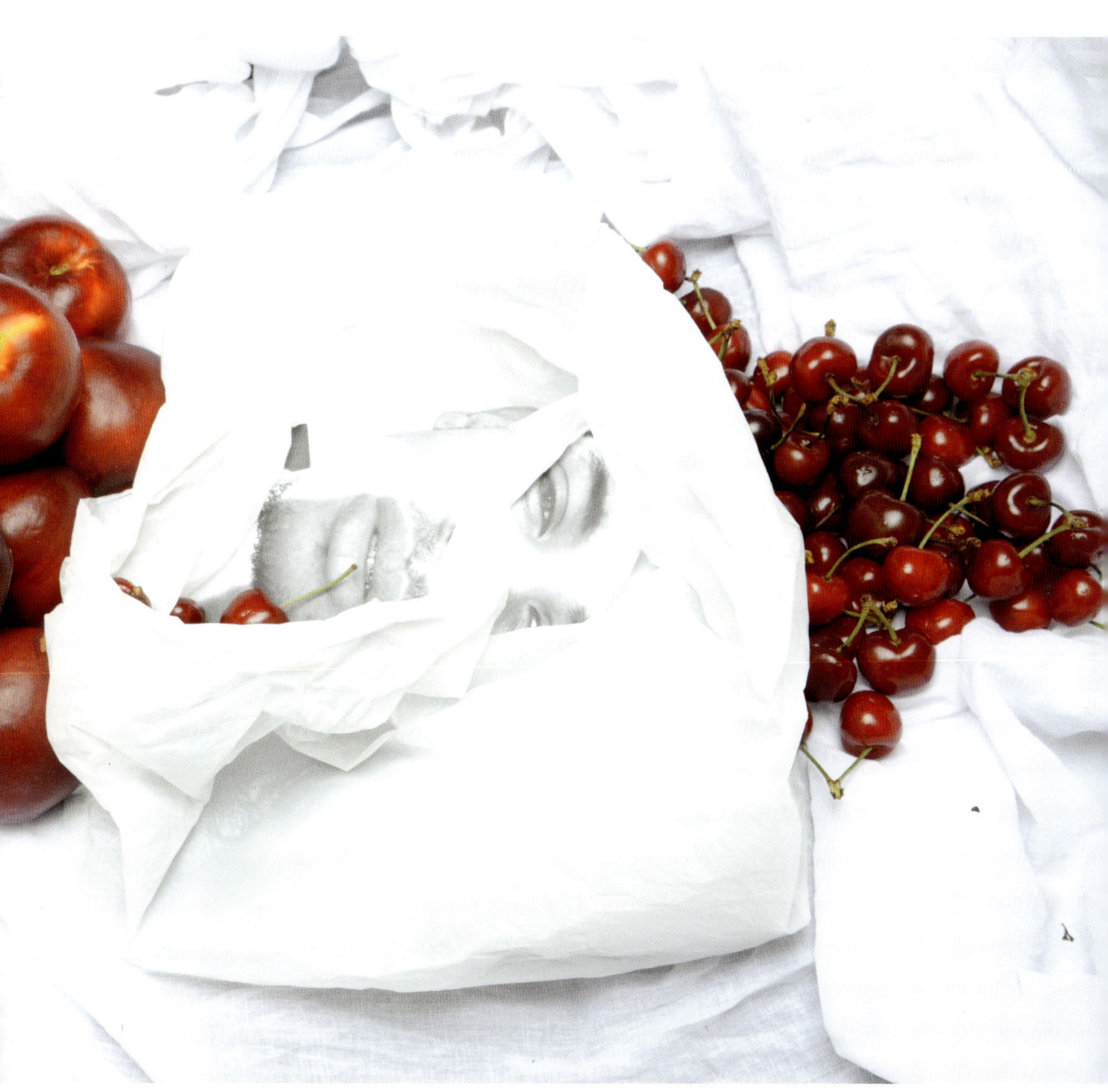

fotofever prize

with dahinden

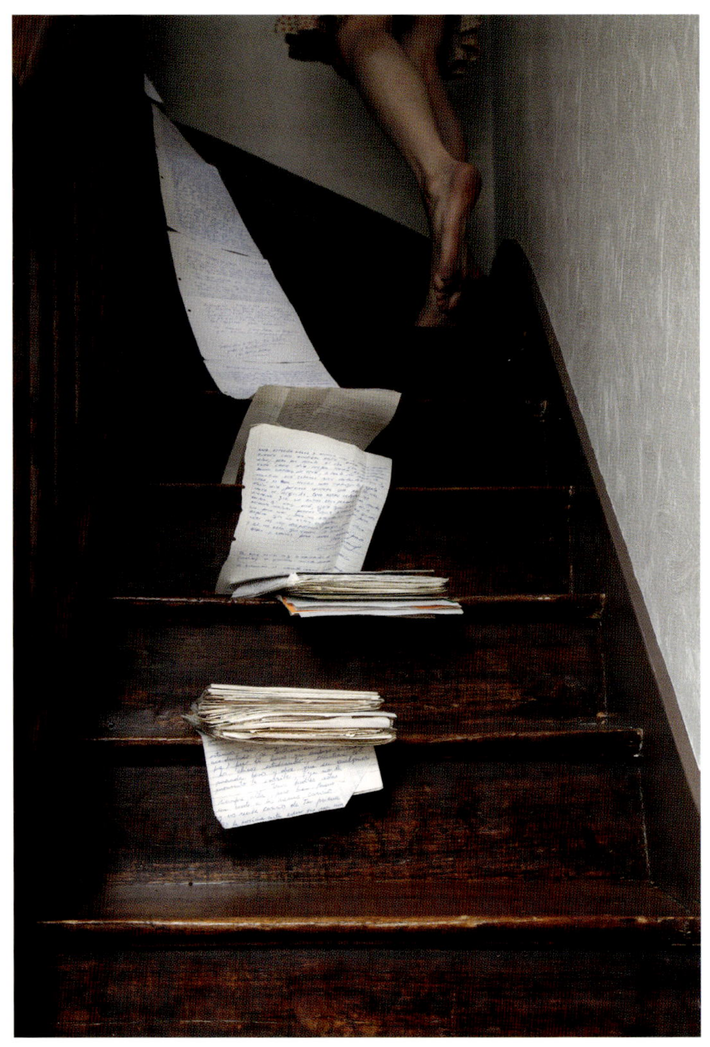

Julia Amarger
Secret n°10, 2015

2019

focus femmes

focus women

Dans le monde de l'art comme ailleurs, les femmes sont sous-représentées : elles sont moins exposées, moins publiées et leurs œuvres sont vendues moins cher. Cette année, avec une équipe exclusivement féminine, nous sommes déterminées à faire progresser la représentation des femmes en commençant par notre propre programmation : de 30% en 2018 à plus de 40% en 2019, nous nous engageons à **atteindre l'égalité en 2020** !

In the art world as elsewhere, women are underrepresented: they are less exhibited, less published and their artworks are sold at a lesser price. Starting this year, with an all-female team, we are determined to increase the representation of women artists through our program: from 30% in 2018 to more than 40% in 2019, we are committed to ***achieving equality in 2020****!*

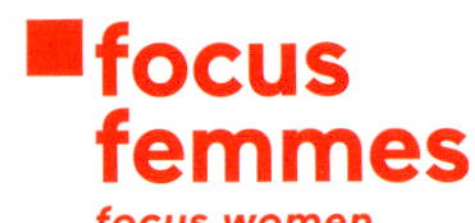

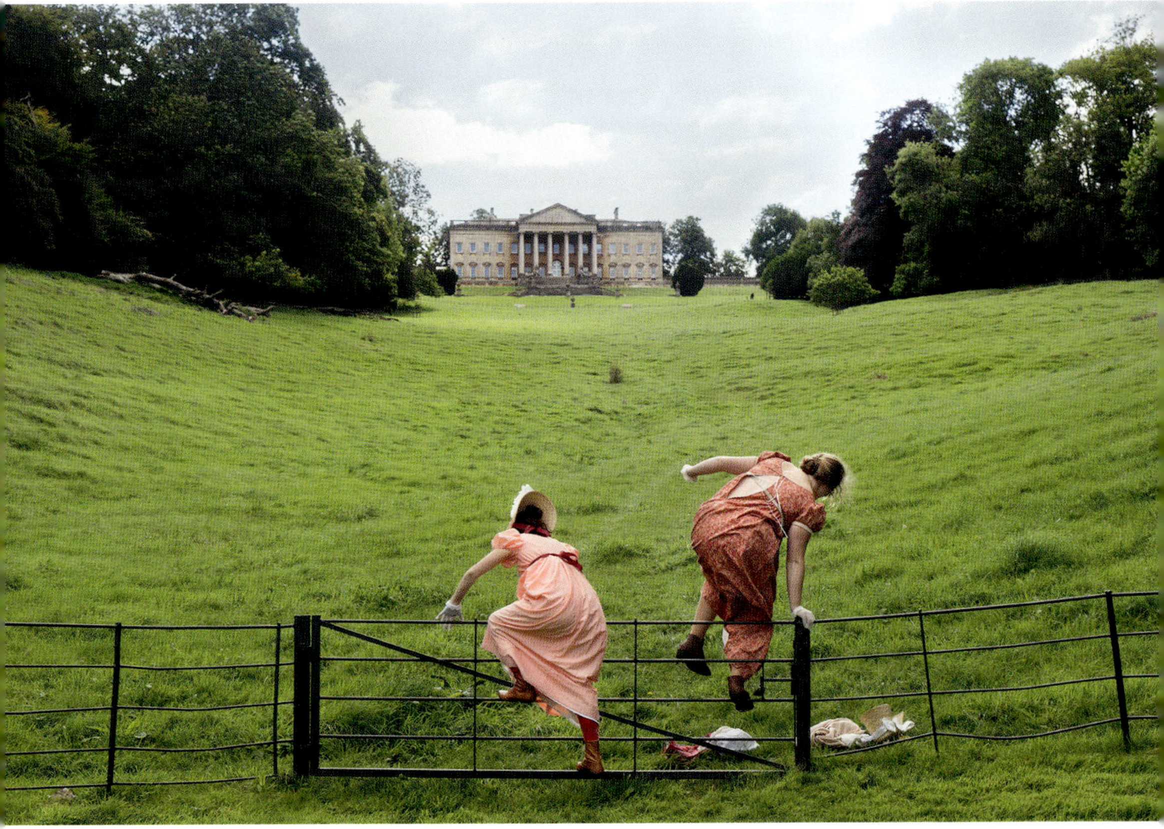

Alejandra Carles-Tolrá
Over the fence, 2016-2018
FIFTY DOTS GALLERY

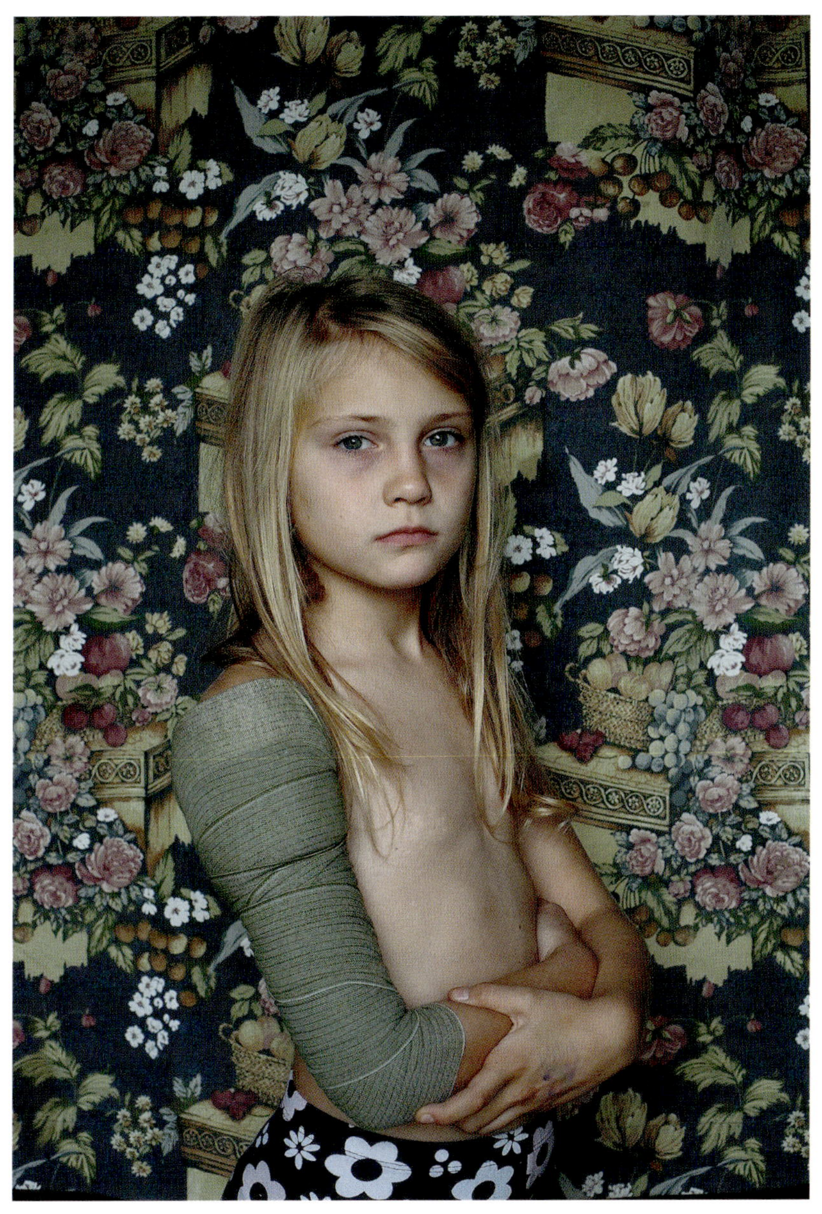

Anna Ajtner
Portrait of my daughter - Sandra's arm, 2017-2019
AJTNER FINE ART GALLERY

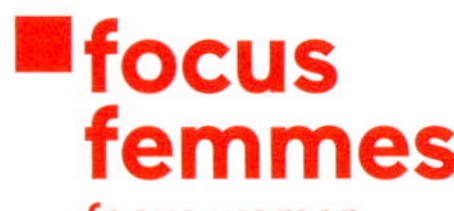

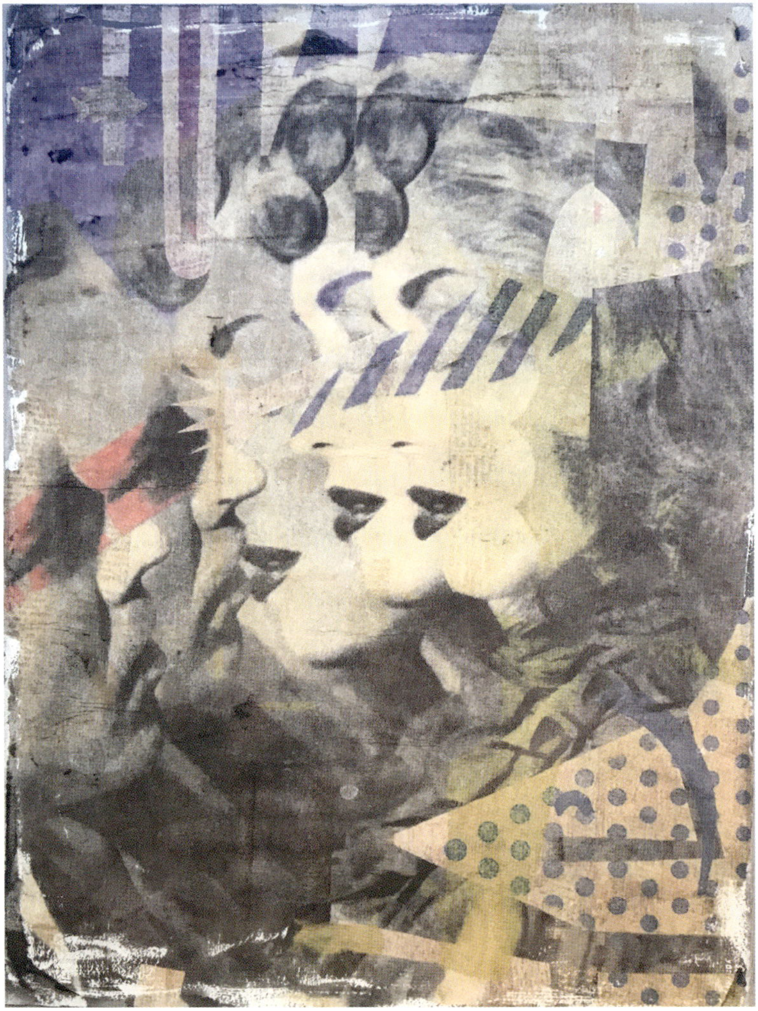

Isabella Accenti
The Kiss, 2019
EXPOWALL GALLERY

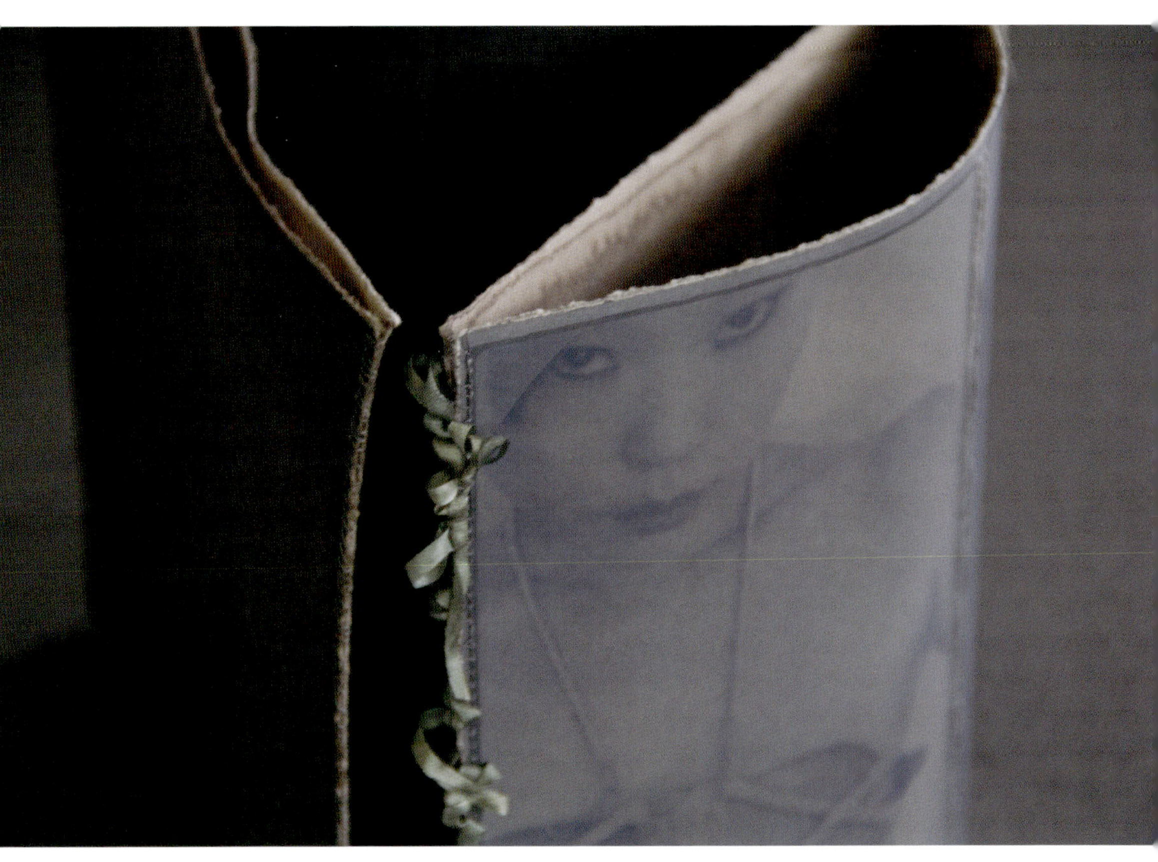

L. Mikelle Standbridge
Rebellious Confinement °2 (in the era of Araki), 2019
CASA REGIS

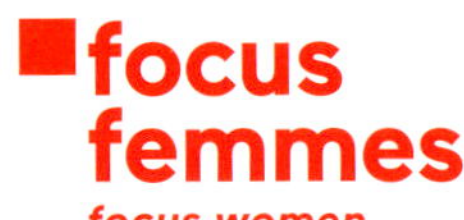

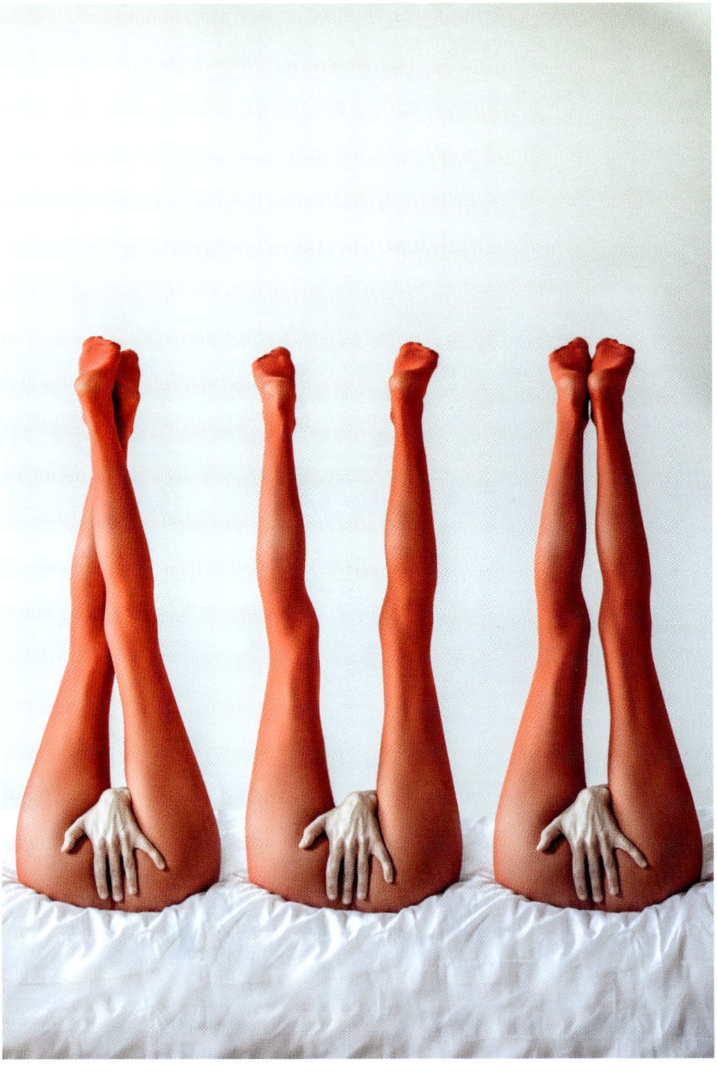

Julie Lagier
Collants, 2019
GALERIE OLIVIER BARRIOL

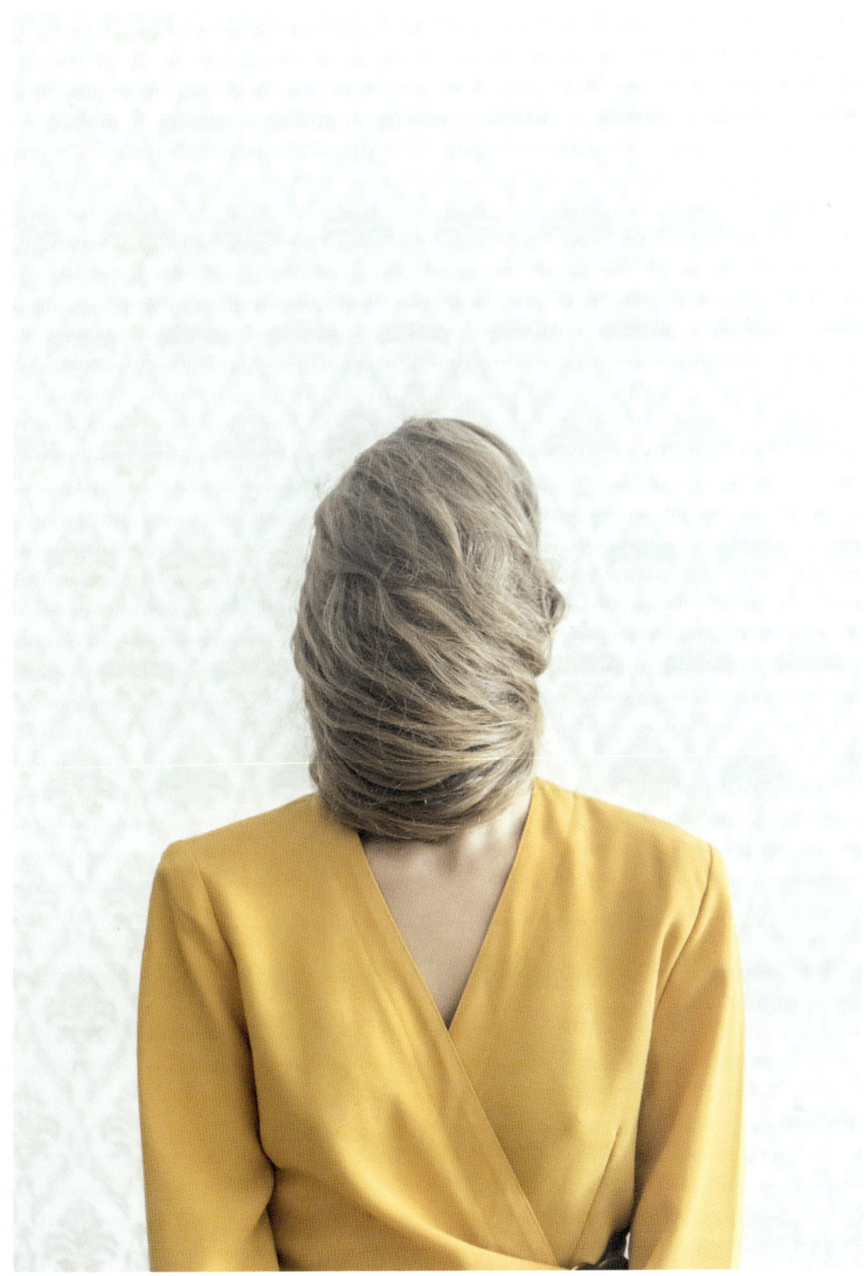

Julie Lagier
Bérénice, 2019
GALERIE OLIVIER BARRIOL

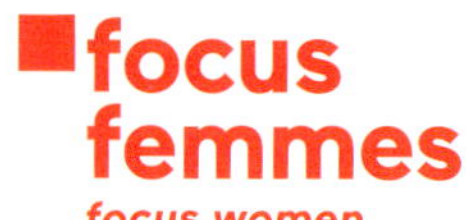

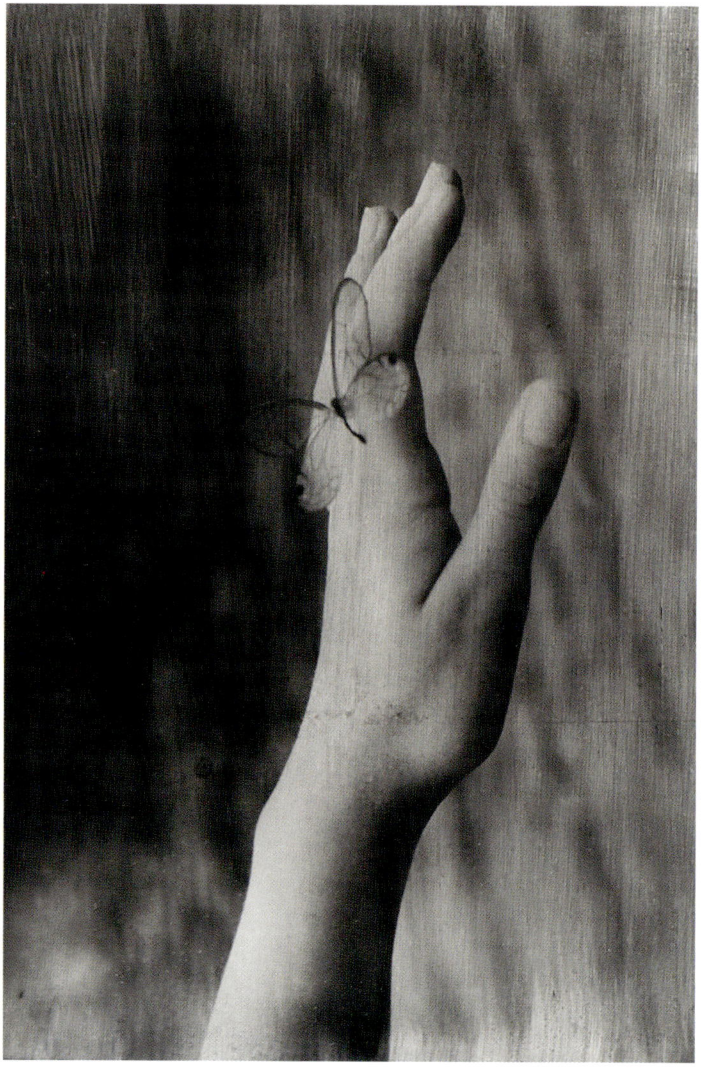

Marie Rameau
La main et le papillon, 2019
GALERIE ALBANE

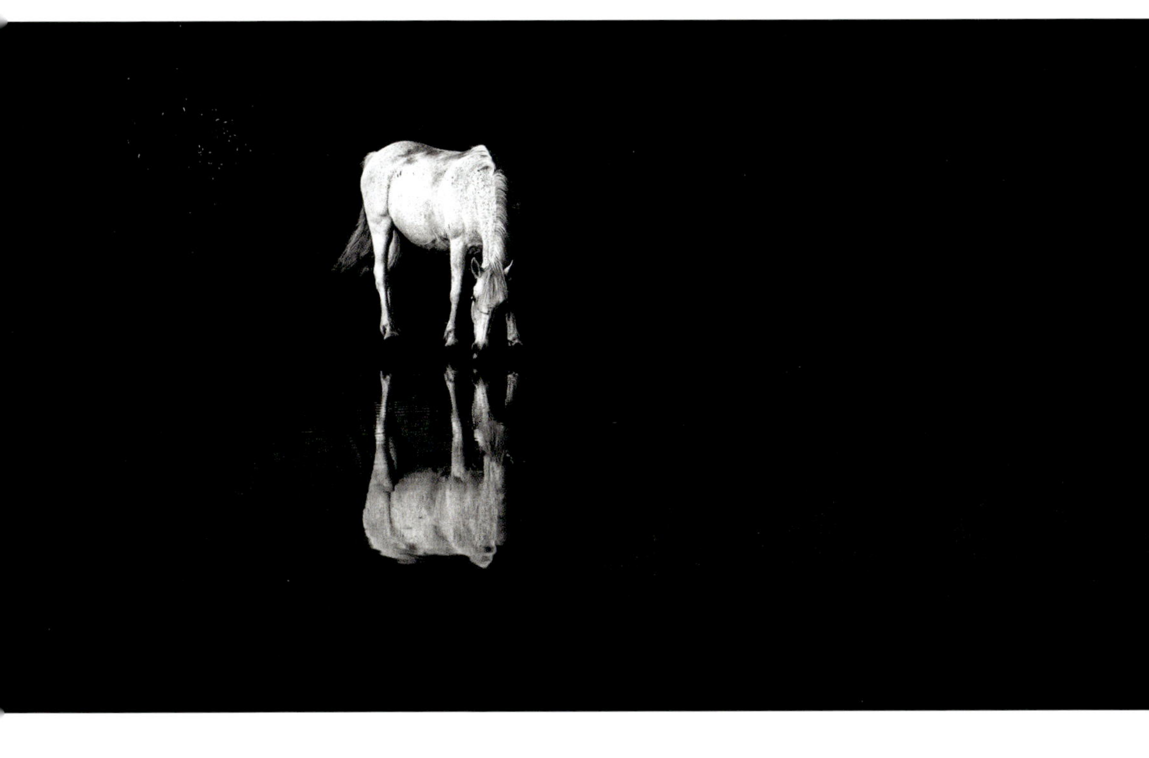

Karen Du Vivier
L'instinct, 2018
GALERIE RASTOLL

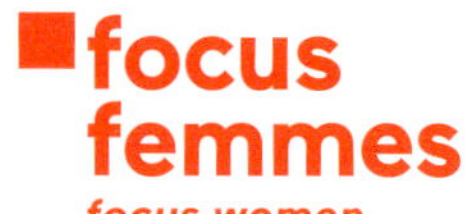

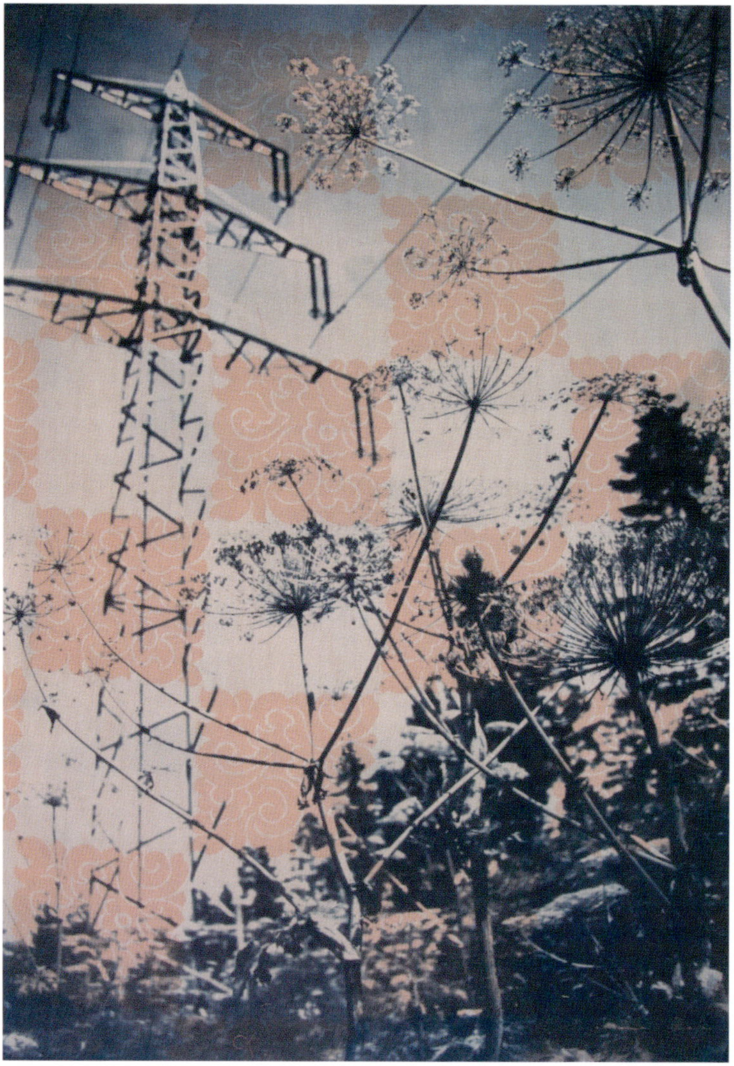

Ramona Czygan
Three meter floral, 2012
GALERIE STP

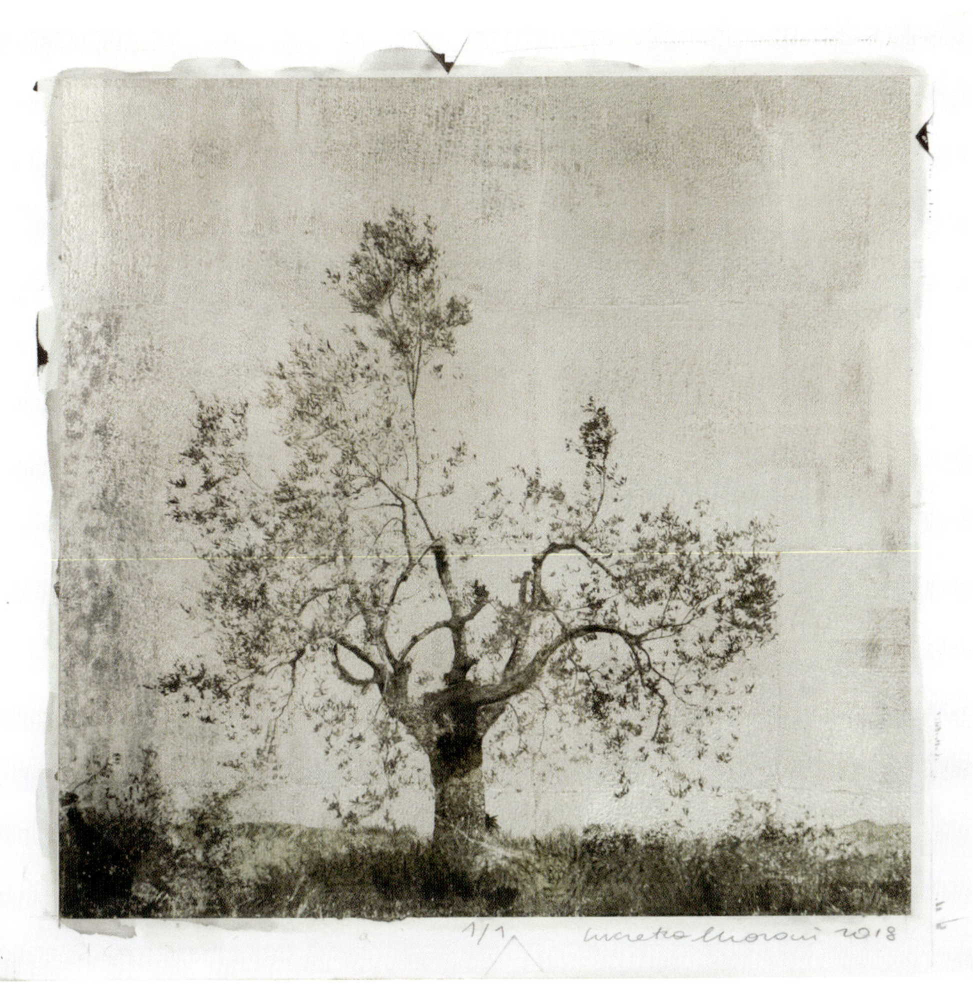

Lucretia Moroni
Olive Tree, 2018
GALLERIA L'AFFICHE

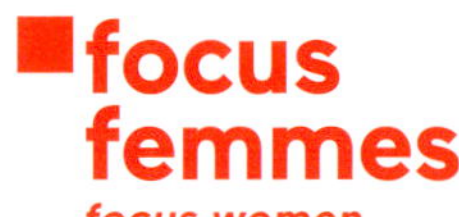

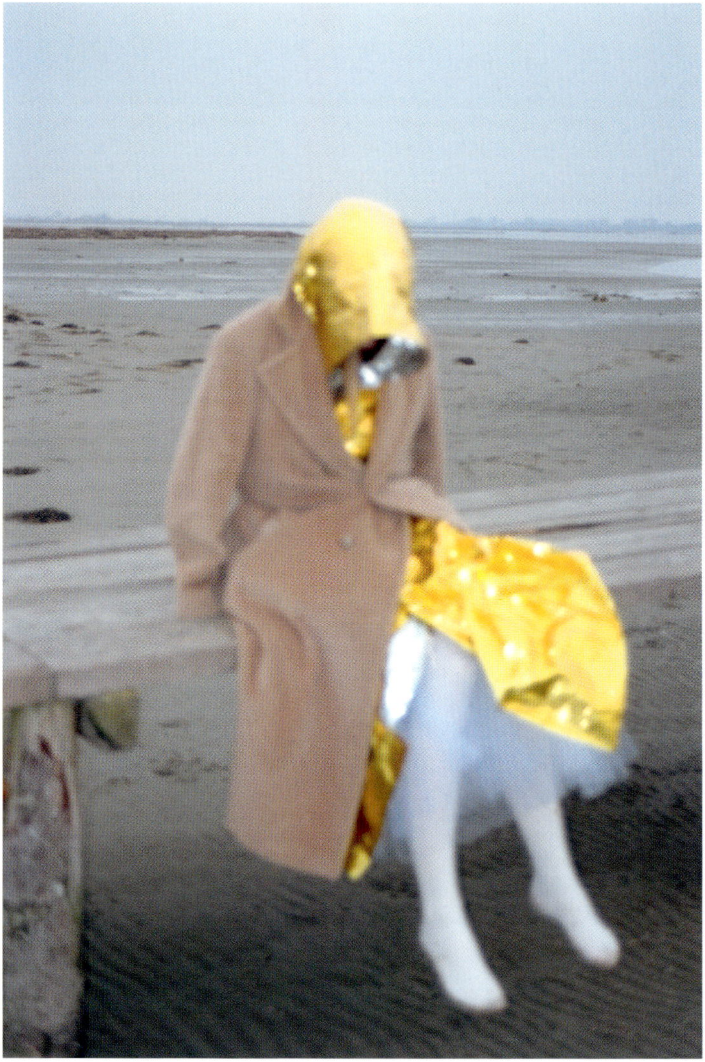

Giulia Agostini
Untitled, 2019
HEILLANDI GALLERY

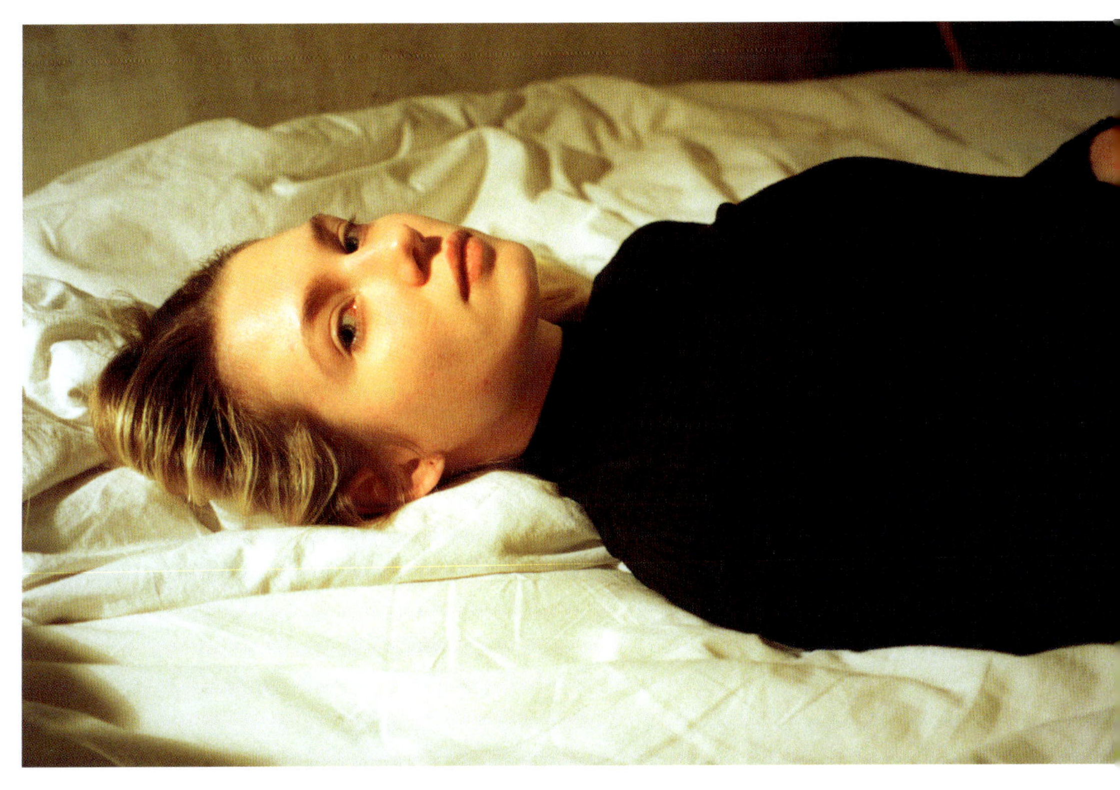

Irene Royo
Bons Nois, 2018-2019
GRISART

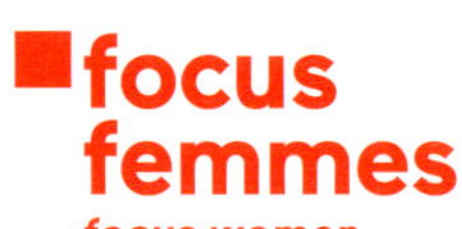

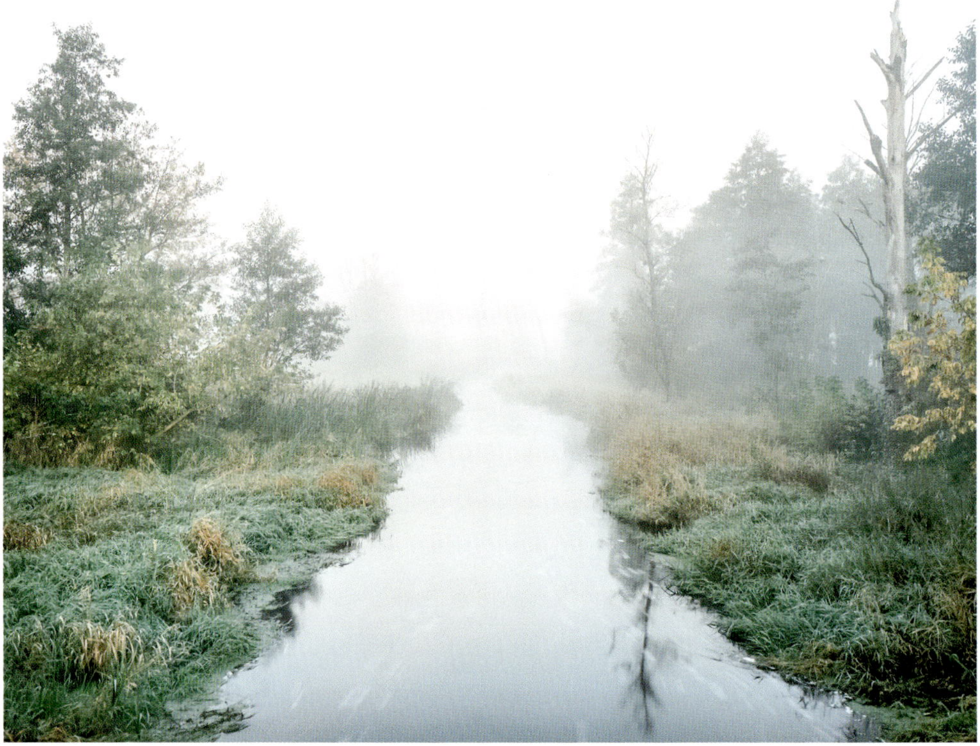

Andrea Olga Mantovani
Narewka, 2017
PRIX OBS LES FEMMES S'EXPOSENT

Tingting Wang →
Contenants du passé, 2018
GALERIE XII

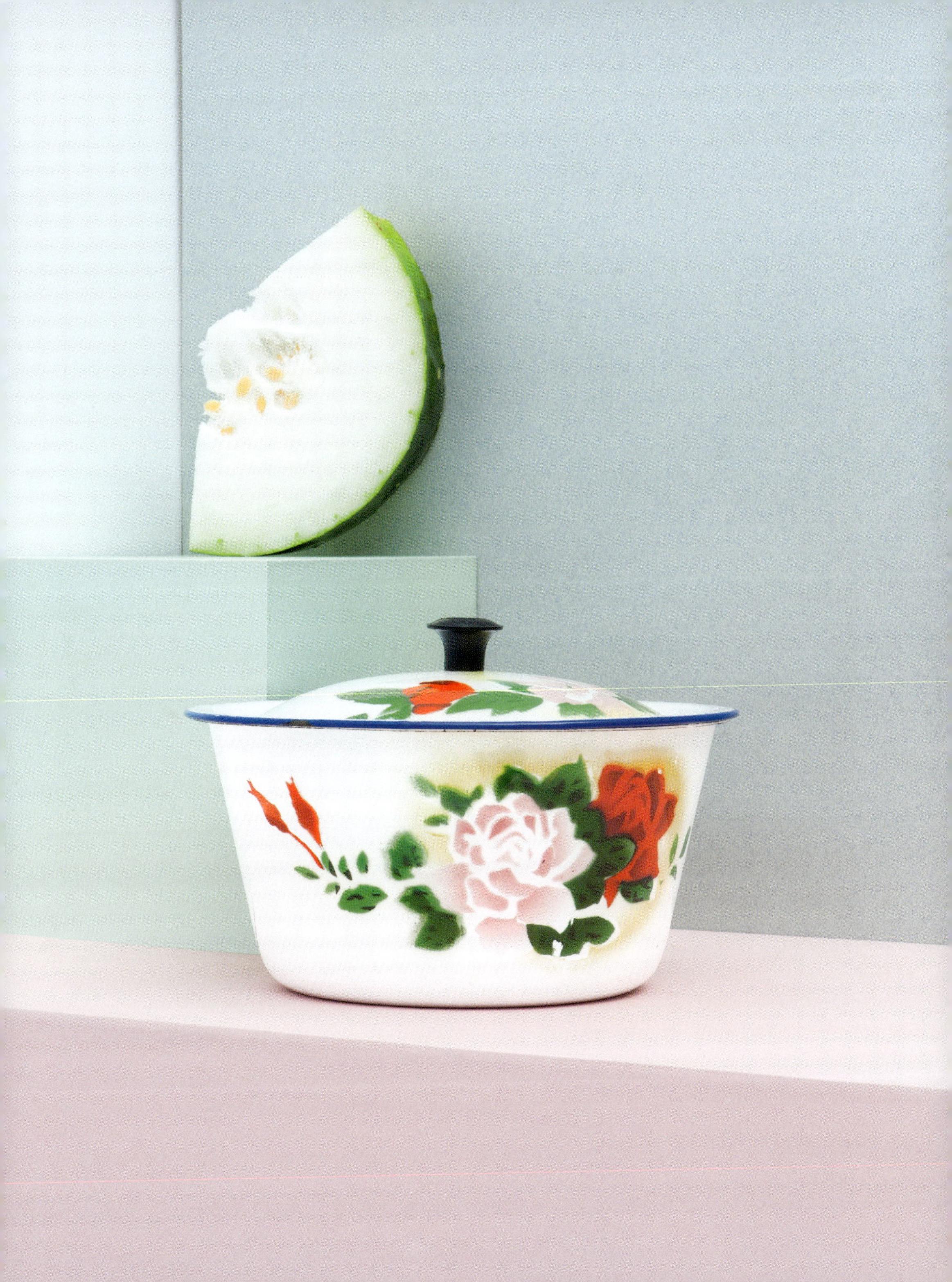

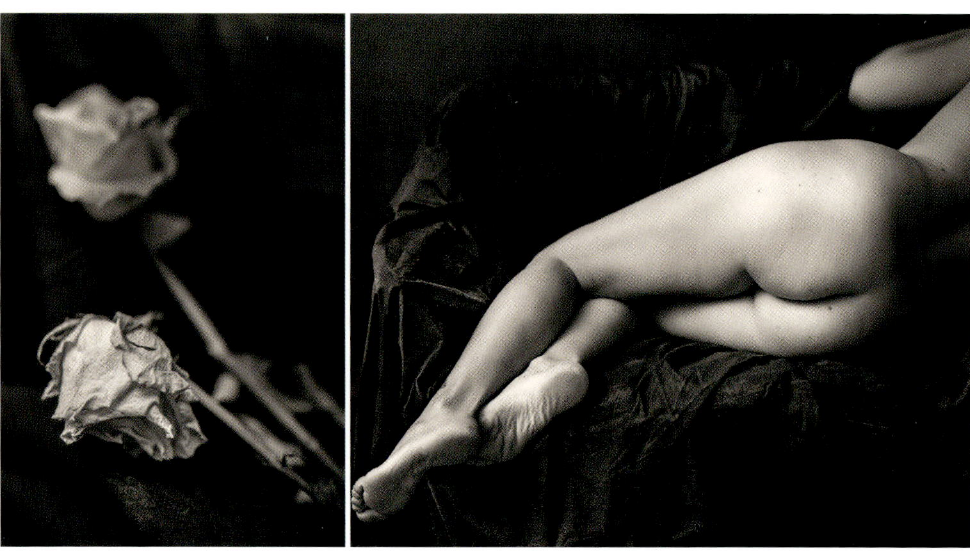

Erica Campanella
Untitled #2, 2018
PODBIELSKI CONTEMPORARY

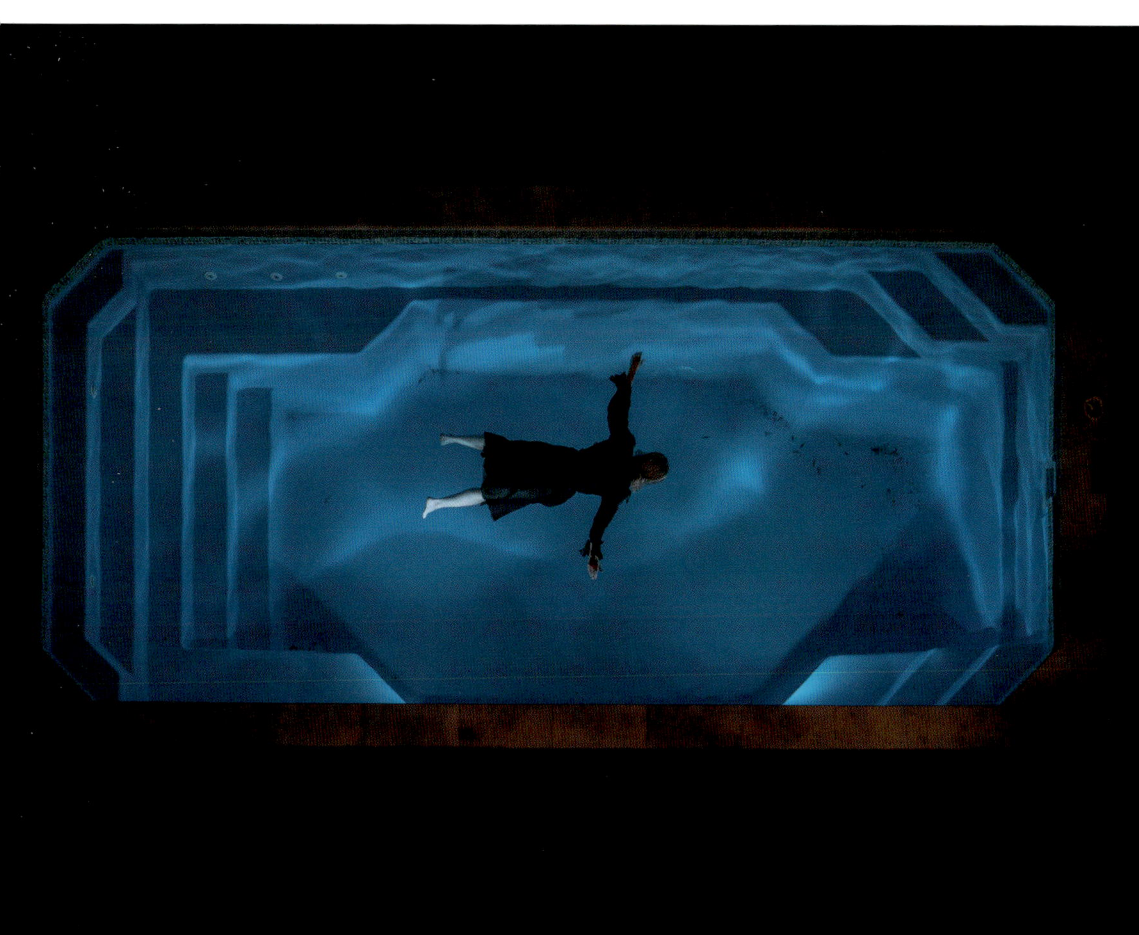

Bootsy Holler
Deadpool, 2018
WALL SPACE CREATIVE

2019

focus france

Le saviez-vous ? 1839 est la date de naissance officielle de la photographie et c'est en France que ça s'est passé ! Pour le 180e anniversaire de l'invention de la photographie, fotofever dévoile l'audace et la créativité de la scène française. Plus de 80 galeries, éditeurs et artistes français ont répondu à notre appel pour fêter cette édition de fotofever unique en son genre avec un parcours inédit, un espace dédié en préambule de la foire, un talk thématique...

Did you know? 1839 is the official date of birth of the photography and it happened in France! *For the 180th anniversary of the invention of photography, fotofever unveils the boldness and creativity of the French scene. More than 80 French galleries, publishers and artists have responded to our call to celebrate this unique edition of fotofever with a themed itinerary and talk, as well as a dedicated exhibition at the entrance of the fair...*

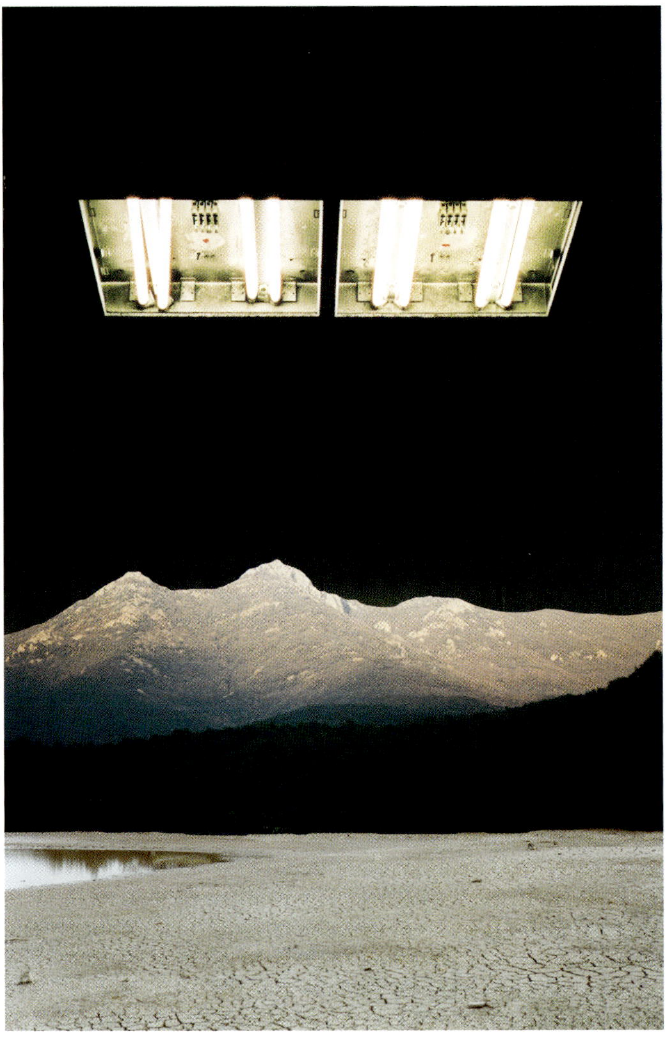

Anaëlle Cathala
Neon lights, 2019
GALERIE ALB

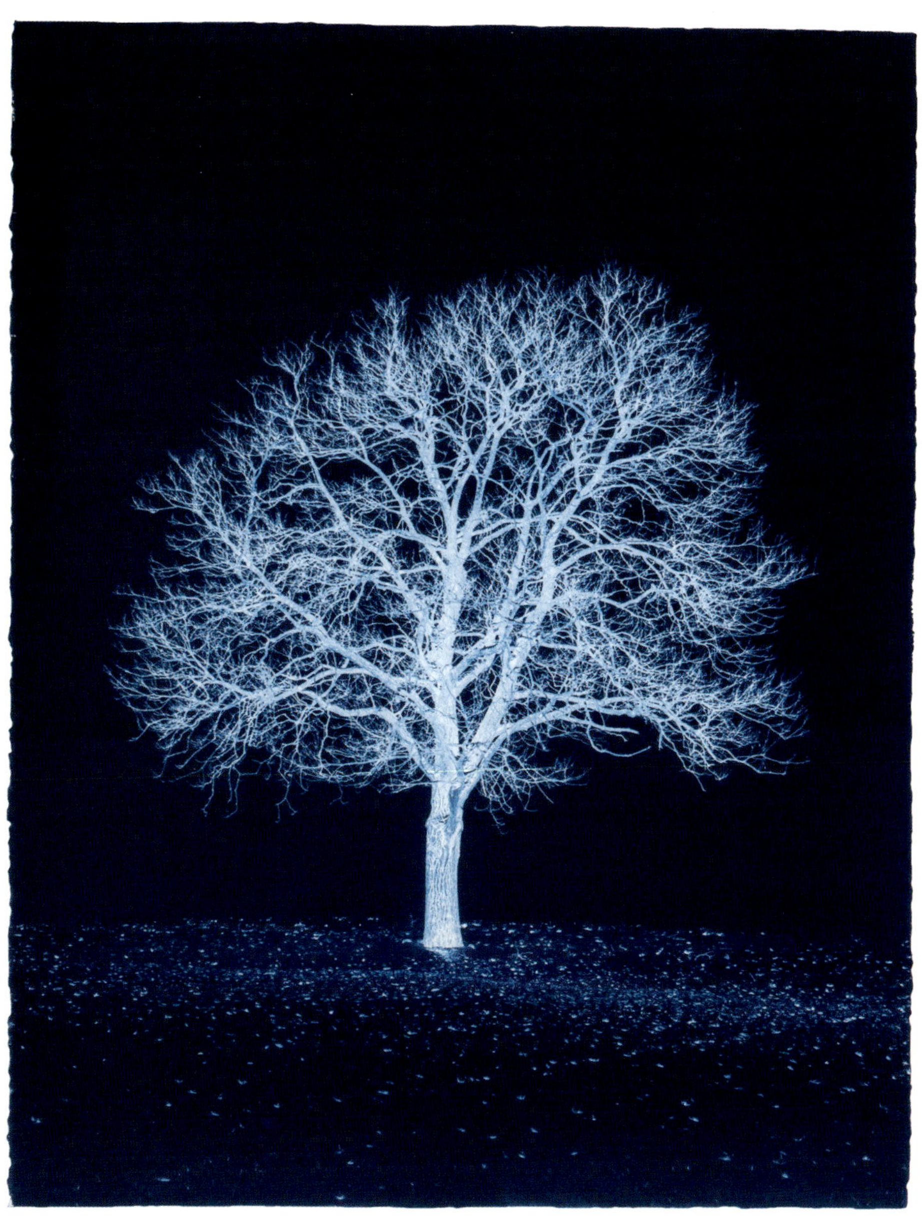

Gilles Lorin
Portrait d'Arbre, Prussian Blue Study no. 1, 2016
JÖRG MAASS KUNSTHANDEL

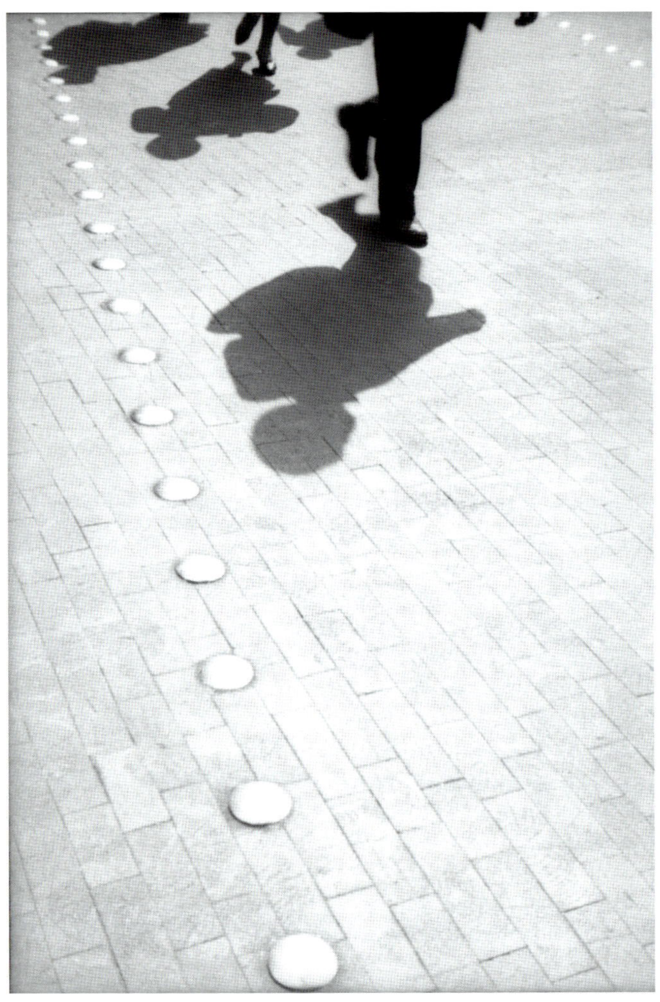

Roger Schall
Paris, 1929
GALERIE ARGENTIC

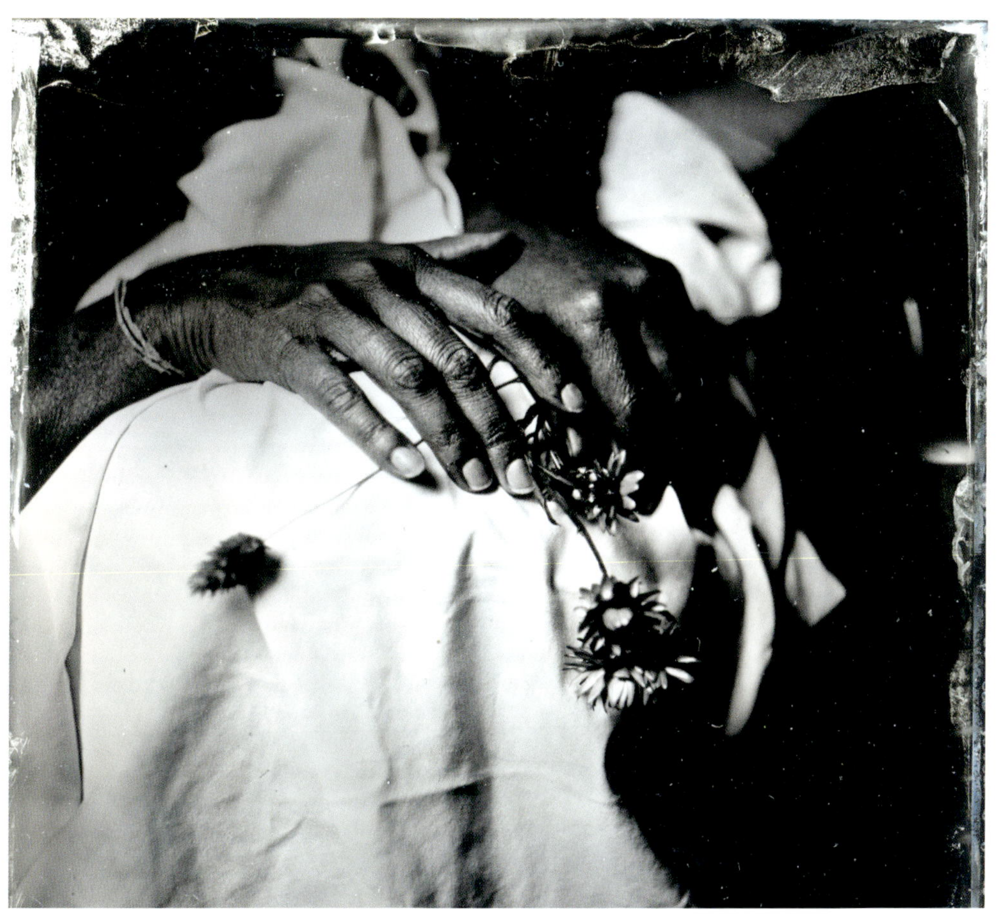

Emmanuel Ligner
Ternura Oscura N°12
GALERIE ALBANE

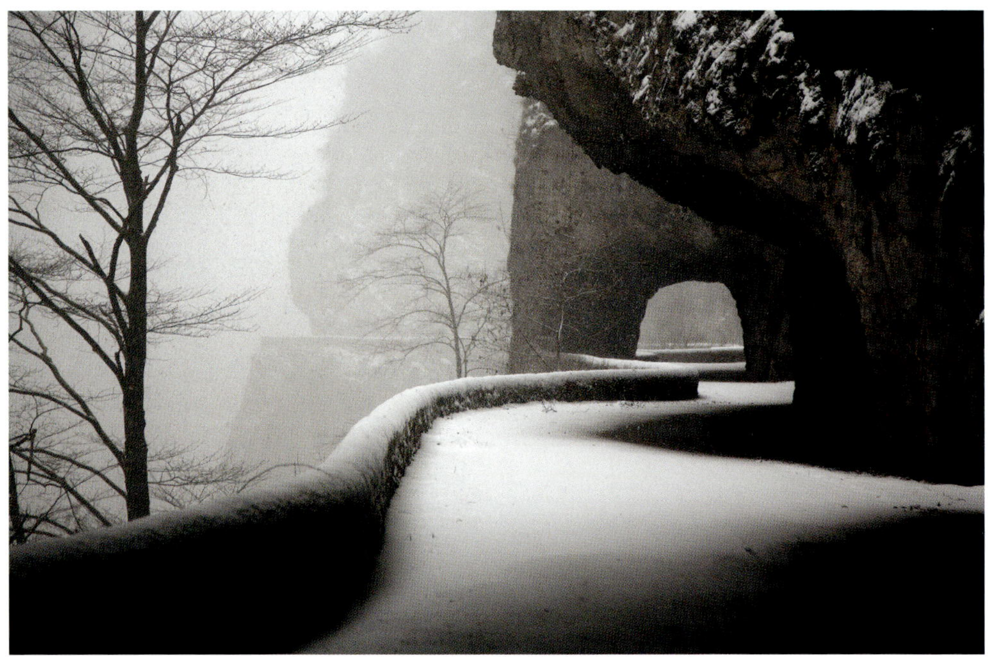

Christophe Jacrot
Tunnels, 2019
GALERIE R/G

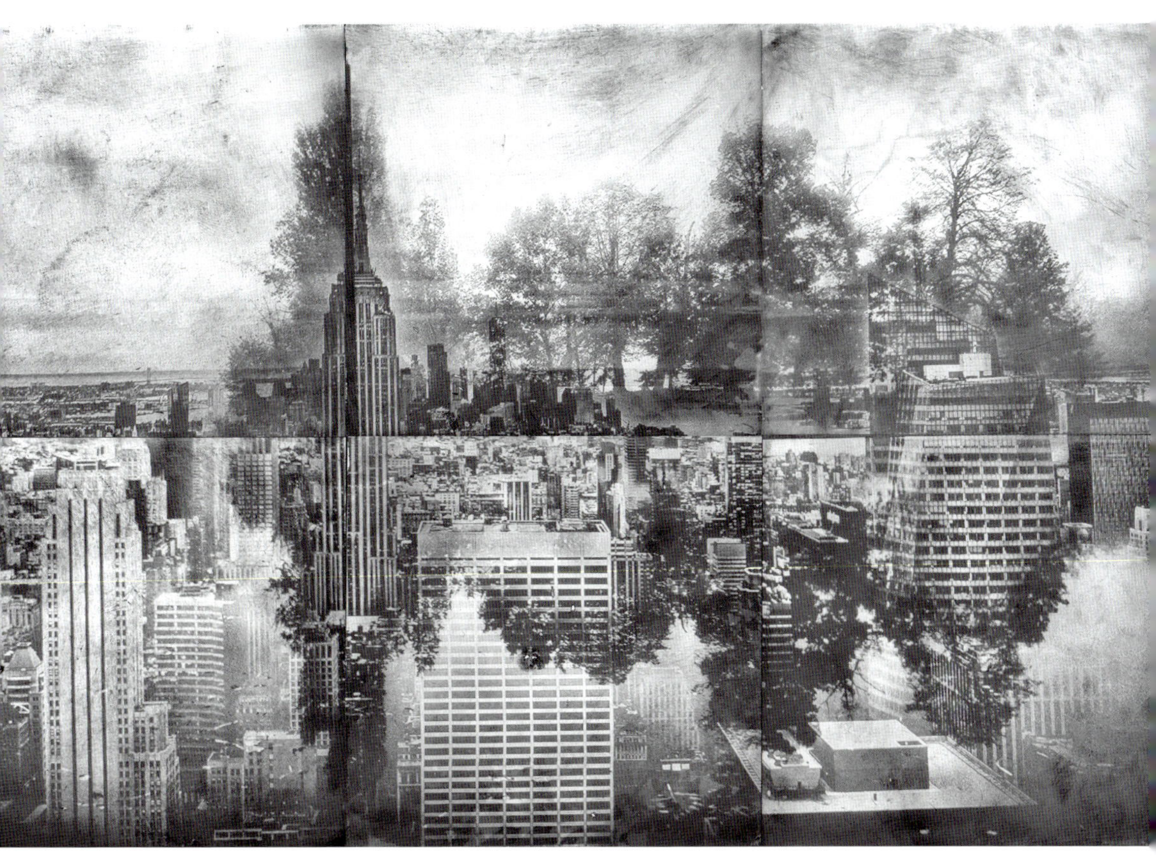

Marjolaine Vuarnesson
Dream'City, 2017
GALERIE RASTOLL

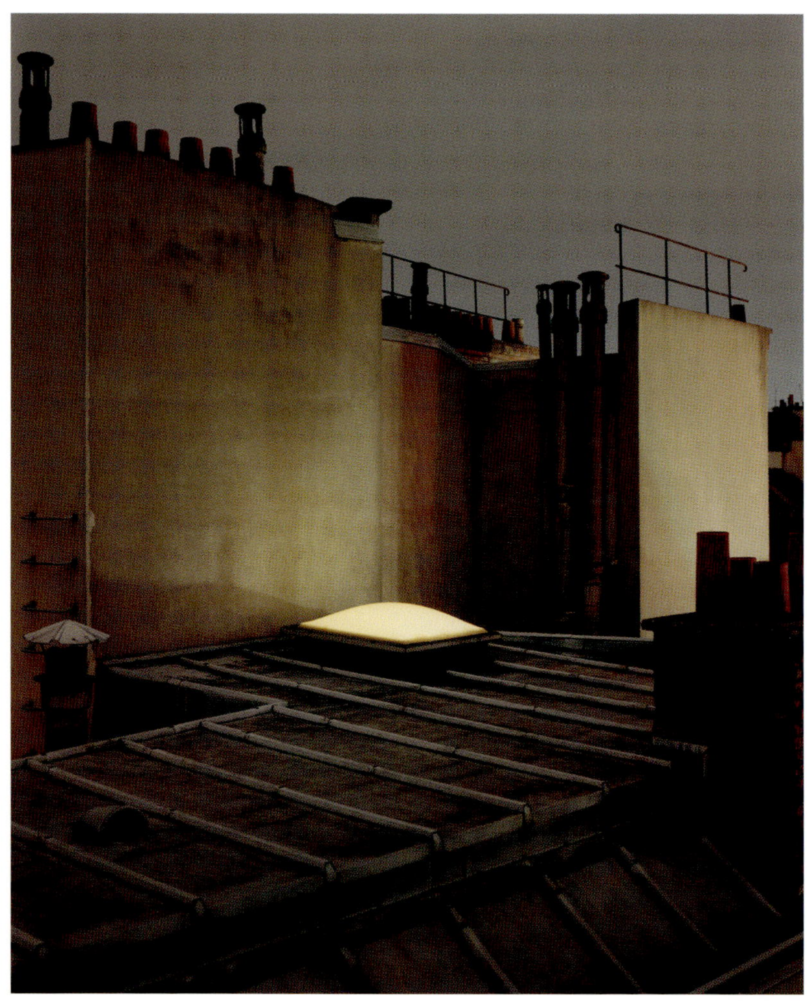

Alain Cornu
Sur Paris #51, 2011
GALERIE STP

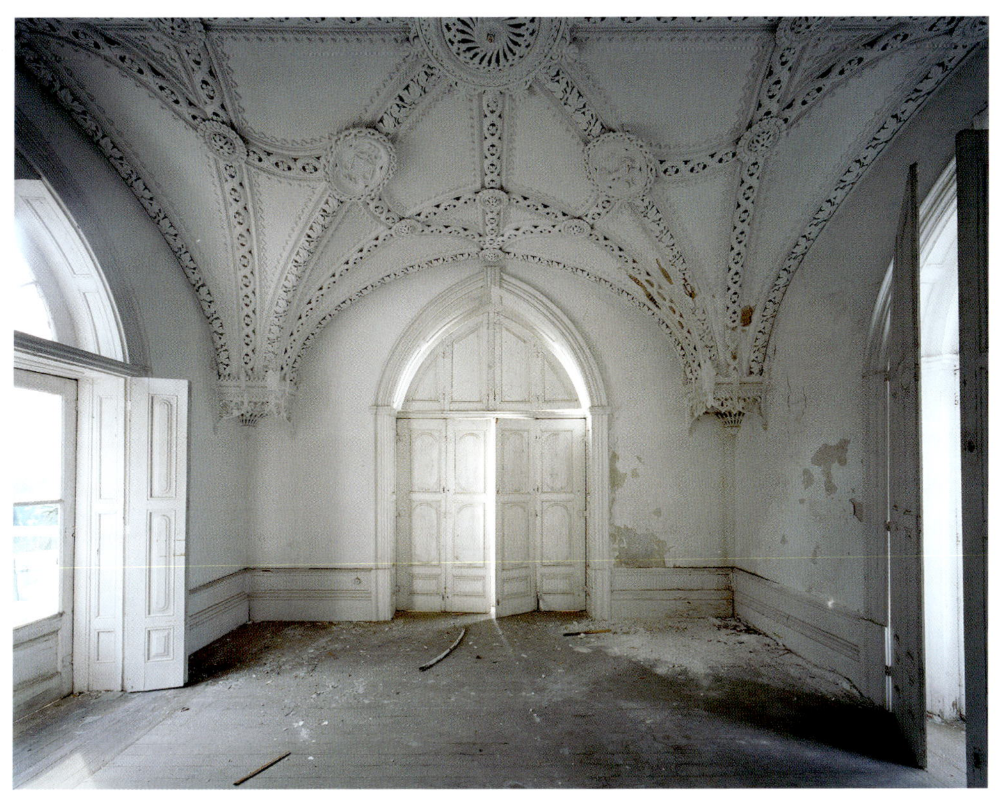

Thomas Jorion
Laço (Portugal), 2017
GALERIE INSULA

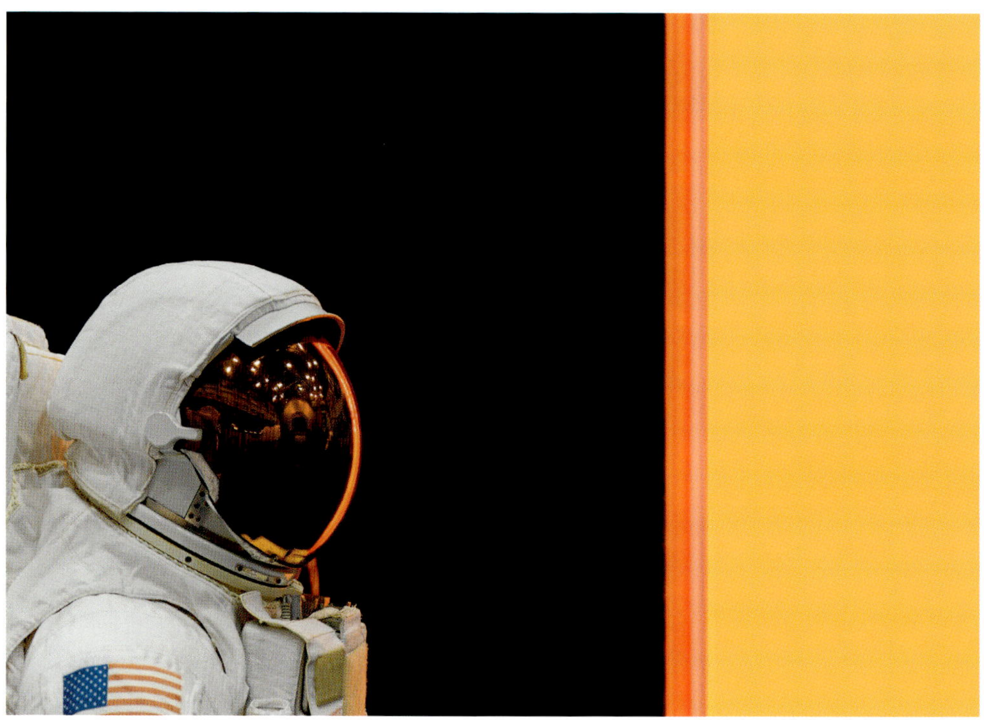

Vincent Fournier
Apollo model A7L spacesuit, Johnson Space Center, Houston, [NASA], U.S.A, 2017
LA GALERIE PARIS 1839

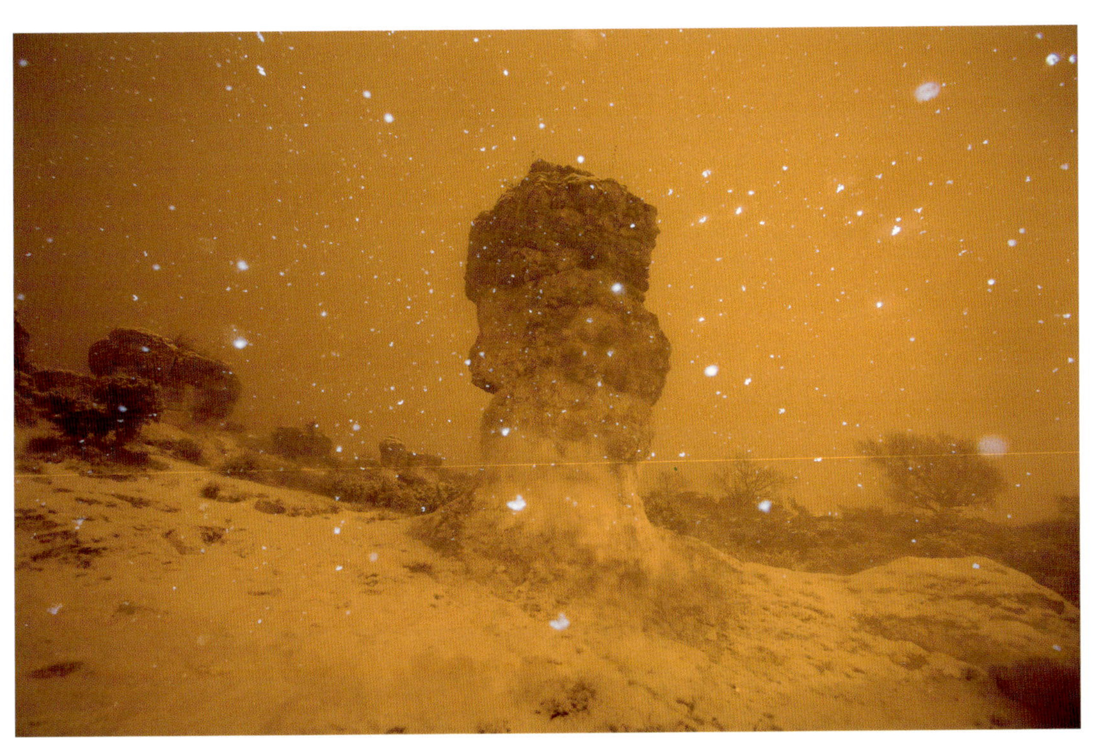

David Tatin
Cosmos #1, 2019
L'ANGLE

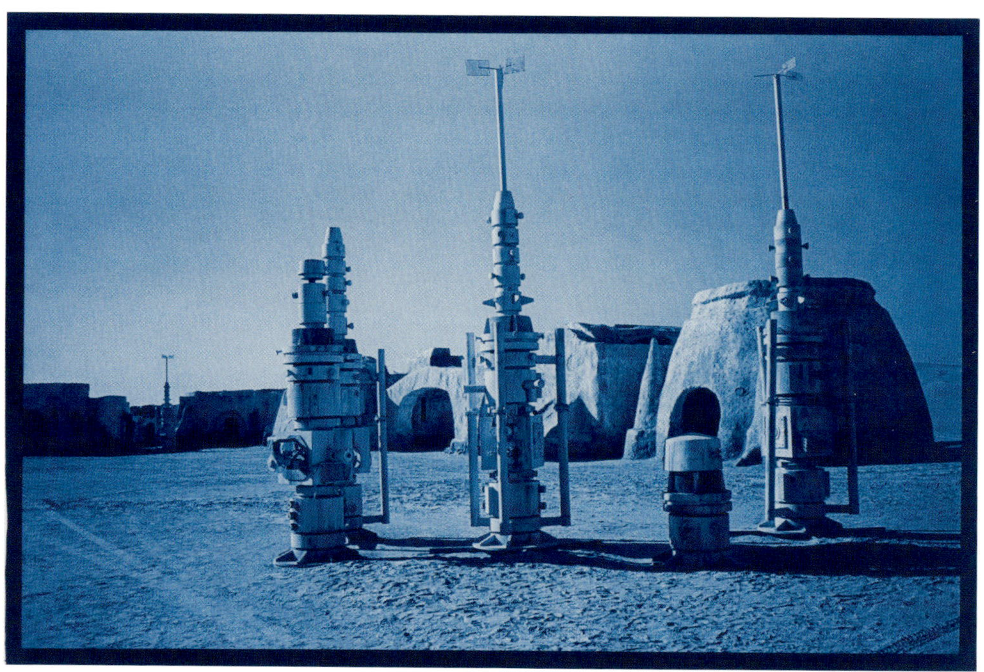

Ludovic Bollo
Vaporateurs, 2000
LIBRAIRIE MICHAEL SEKSIK

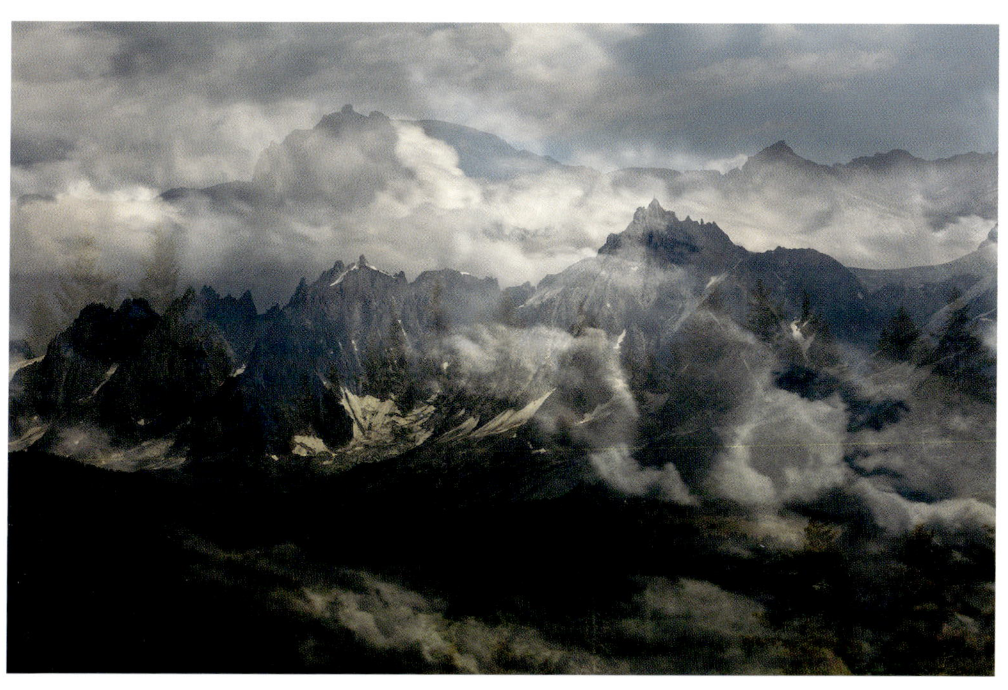

Edouard Mazaré
L'aiguille, 2019
GALERIE MONA LISA

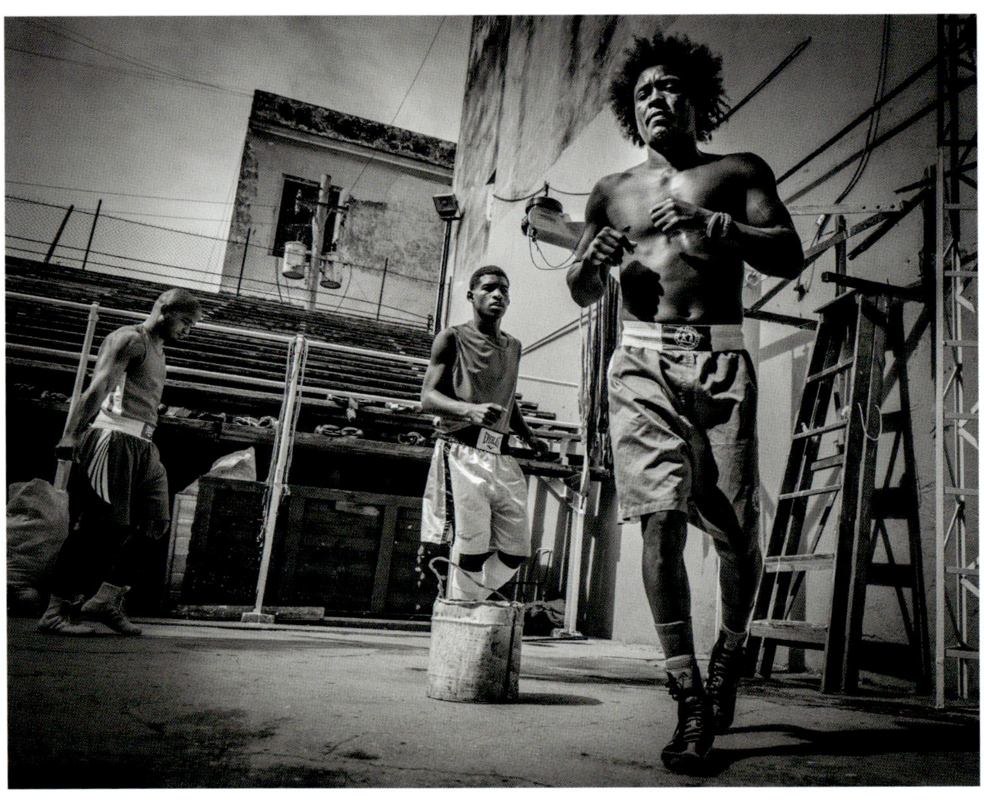

Jérémy Garamond
Training 1, 2018
VM FOR ART

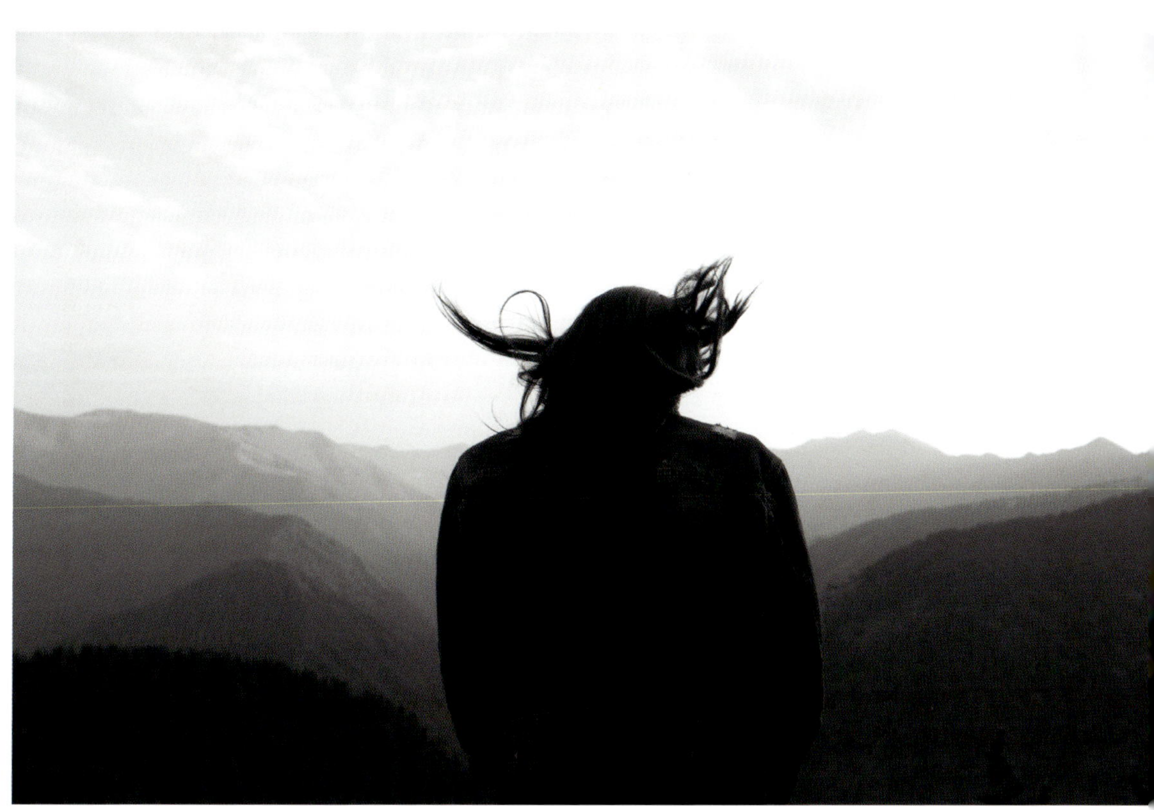

Tendance Floue
Géorgie, 2018

2019

éditeurs
publishers

Parce que l'édition est inhérente à la photographie et que de nombreux collectionneurs ont démarré avec l'acquisition de livres photo, fotofever accueille une **sélection d'éditeurs français et internationaux** présentant une sélection exceptionnelle de publications. Pour la première fois cette année, la librairie parisienne La Comète sera présente pour mettre notamment en avant la scène française, les femmes photographes et l'histoire de la photographie, avec une sélection originale de monographies, catalogues, revues, éditions de tête et objets d'artiste.

Because publishing is an intrinsic part of photography and numerous collectors have started with the purchase of photographic books, fotofever welcomes a ***selection of French and international*** *publishers presenting a wide array of books. For the first time, the Parisian bookseller La Comète will be present with a pop up bookstore with publications highlighting the French scene, women photographers and the history of photography*

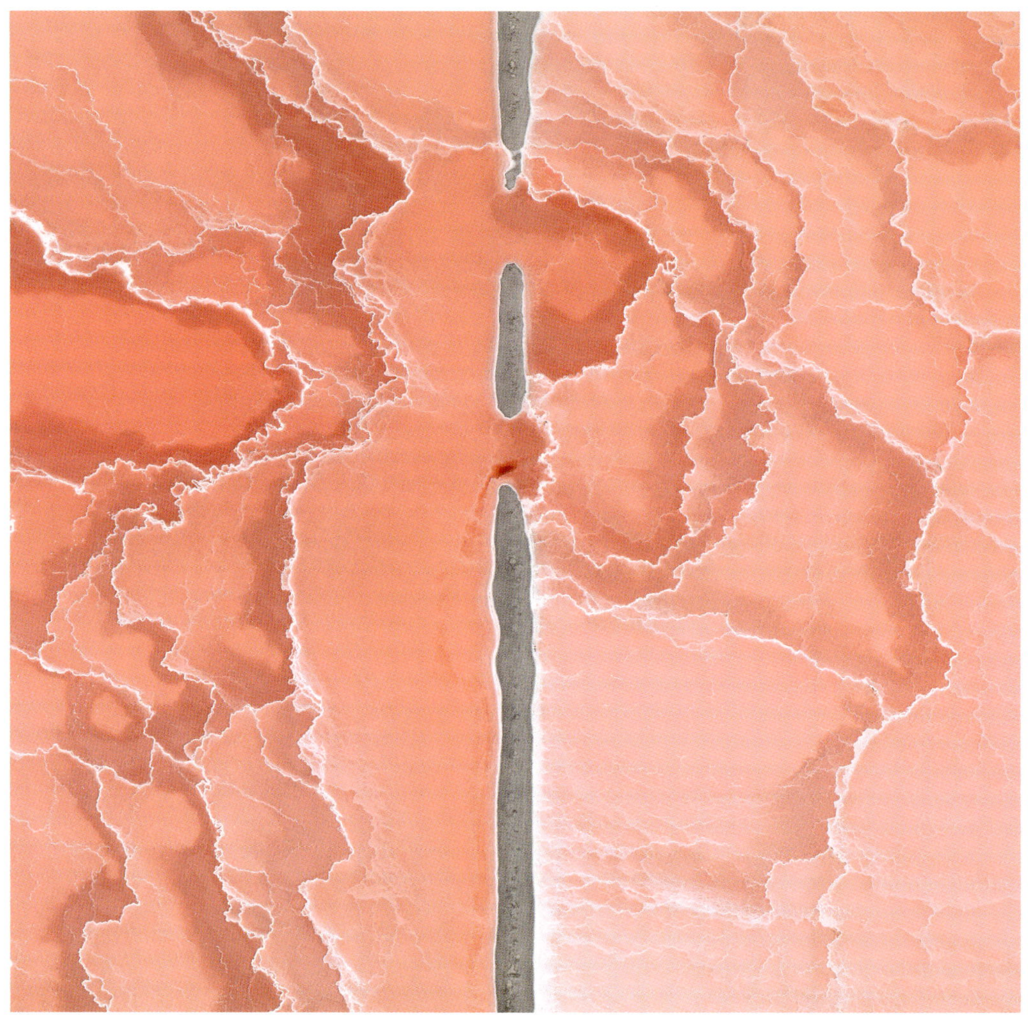

Jérémie Lenoir
#6561087, Salt Lake, 2017
ÉDITIONS LIGHT MOTIV

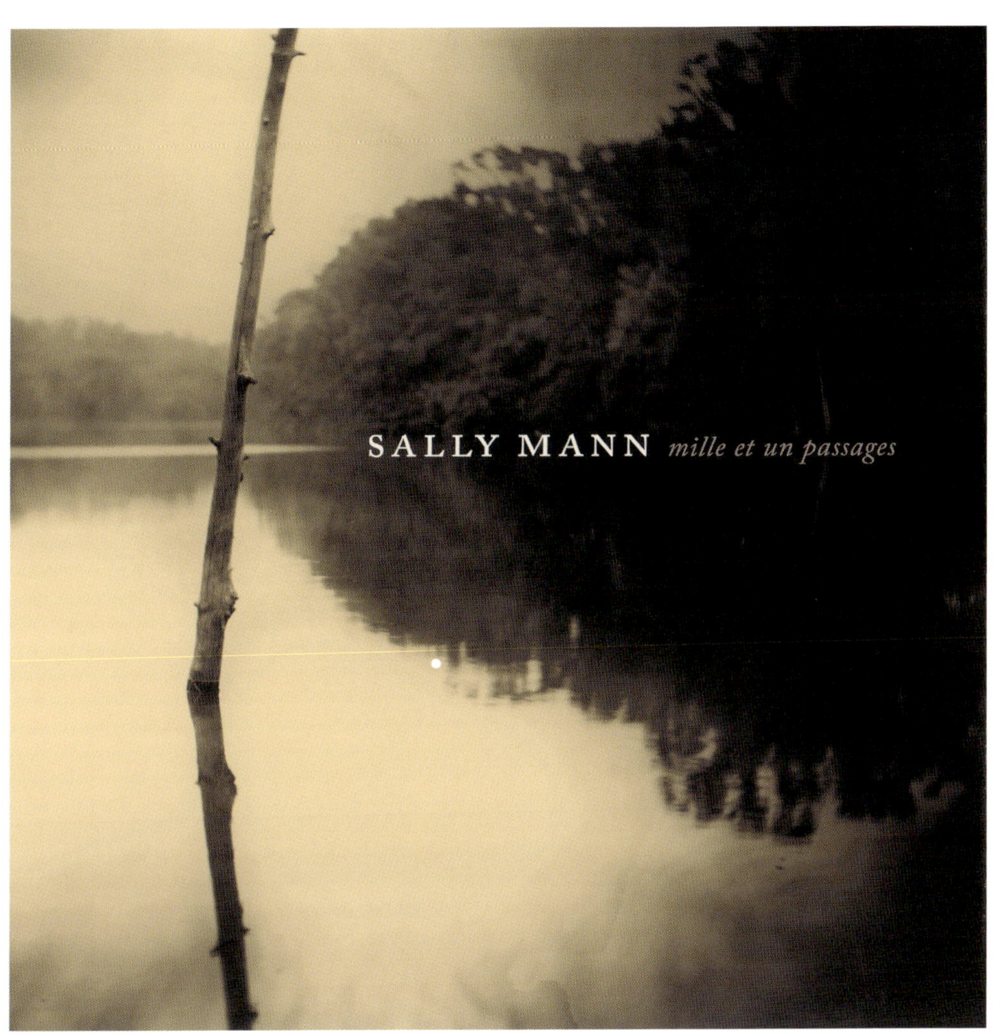

Sally Mann
Mille et un passages, Éditions Xavier Barral
LIBRAIRIE LA COMÈTE

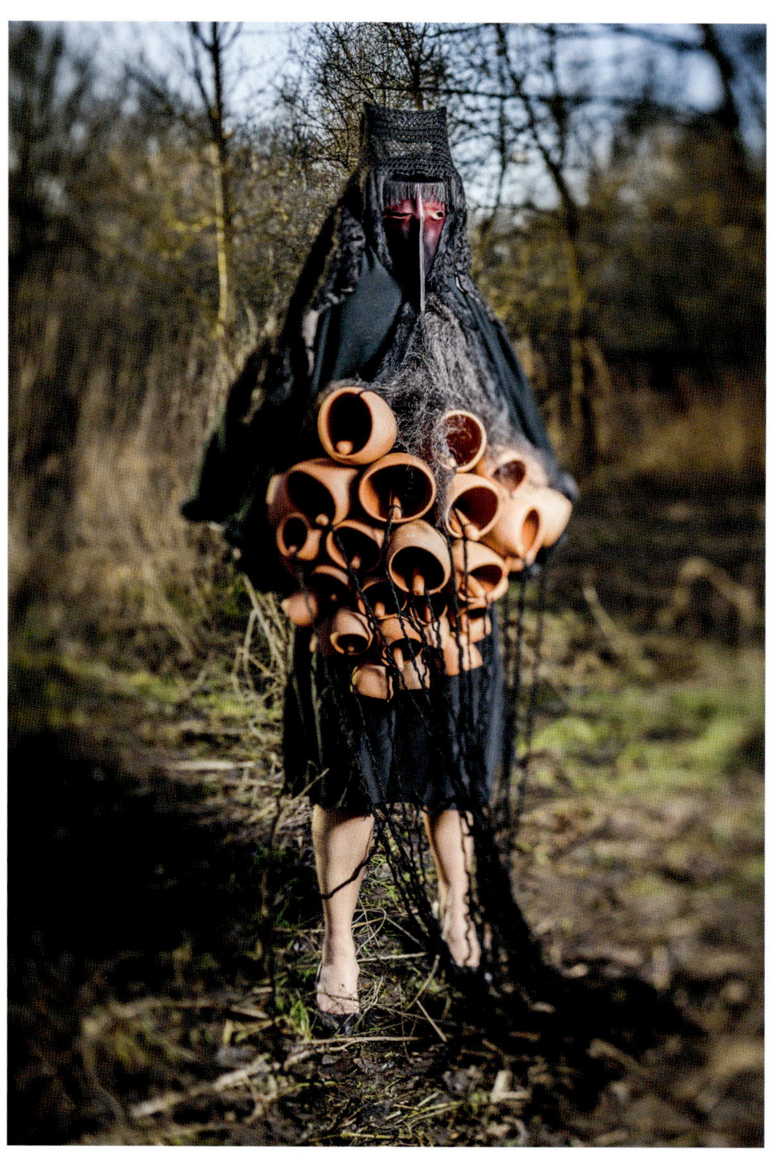

Pierre Redon
Femme Cloche, 2015
LES SOEURS GRÉES

Shuhei Nakamura →
Pass By, 2019
EINSTEIN STUDIO

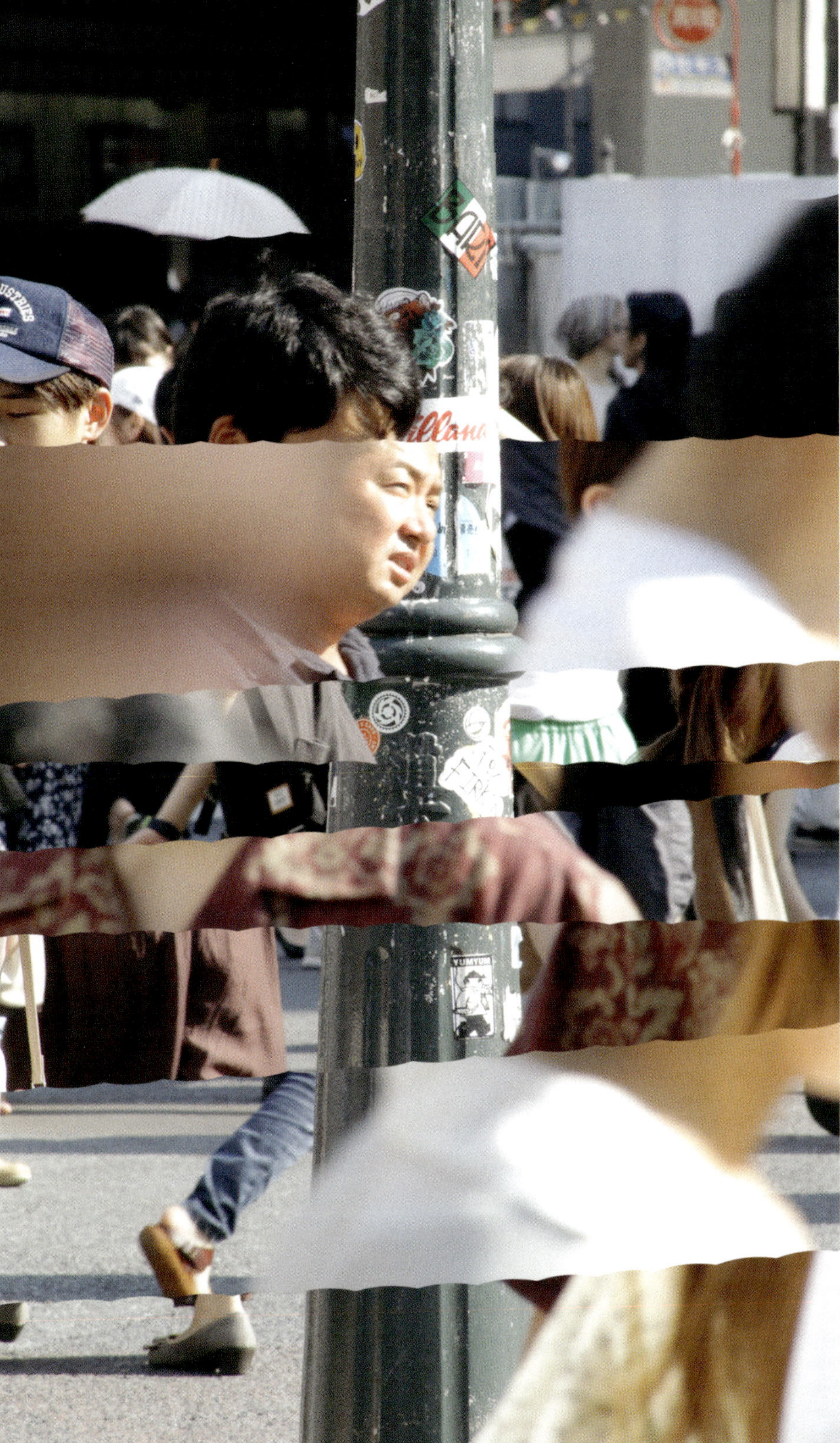
YUMYUM

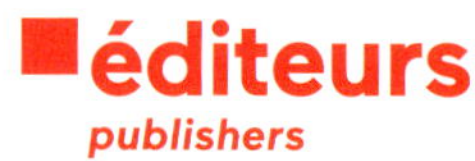

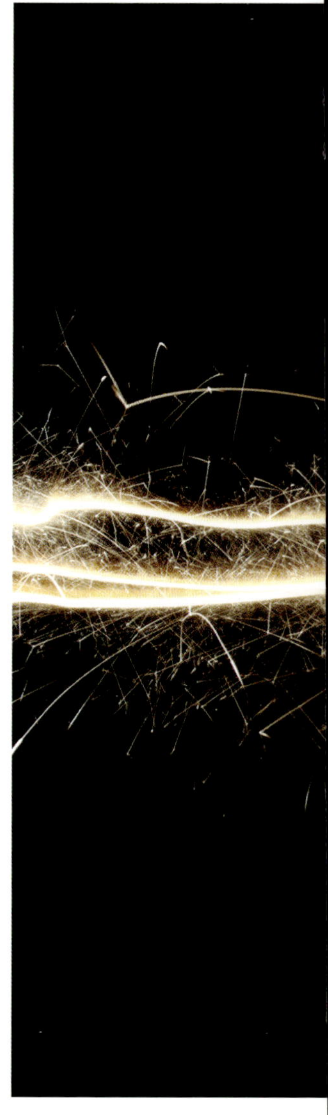

Flore-Aël Surun
Chamane-Lumière, 2015
LES ÉDITIONS DE JUILLET

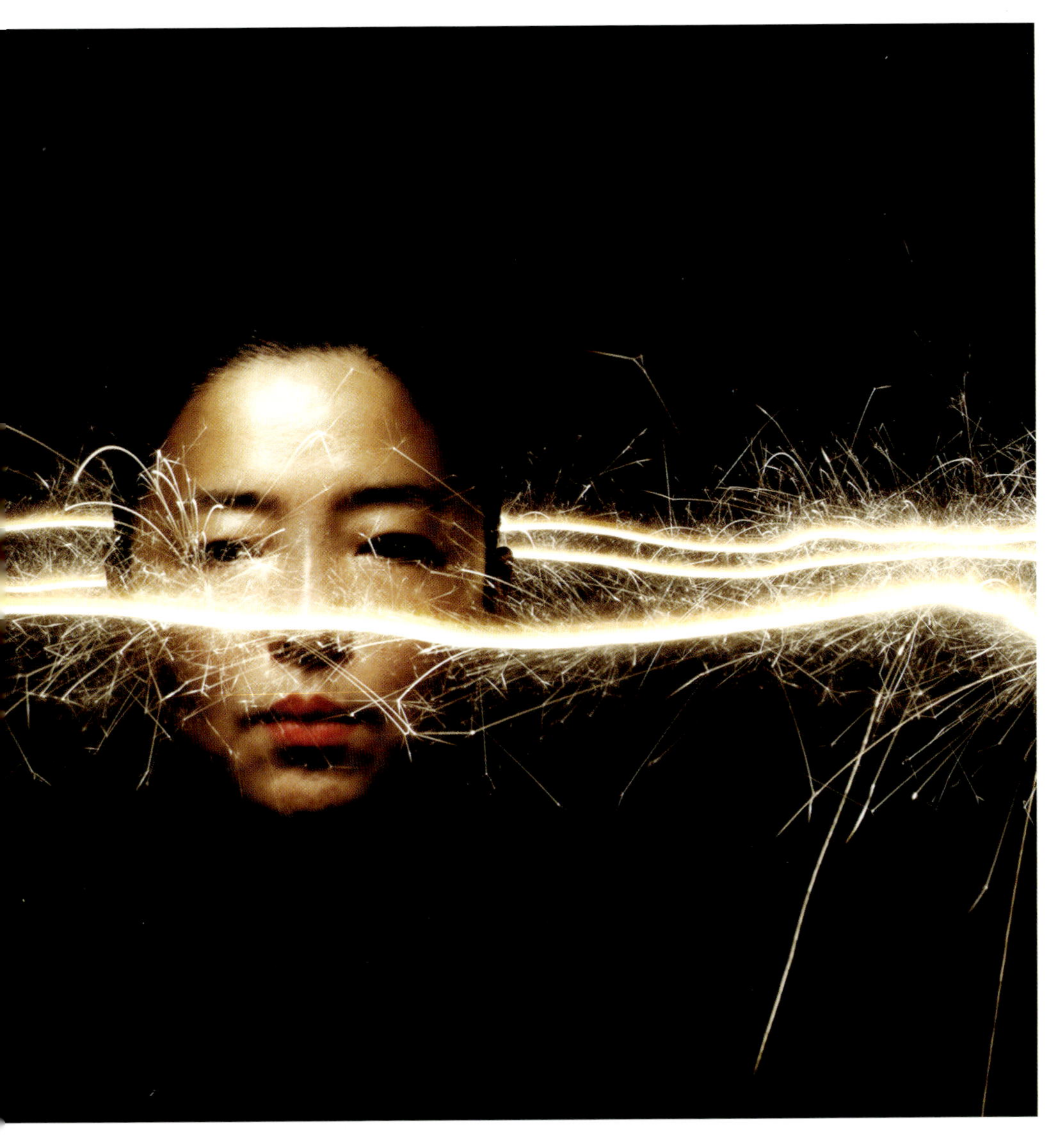

2019

galeries

galleries

Pour sa 8e édition à Paris, fotofever accueille des galeries de 20 pays différents. Venues d'Europe, d'Amérique ou d'Asie, elles présentent un panorama de la photographie contemporaine avec 200 artistes émergents, dont plus de 40 solos shows notamment dans la section dédiée La Ruche. Une occasion unique de communiquer avec des galeries dont les programmes d'exposition démontrent une forte prédilection pour **l'audace et la créativité**.

*For its 8th edition in Paris, fotofever welcomes galleries from 20 different countries. Coming from Europe, America and Asia, they present the latest landscape of contemporary photography with 200 emerging artists, including over 40 solo shows notably in the dedicated section The Hive. A unique opportunity to connect with galleries with an **exciting artistic program**.*

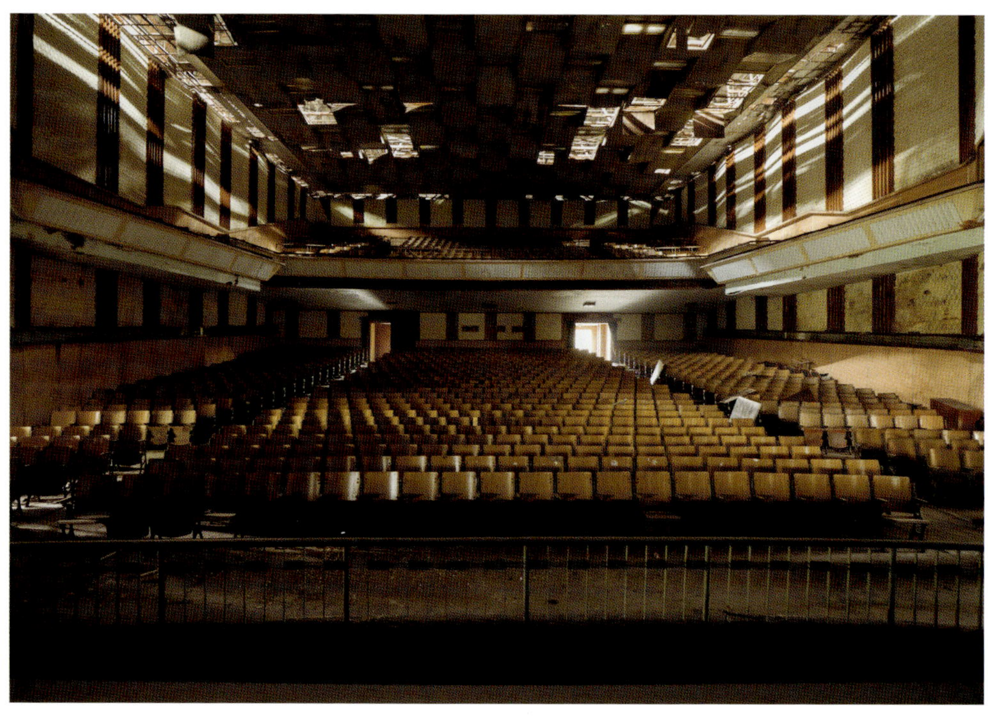

Mingxi Fan
Theatre I, 2018
24P STUDIO

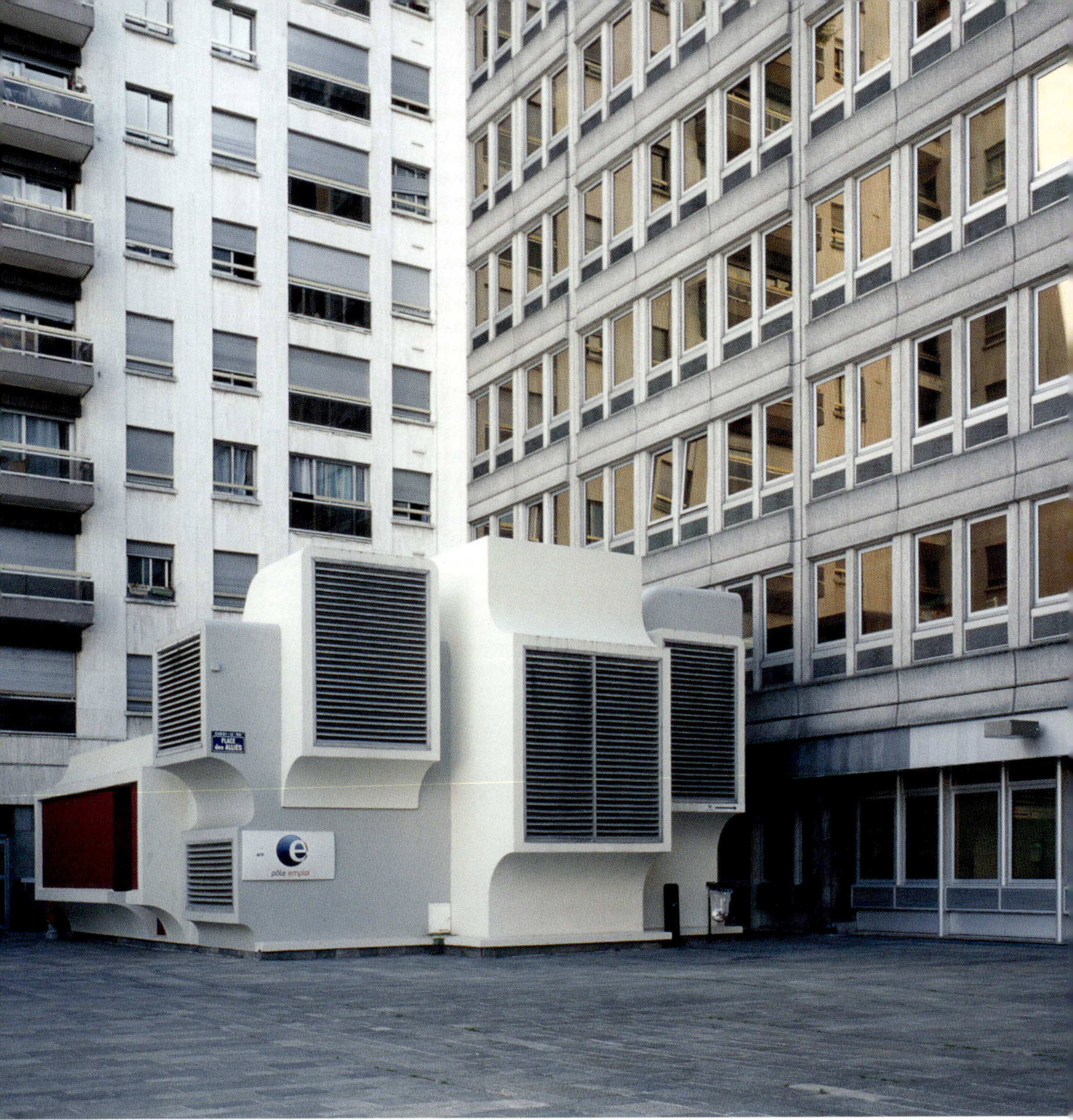

Nanjing Tang
Sans Titre, 2019
24P STUDIO

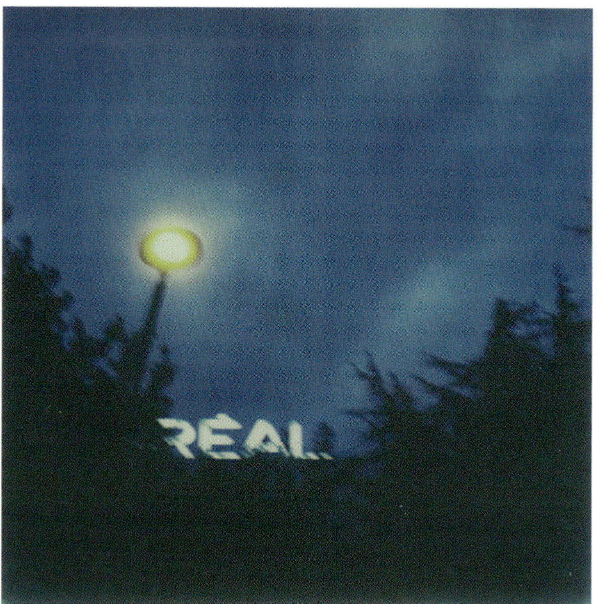

Maxime Touratier
L'Orèal
55BELLECHASSE

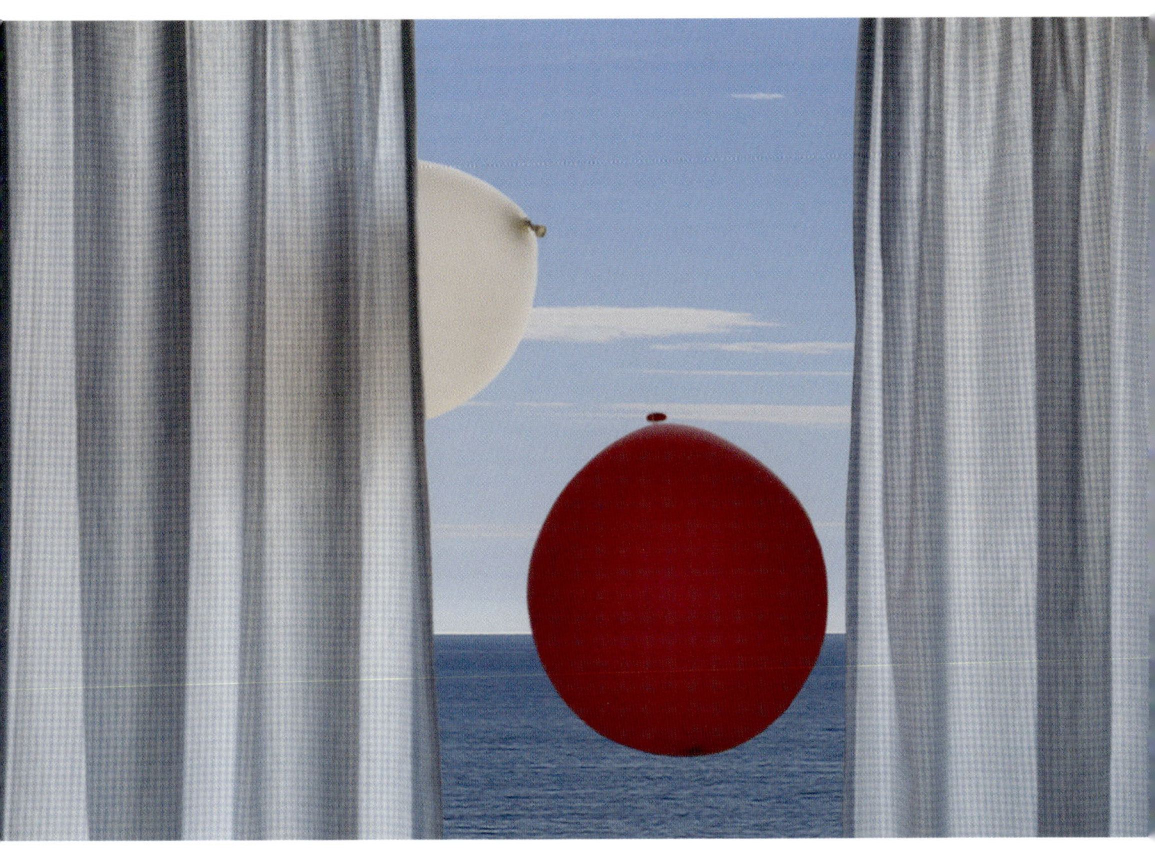

Niloufar Banisadr
Hommage à Magritte No 4, 2017
55BELLECHASSE

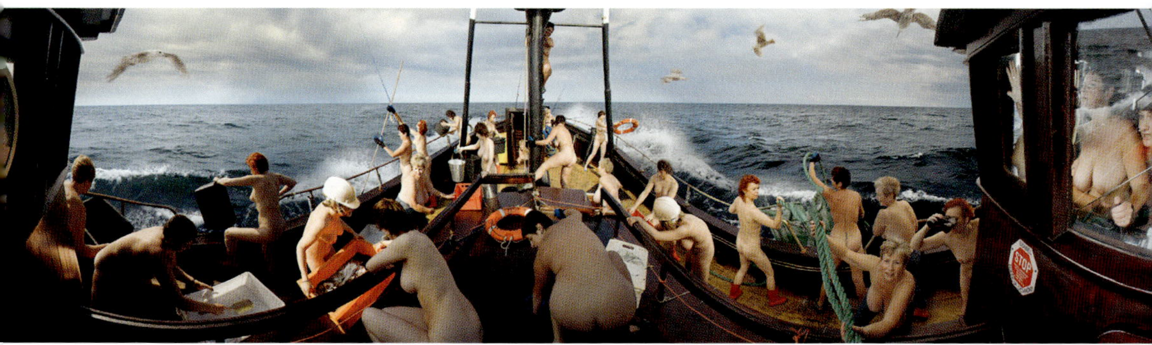

Łódź Kaliska Art Group
Fisherman, 2008
6x7 GALLERY

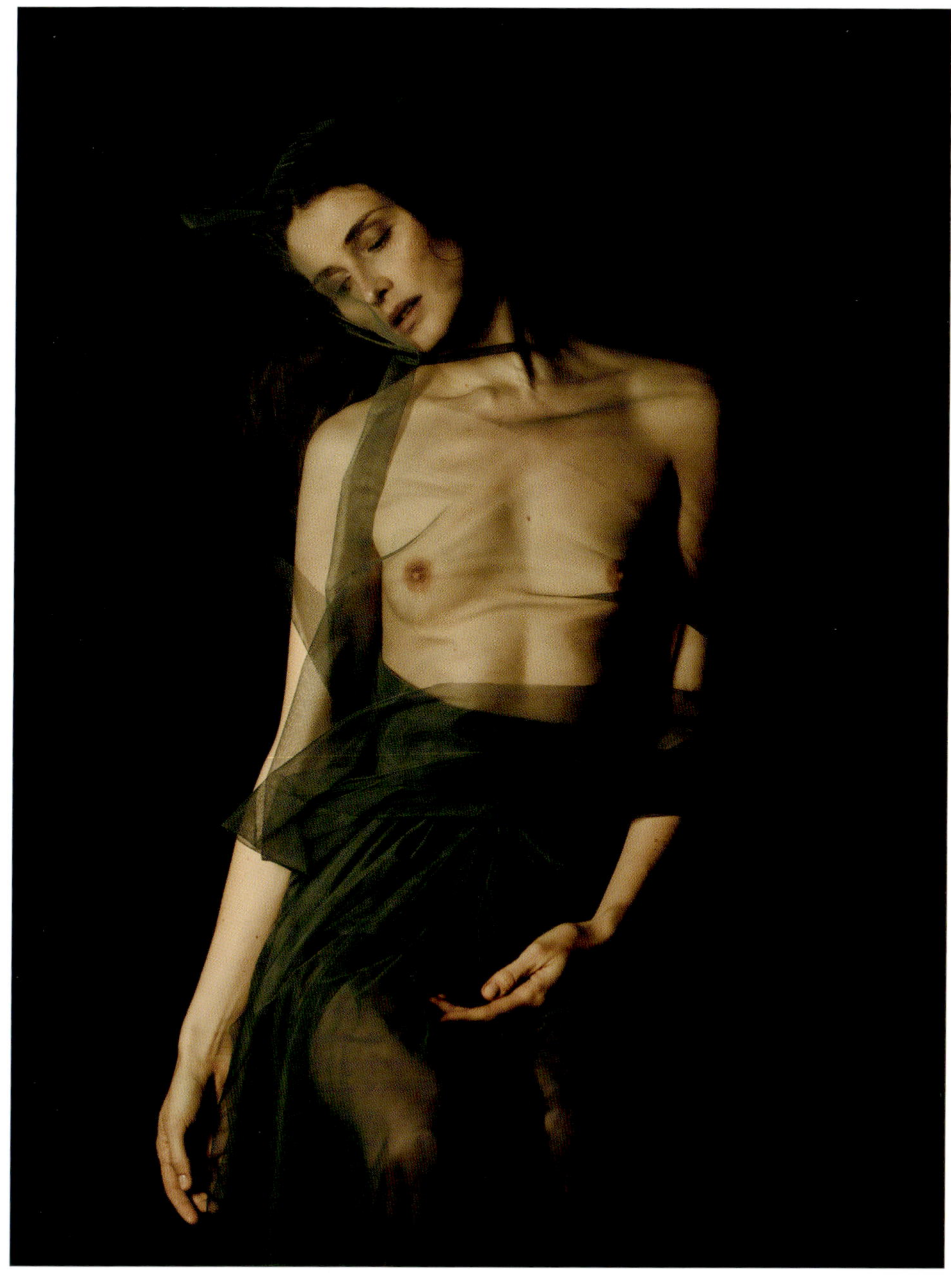

Sonia Szóstak
Allegory, 2016
6x7 GALLERY

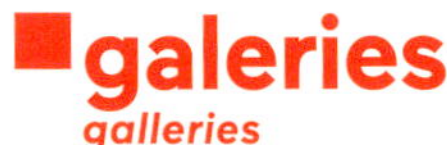

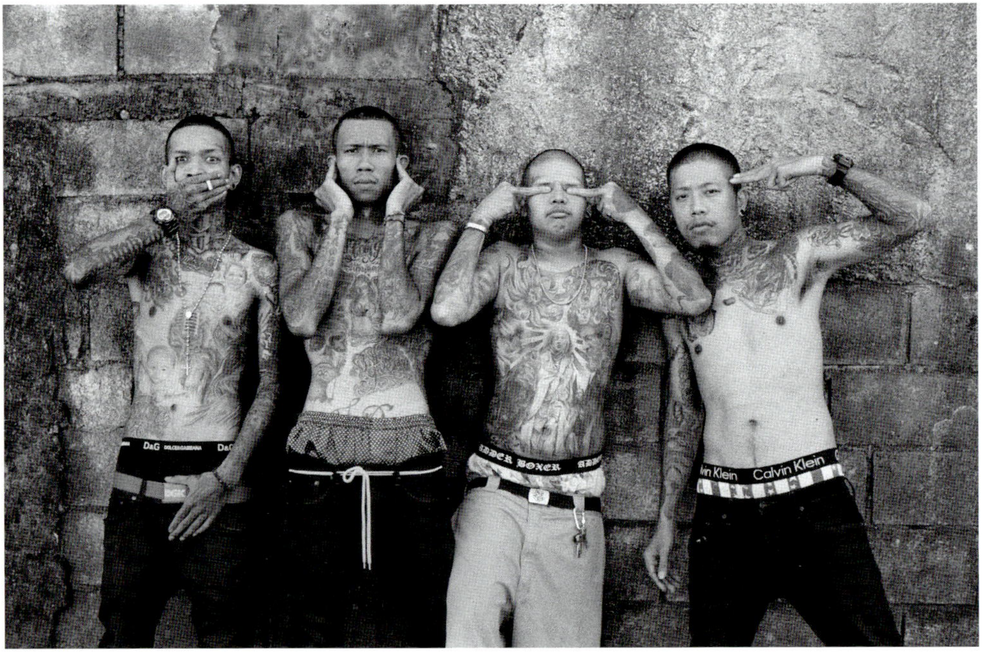

Samuel Cueto
4 Boys, 2014
193 GALLERY

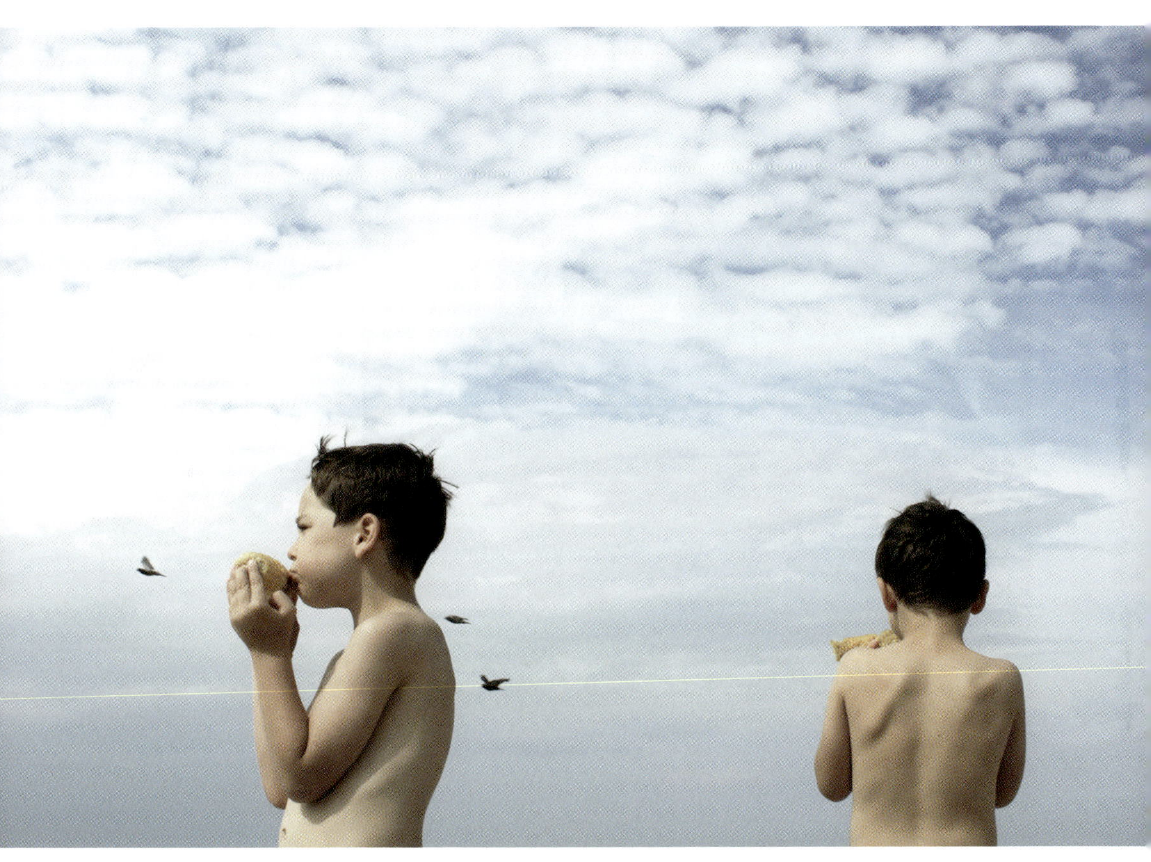

Beata Kilichowska
Twins with corn, 2017-2019
AJTNER FINE ART GALLERY

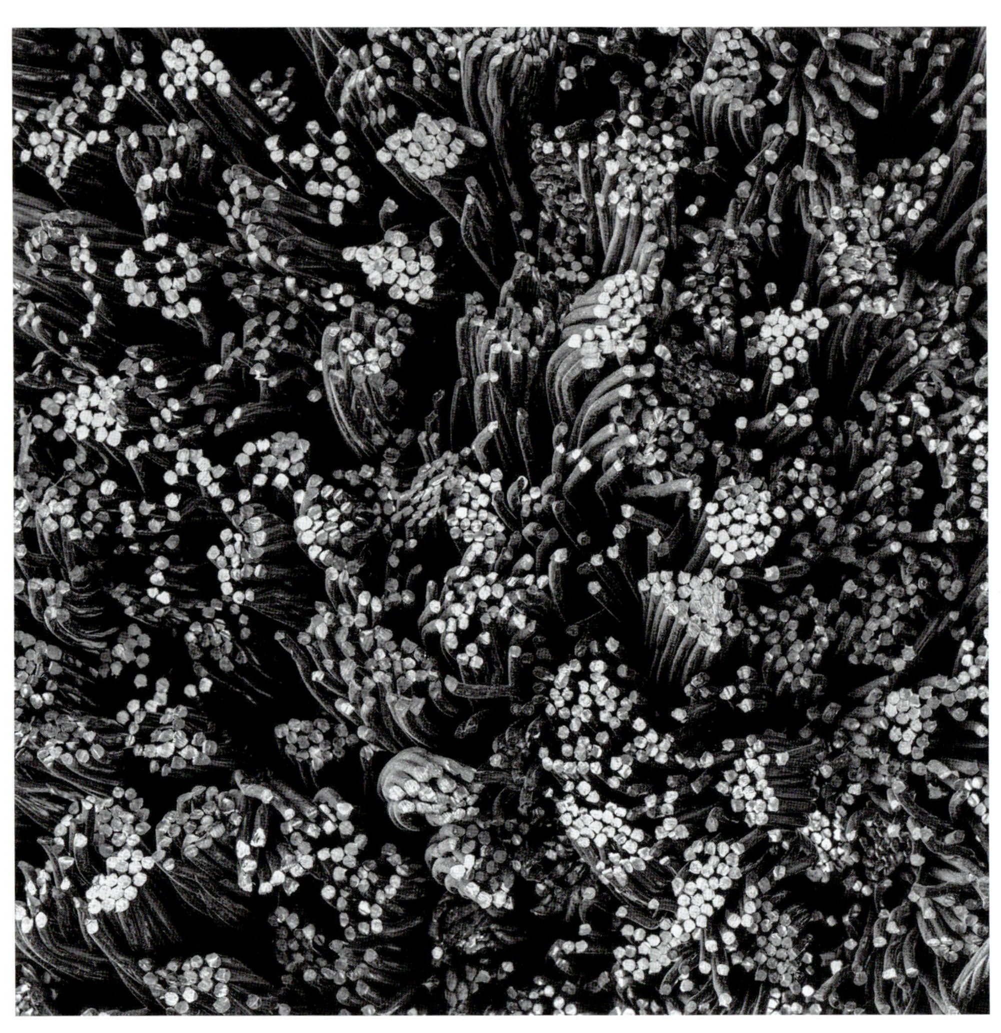

Haejung Park
Steel Light, #05, 2006
AN INC.

Seunghan Kim
SHAPE #9, 2011
AN INC.

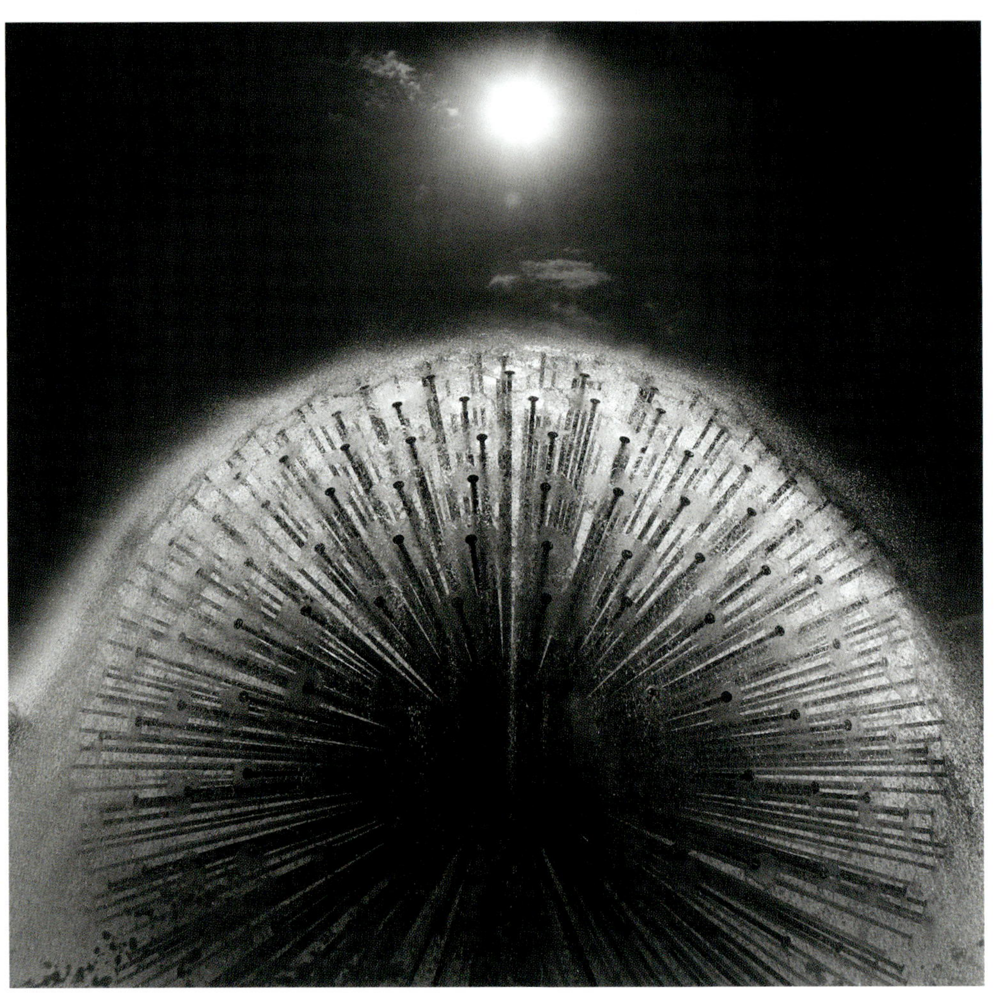

Heesang Lee
#05, Osaka, 1989
AN INC.

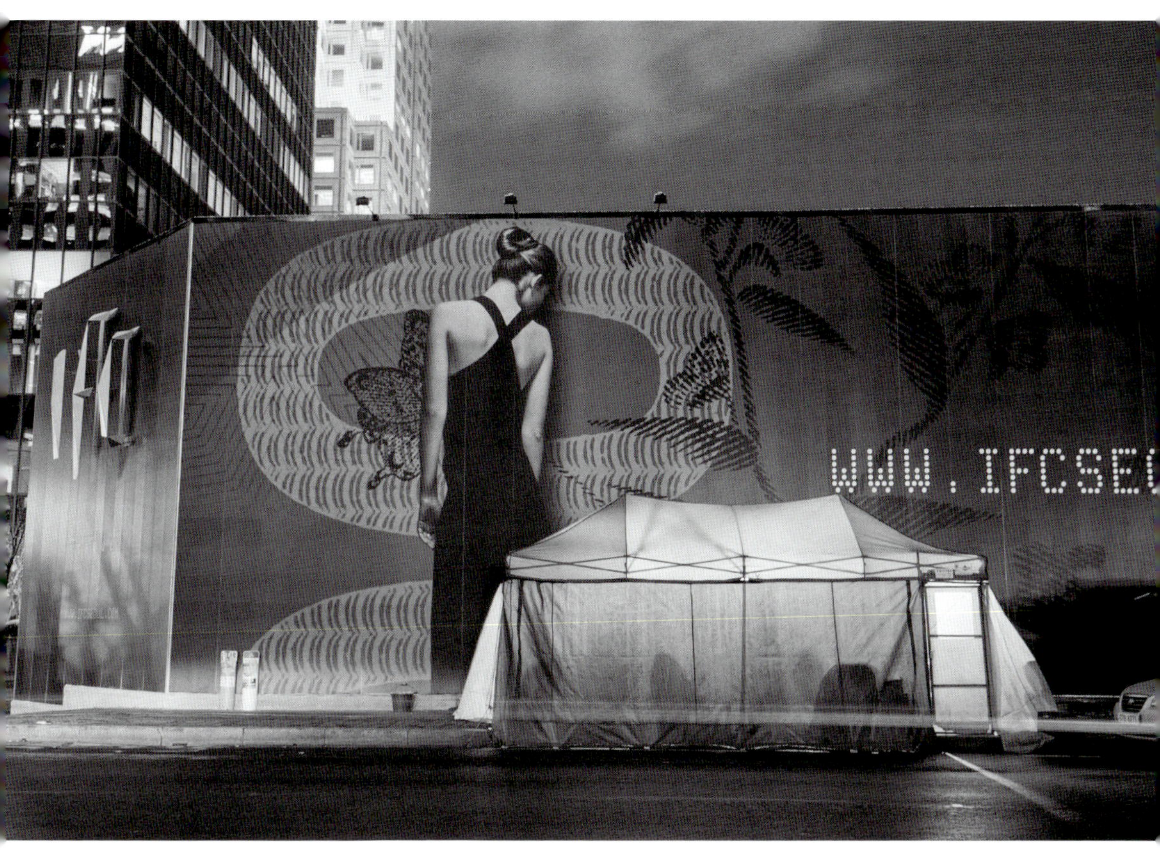

Suna Yu
#02, Yeoeuido, 2007
AN INC.

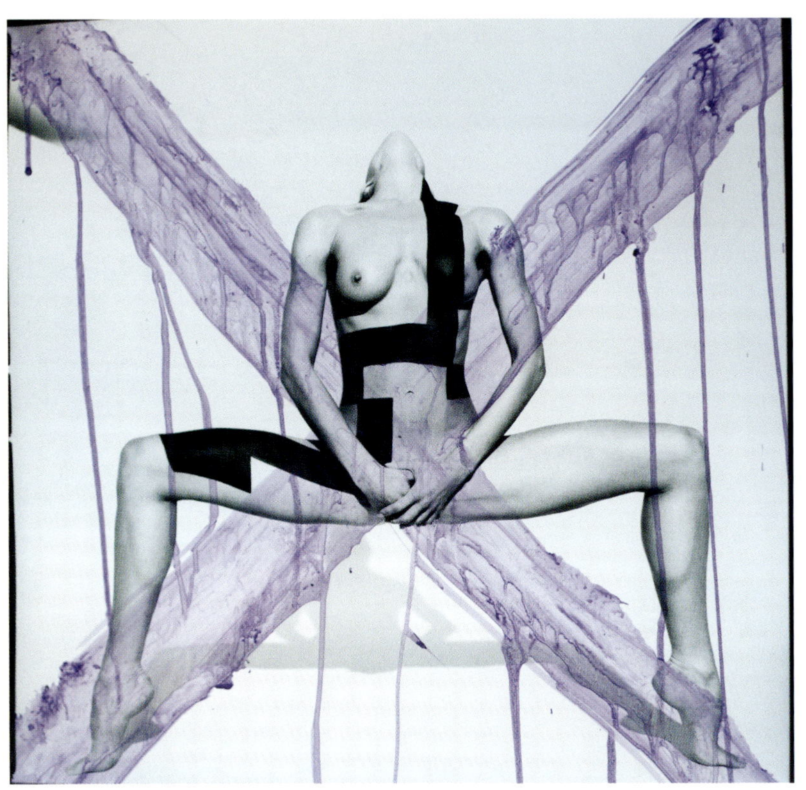

Ewa-Mari Johansson
Purple Birth, 2011
ALL YOU CAN ART

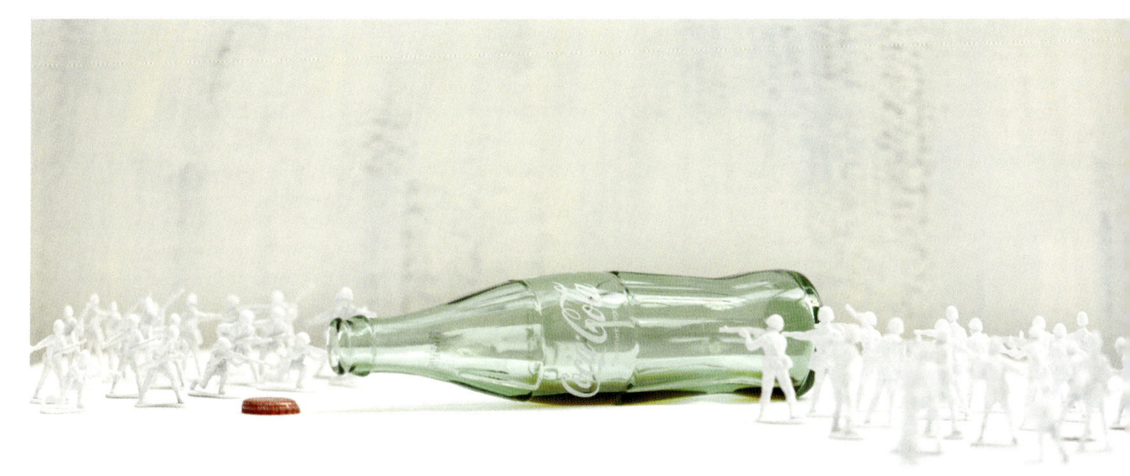

Anna Lim
Romantic Soldiers #10, 2011
AN INC.

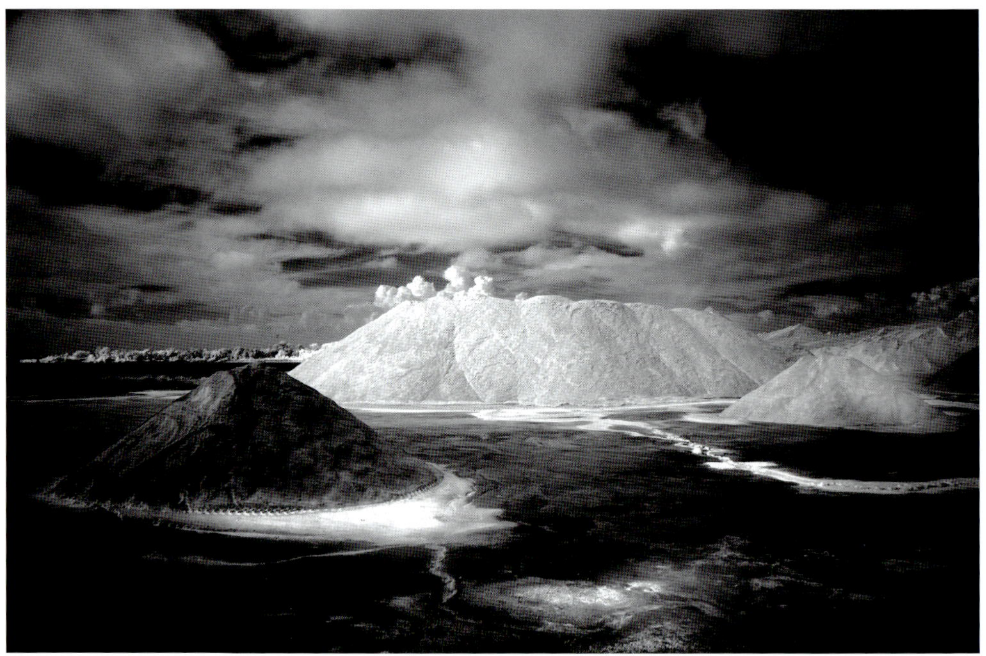

Claudio Argentiero
Paysage, Passage, 2016-2019
ARCHIVIO FOTOGRAFICO ITALIANO

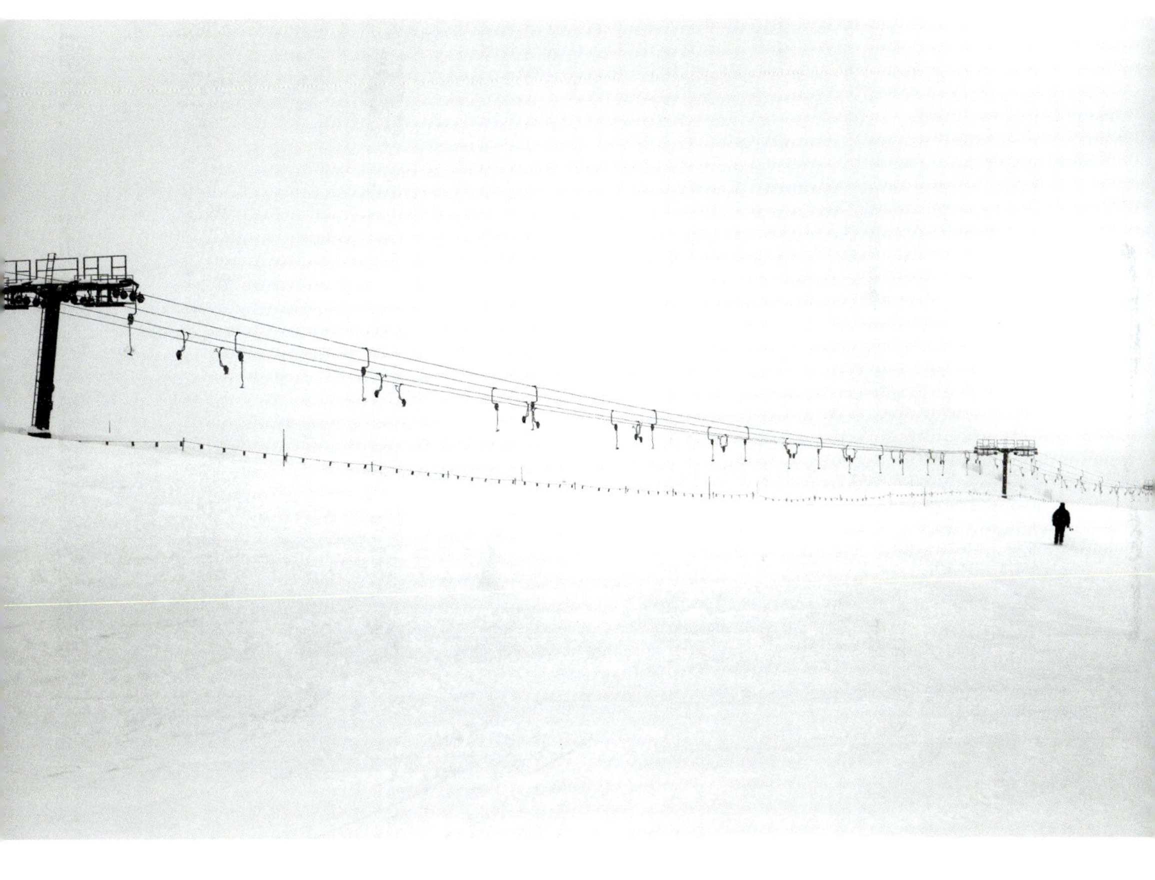

Mario Vidor
Paysage, 2014
ARCHIVIO FOTOGRAFICO ITALIANO

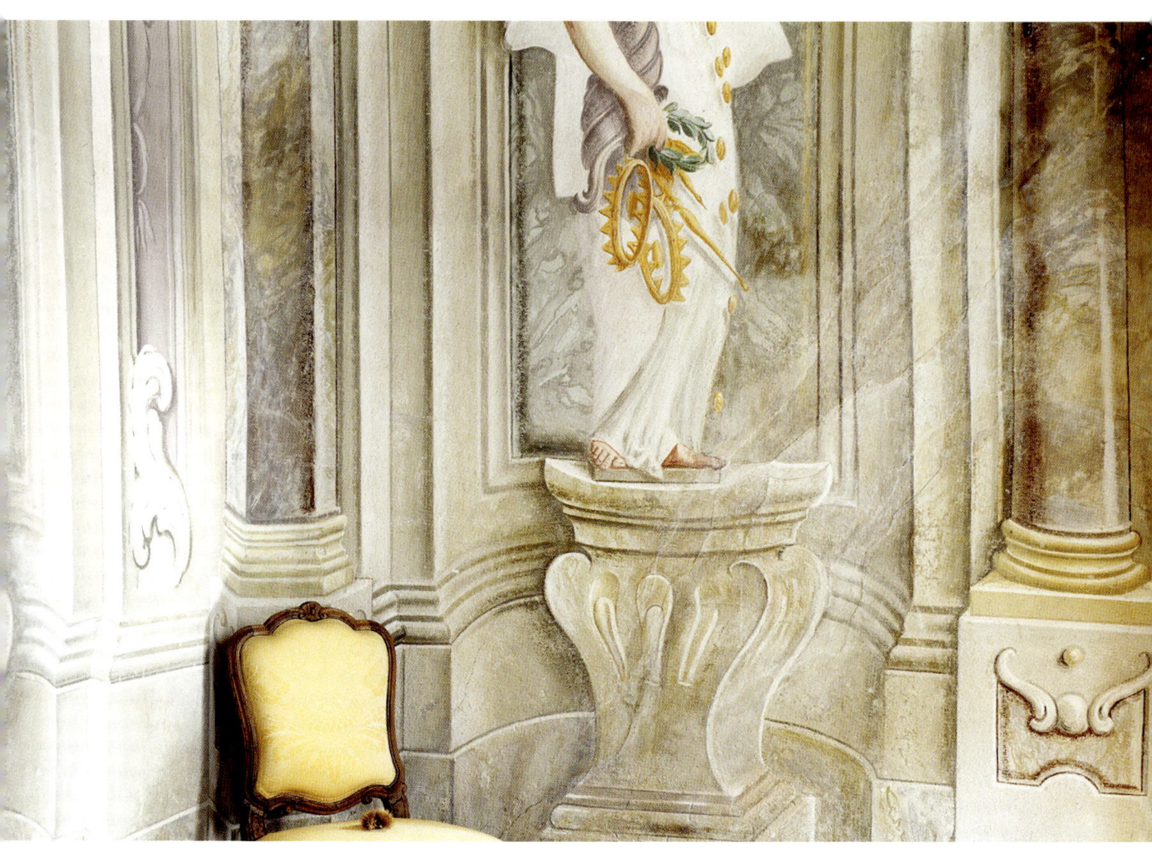

Roberto Bosio
Intérieur, 2018-2019
ARCHIVIO FOTOGRAFICO ITALIANO

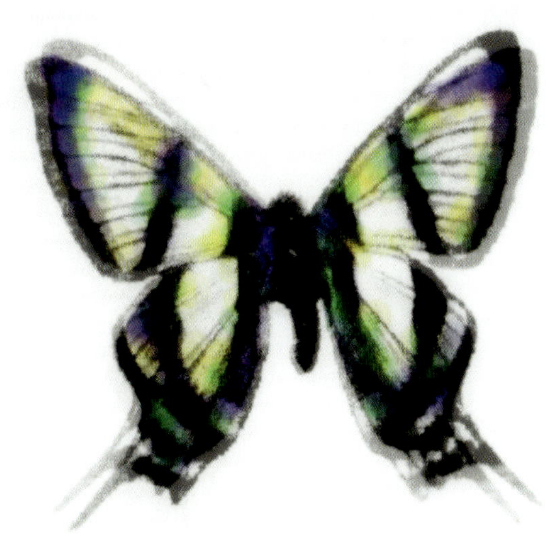

Stefania Ricci
Archetipo farfalla, 2017
ARCHIVIO FOTOGRAFICO ITALIANO

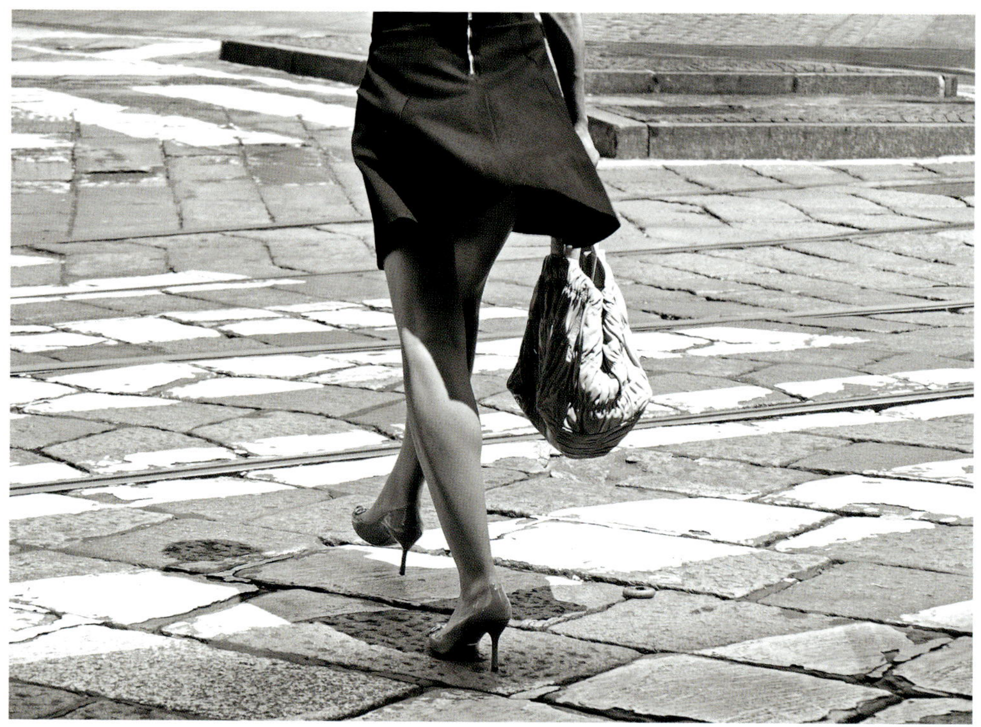

Claudio Montecucco
Inseguendo (Following), 2015
ART D2

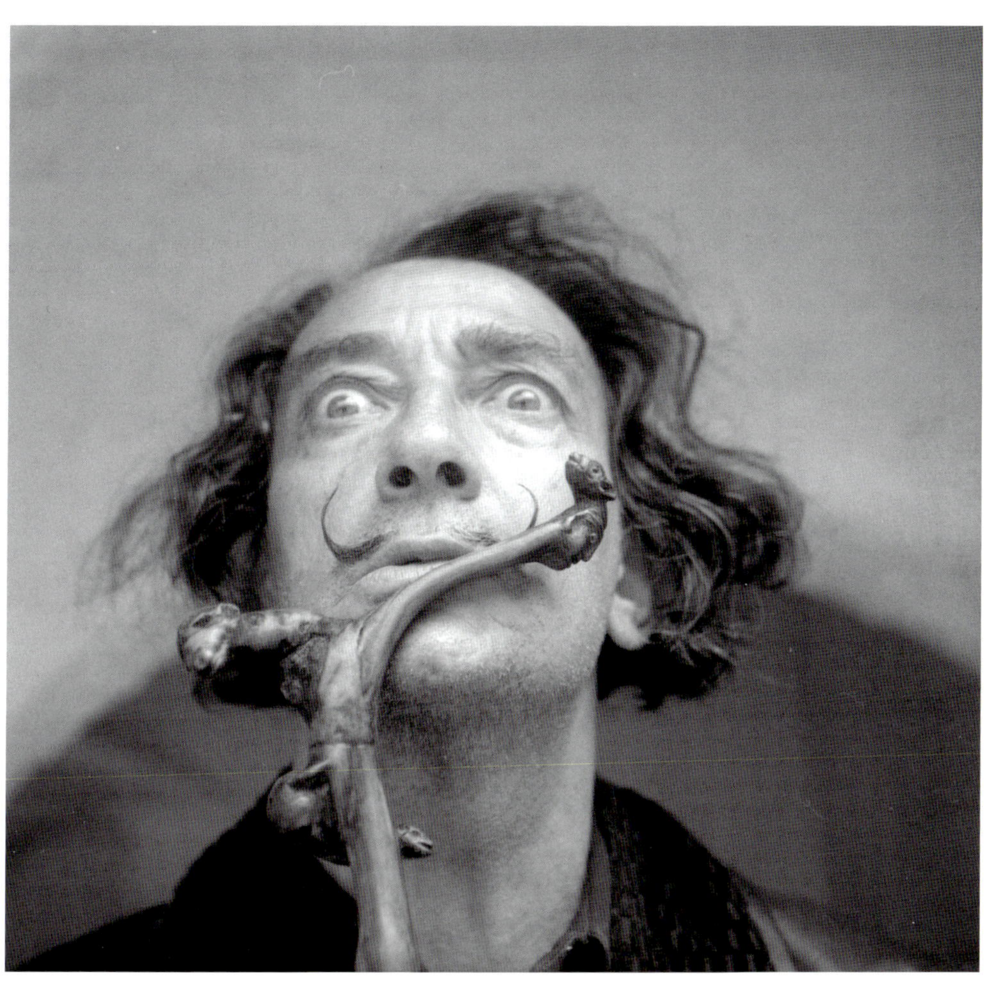

Mimmo Dabbrescia
Salvador Dalì - Port Lligat 1963, 1963-2017
ART D2

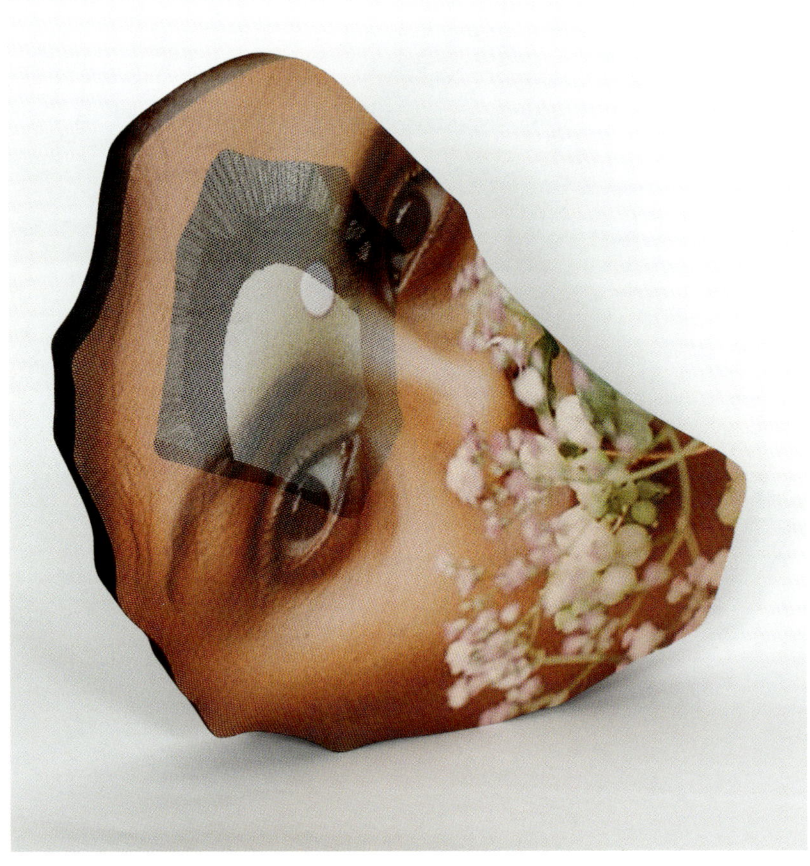

Georgia Clemson
One thing I do remember, 2019
ARTE GLOBALE

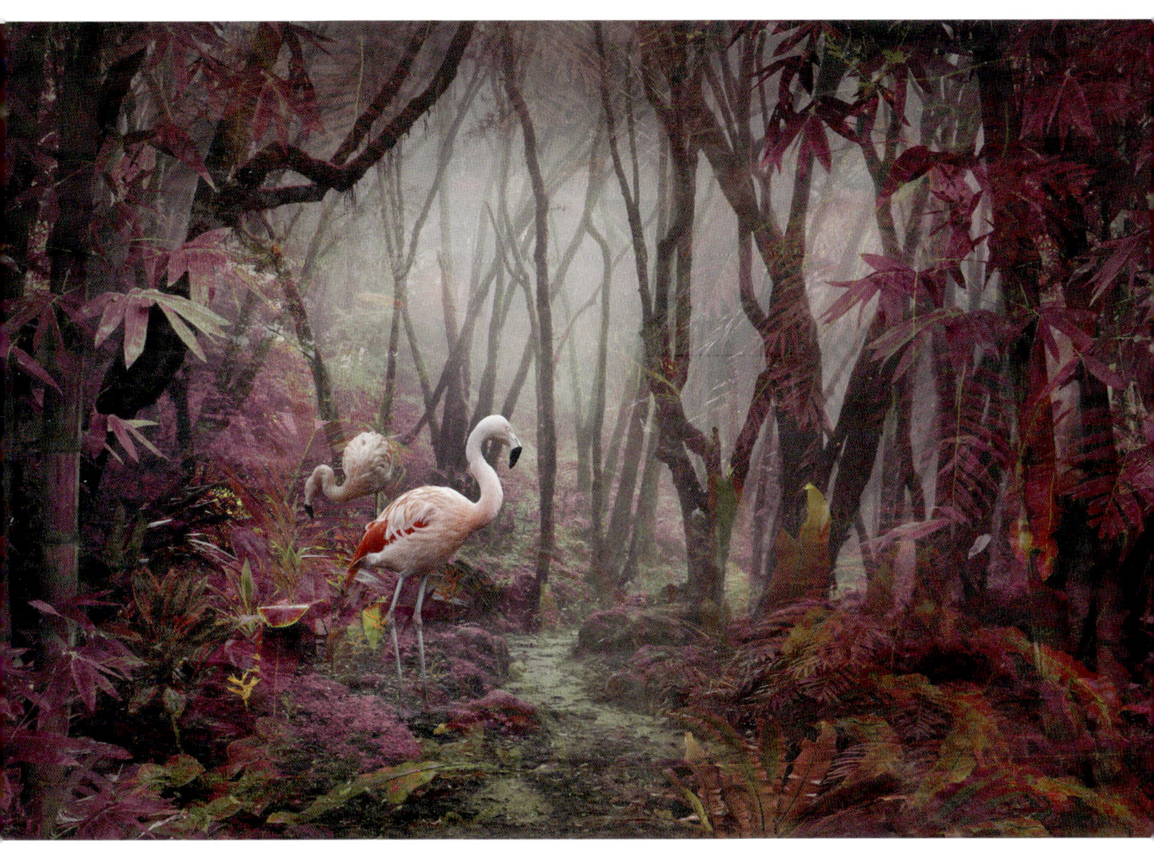

Eriko Kaniwa
Another tropic, 2019
ARTE GLOBALE

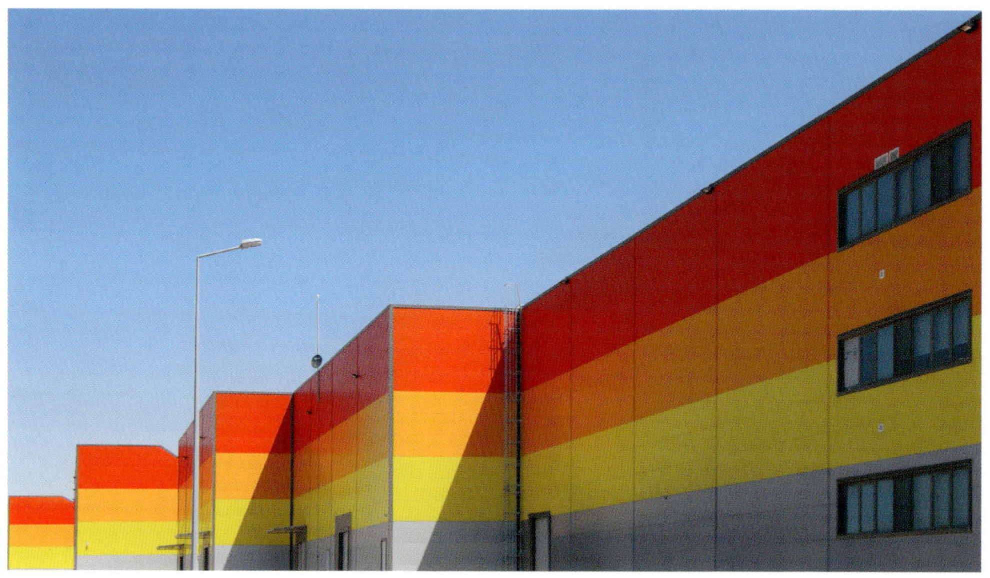

Yener Torun
Train on fire, 2019
ARTE GLOBALE

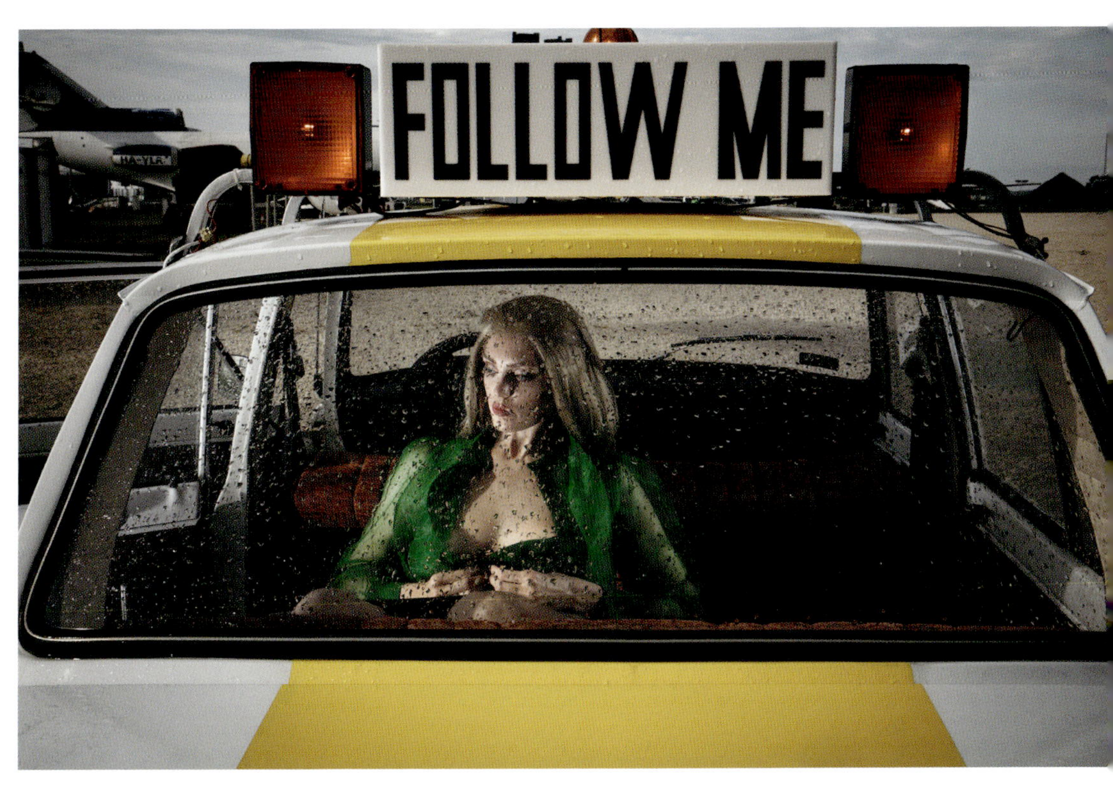

Formento + Formento
Anastasia - Follow me, 2019
ARTYARD GALLERY

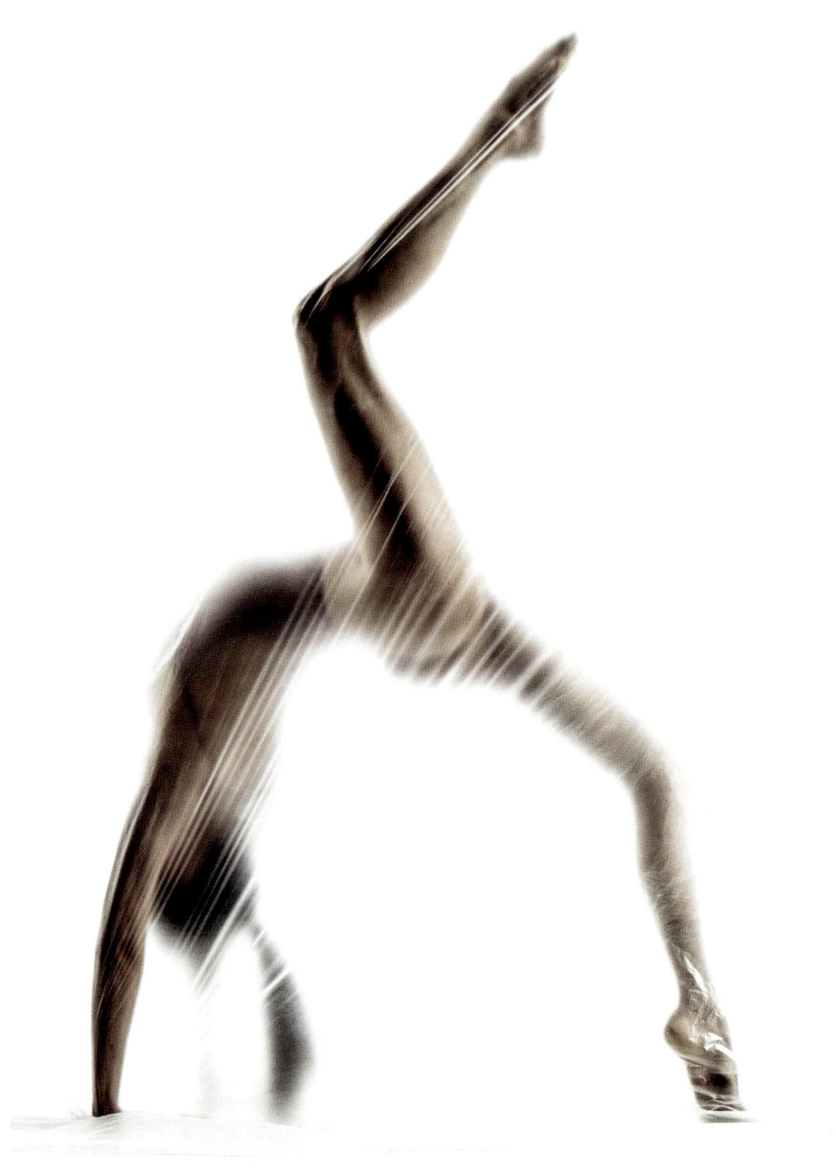

Veronica Lam
Yoga Pose III, 2019
ARTIFY GALLERY

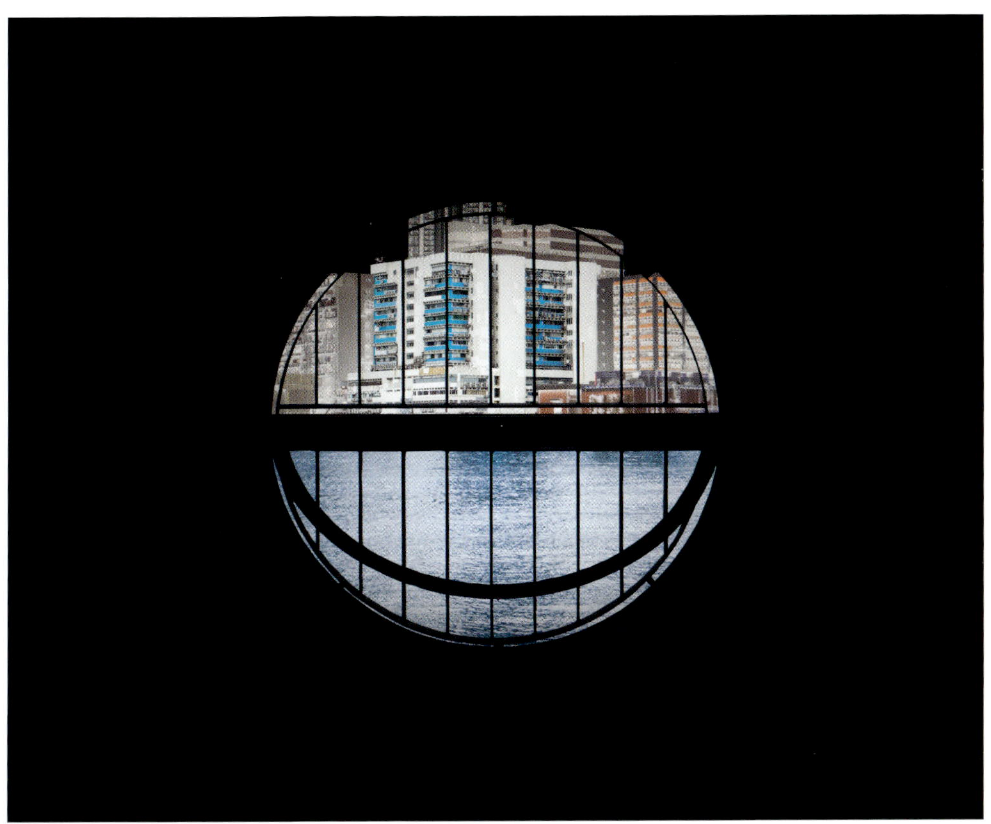

Yick Kan Cheung
No Place Like Home, 2017
ARTIFY GALLERY

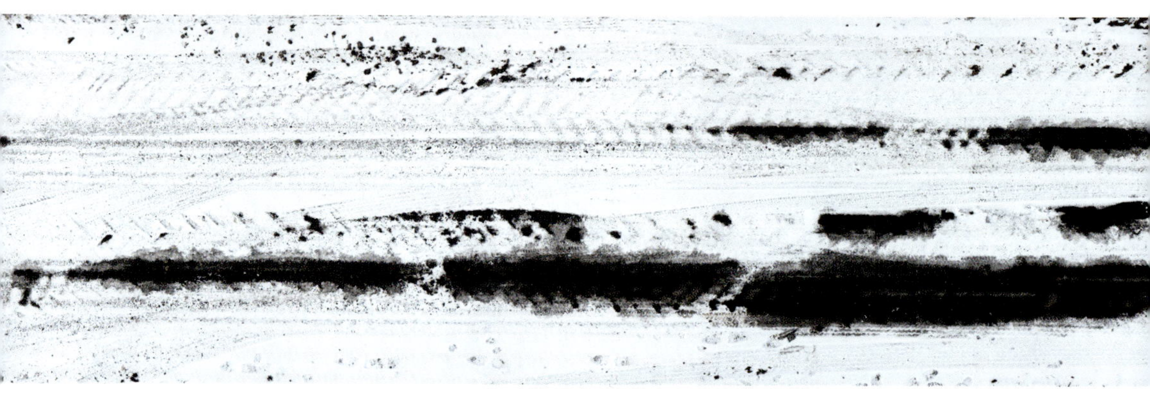

Bence Bakonyi
we're all right here..., 2017
ARTIFY GALLERY

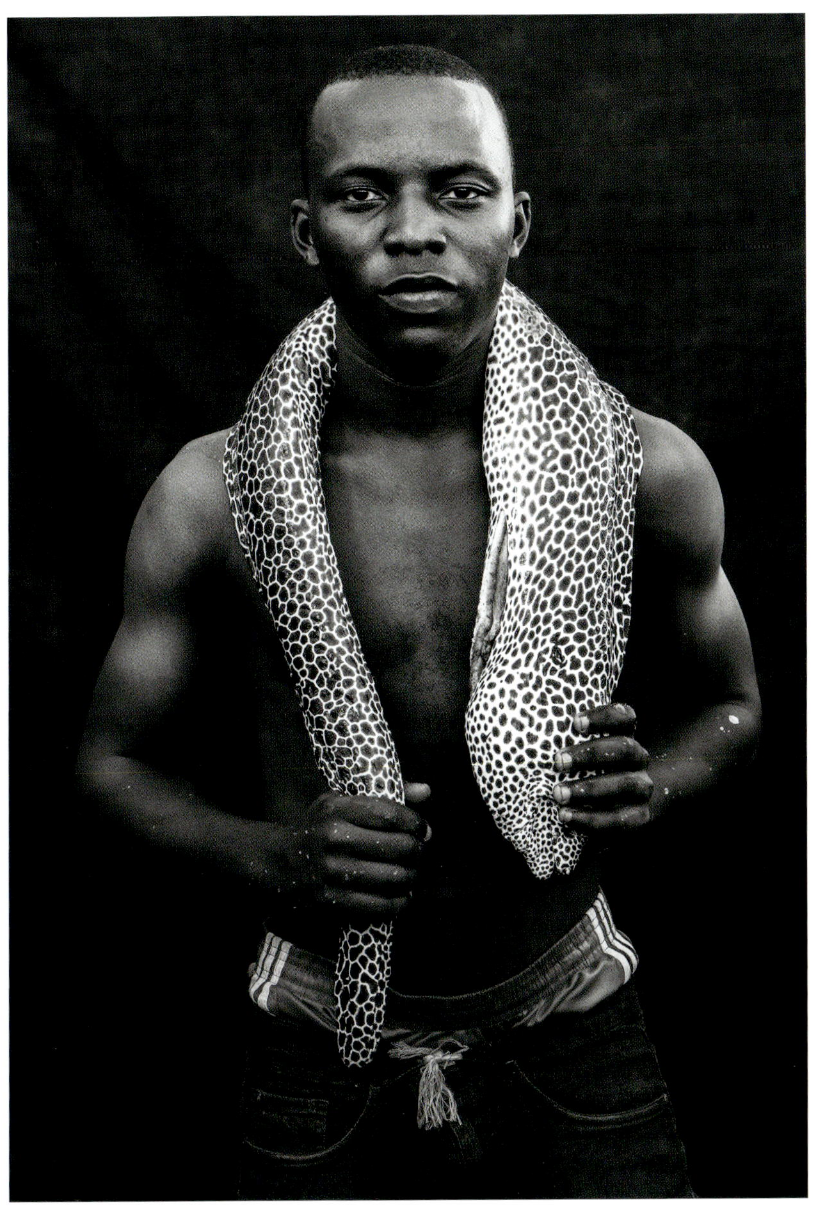

Carlo Mari
Passage through Dar, 2018
CARLO MARI GALLERY

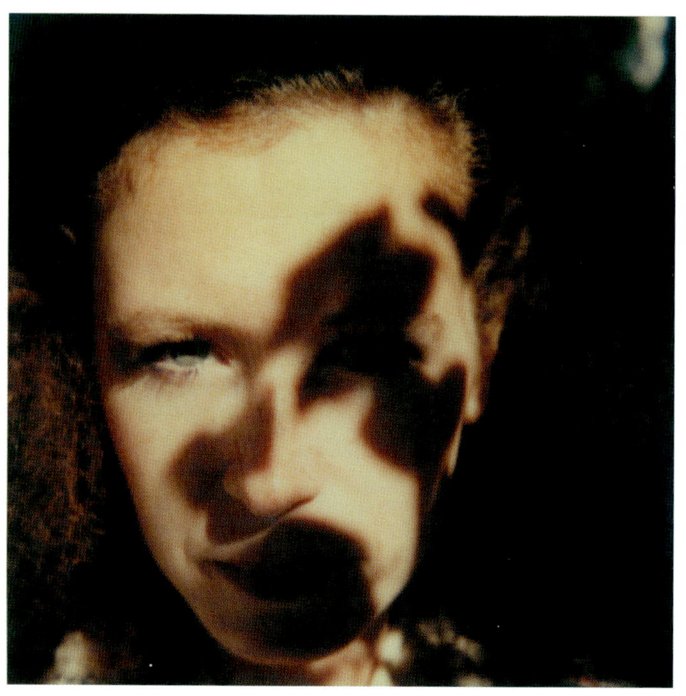

J.K. Lavin
October 30, 1981-2019
WALL SPACE CREATIVE

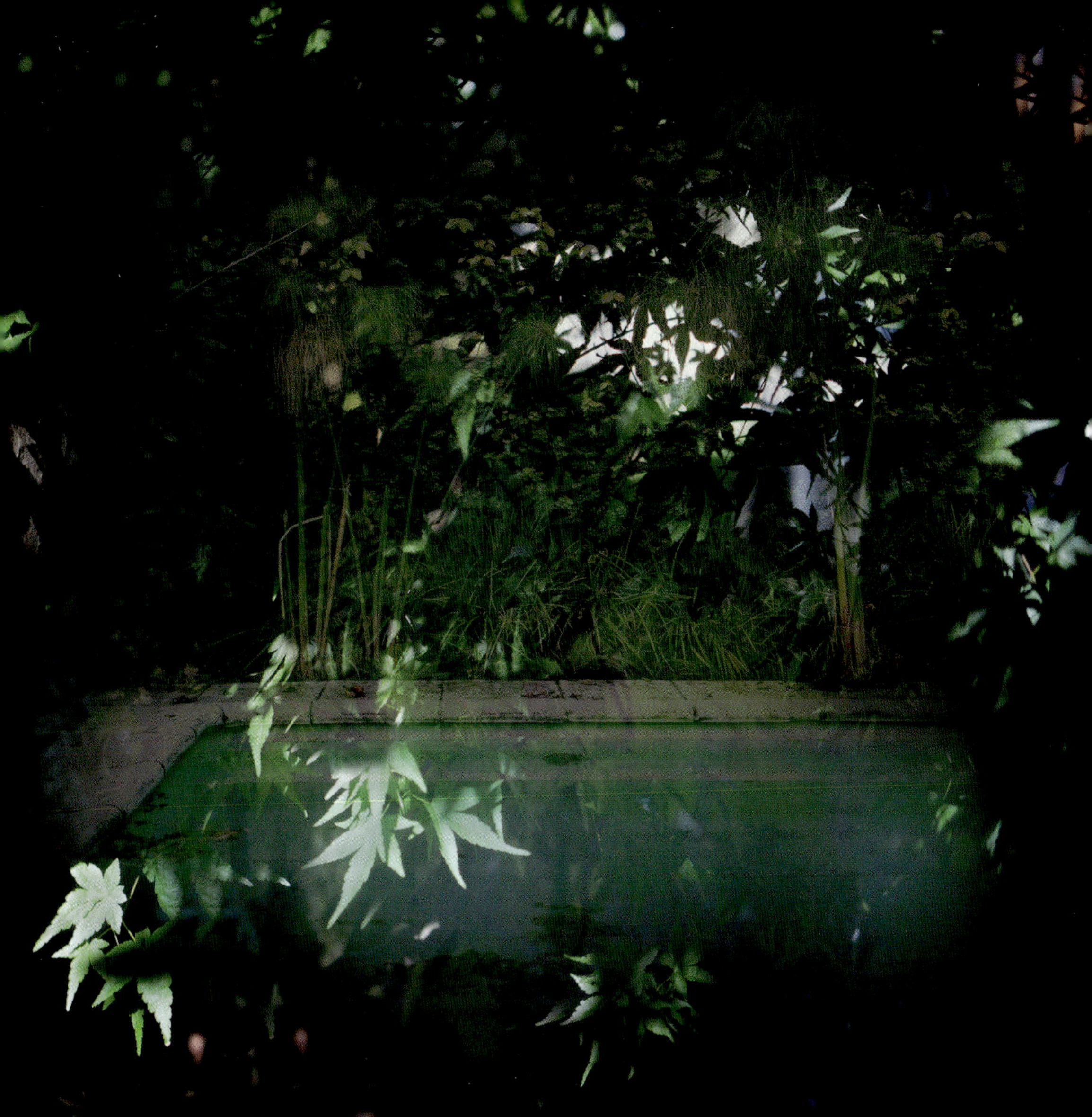

Eleonora Ronconi
Tarde de verano, 2018
WALL SPACE CREATIVE

Marian Crostic
Awakening, 2017
WALL SPACE CREATIVE

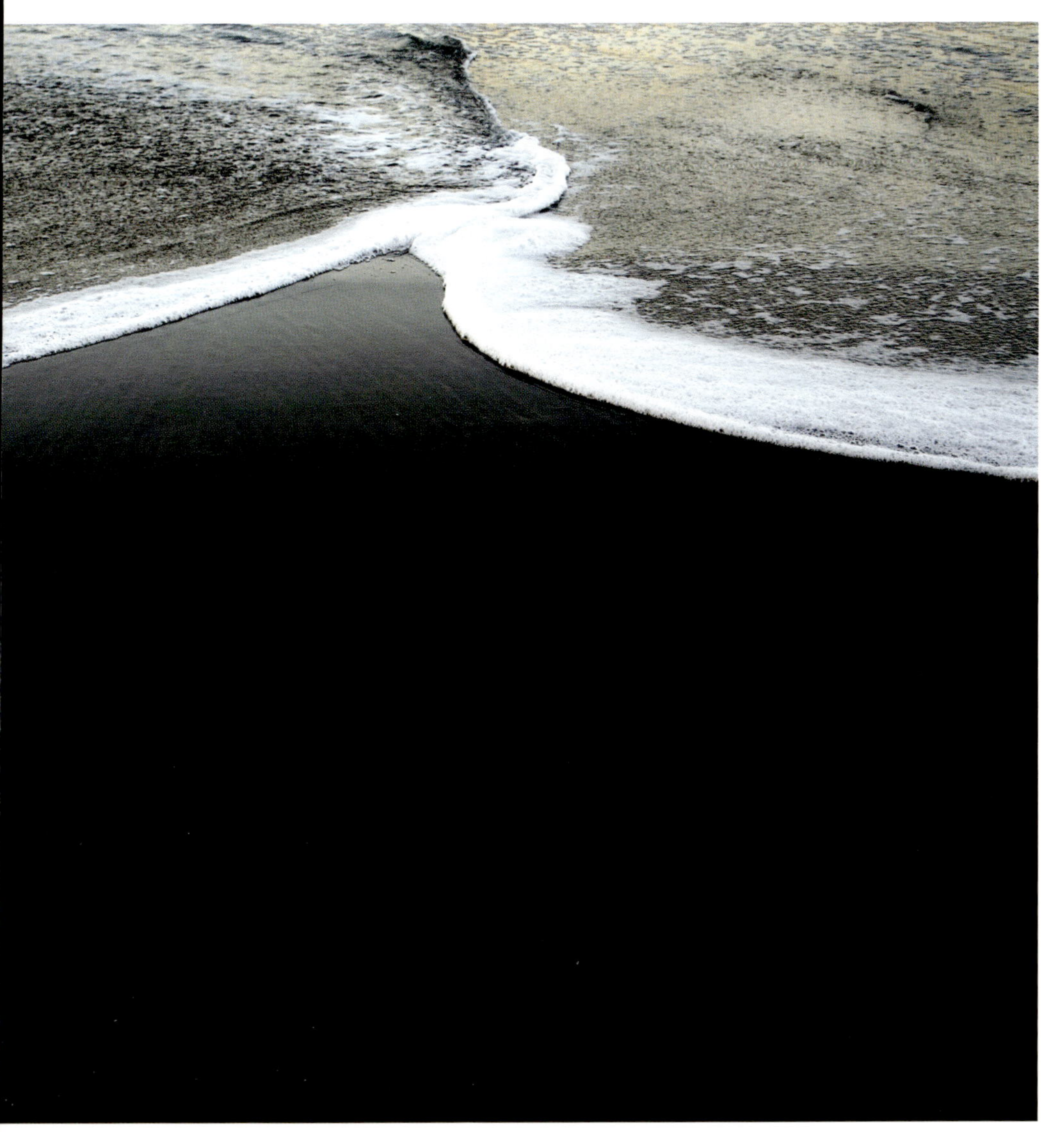

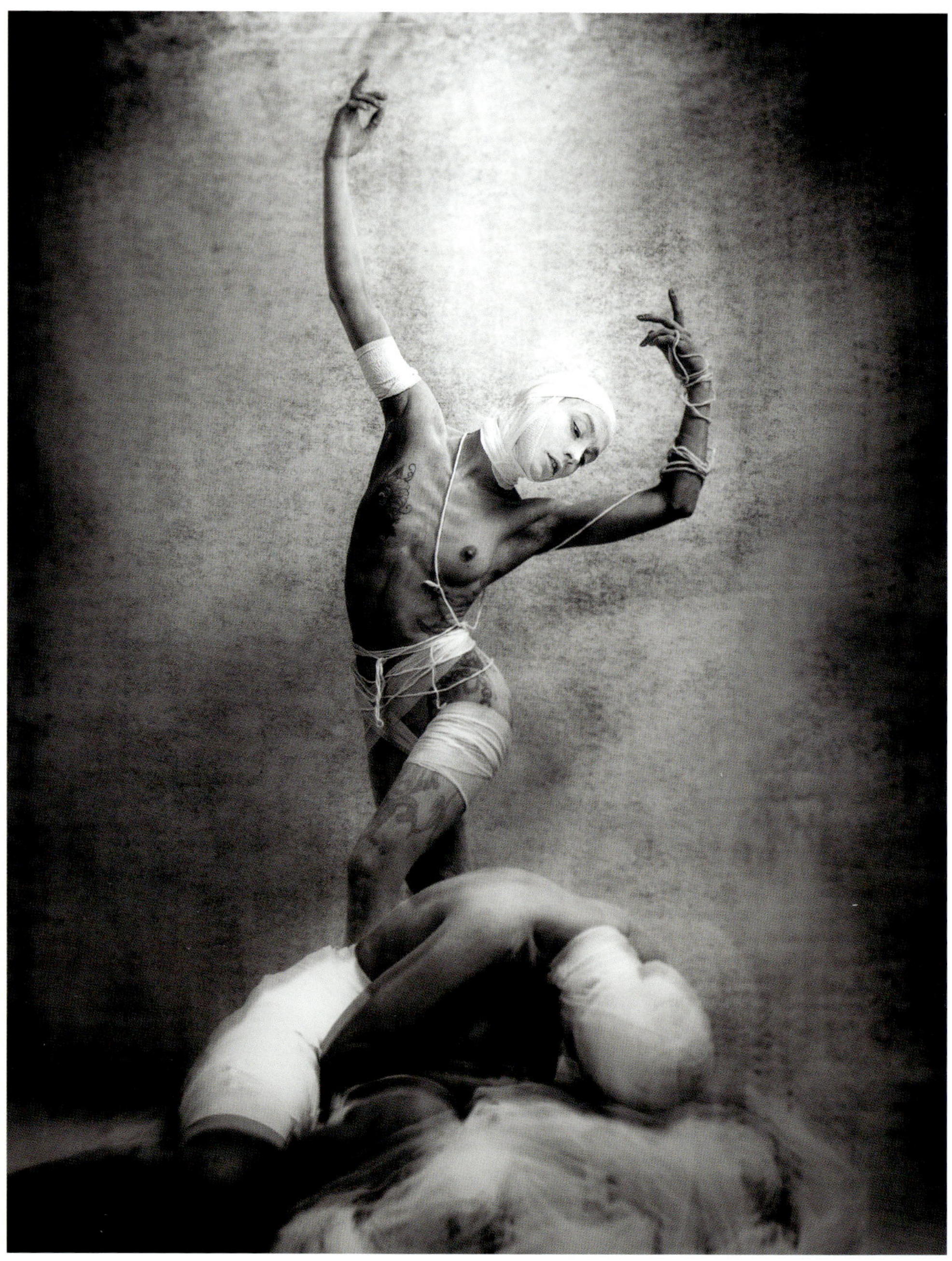

Luciano Corti
Agnus Dei, 2018
CASA REGIS

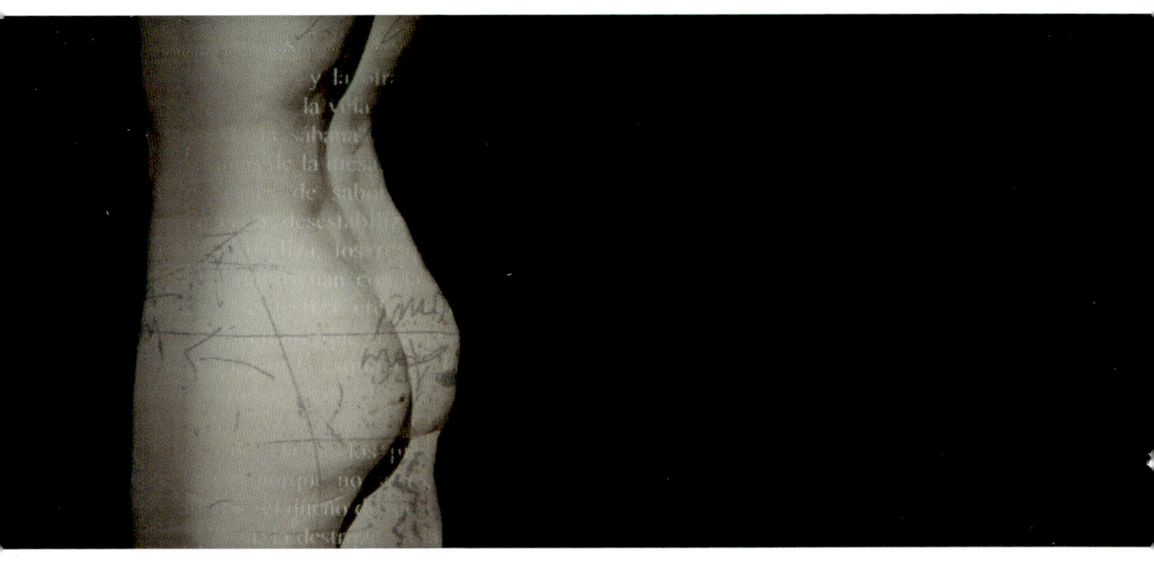

Fabiola Ubani
Deseo, 2000-2019
CASA REGIS

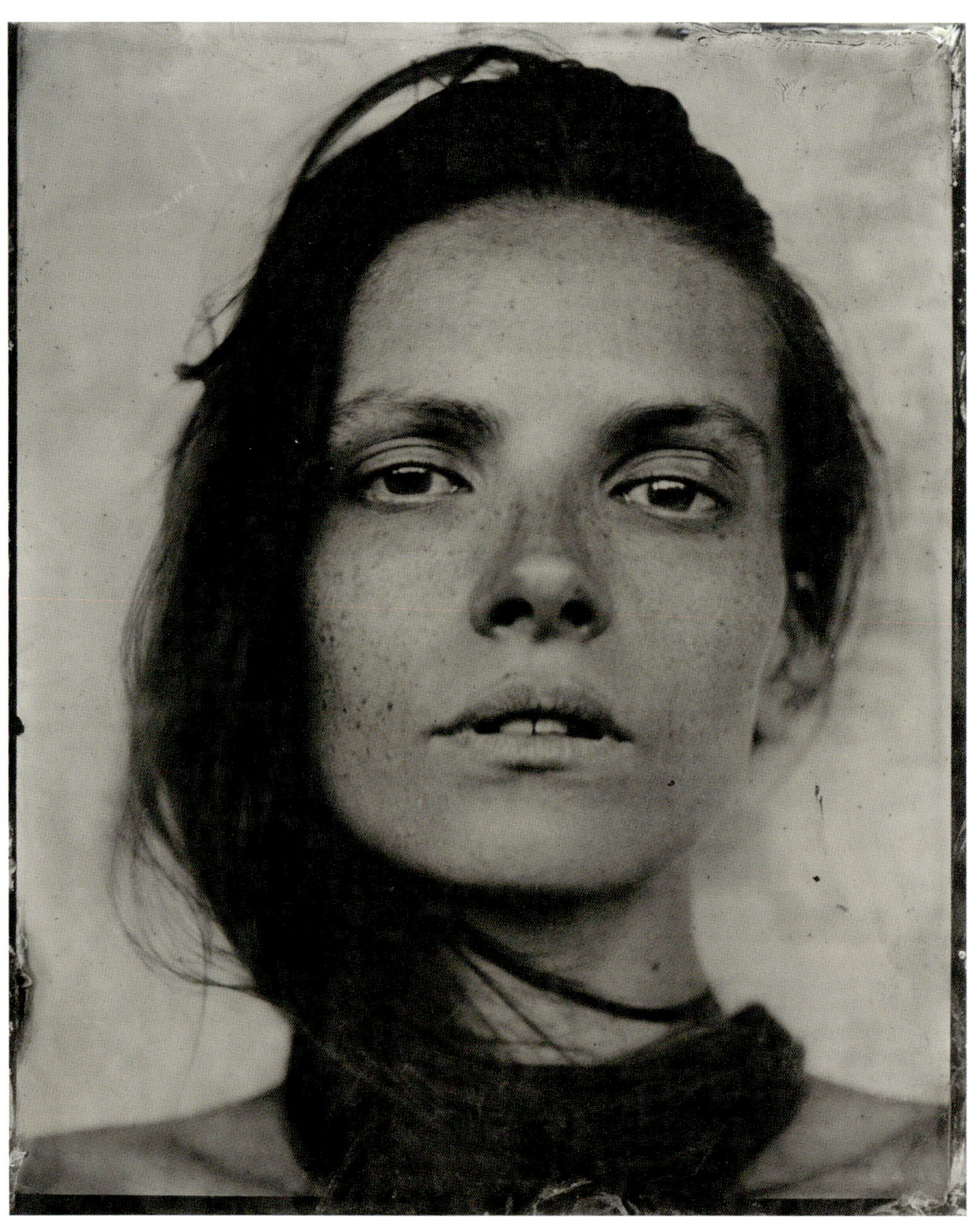

Erica Shires
Nikola, 2019
CASA REGIS

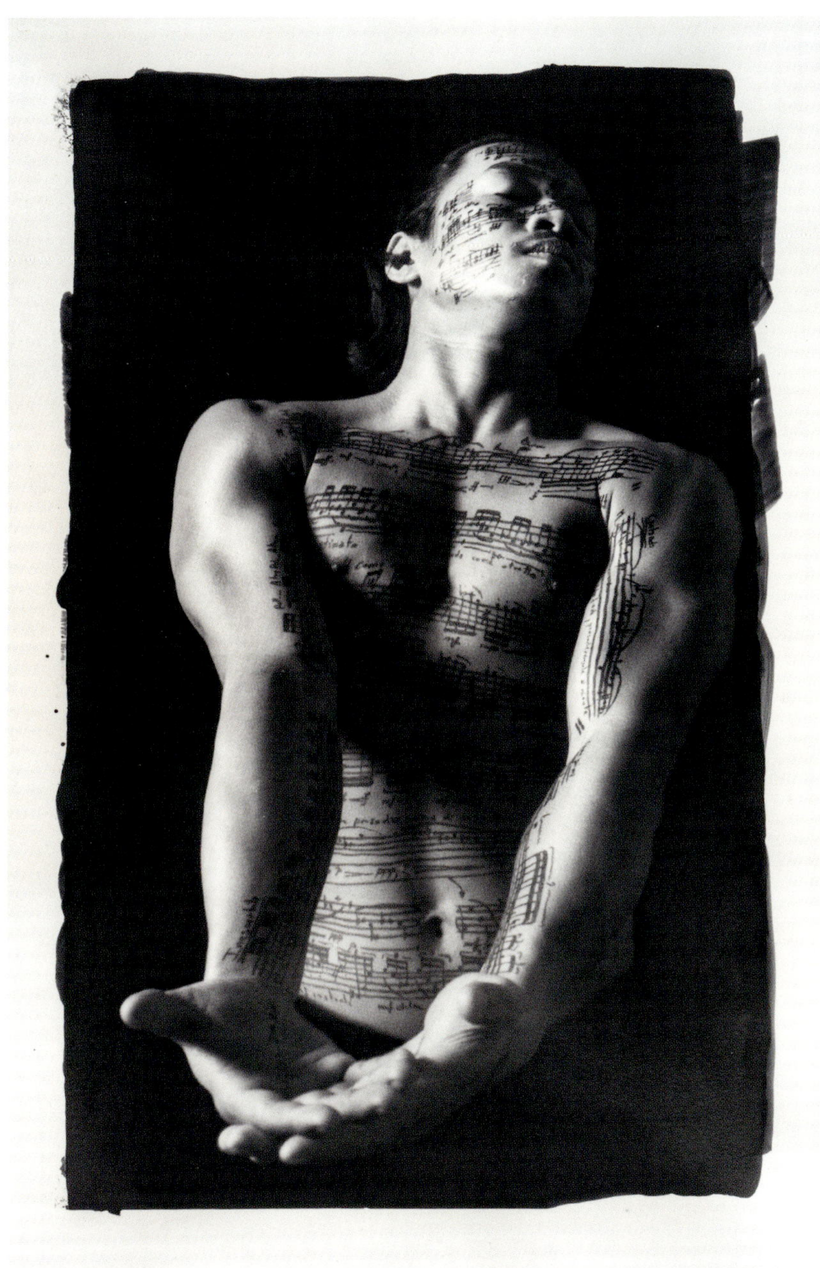

Jacopo Baboni Schilingi
Py-Esquisse, 2018
COLLECTIF DU HÉRISSON

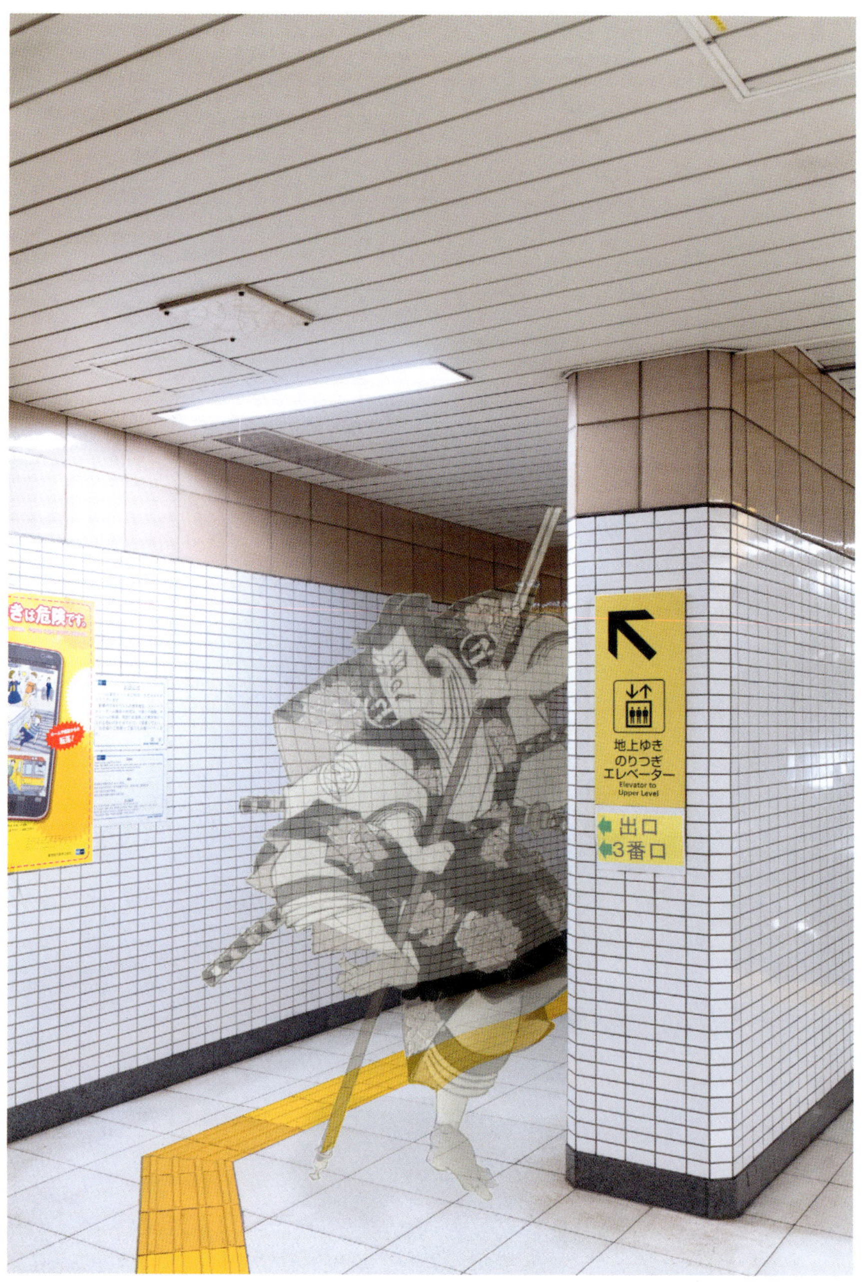

Philippe Charlot
Tokyo, Métro, 2018
DEUX6

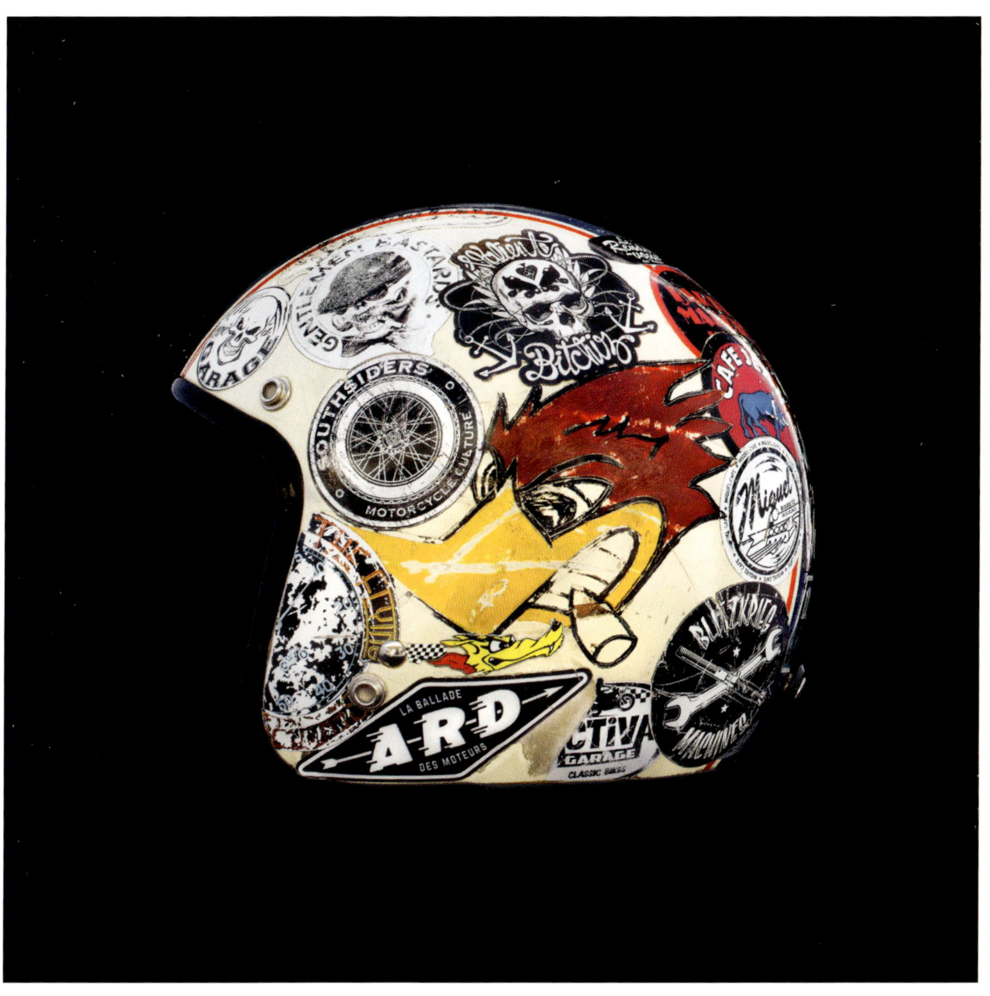

Dur Comme Fer
Smoky Woody, 2017
DEUX6

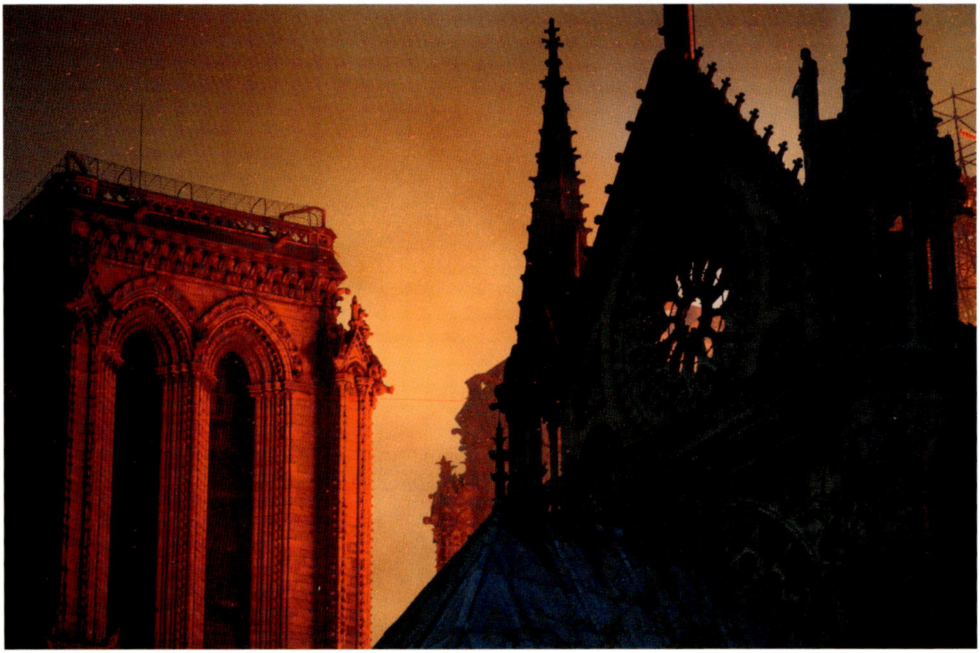

Maxime Hibon
L'incendie, 2019
DEUX6

François Roelants →
Le chignon de Marie-Liliane Lédée, Petit Cul de Sac, 2018
DEUX6

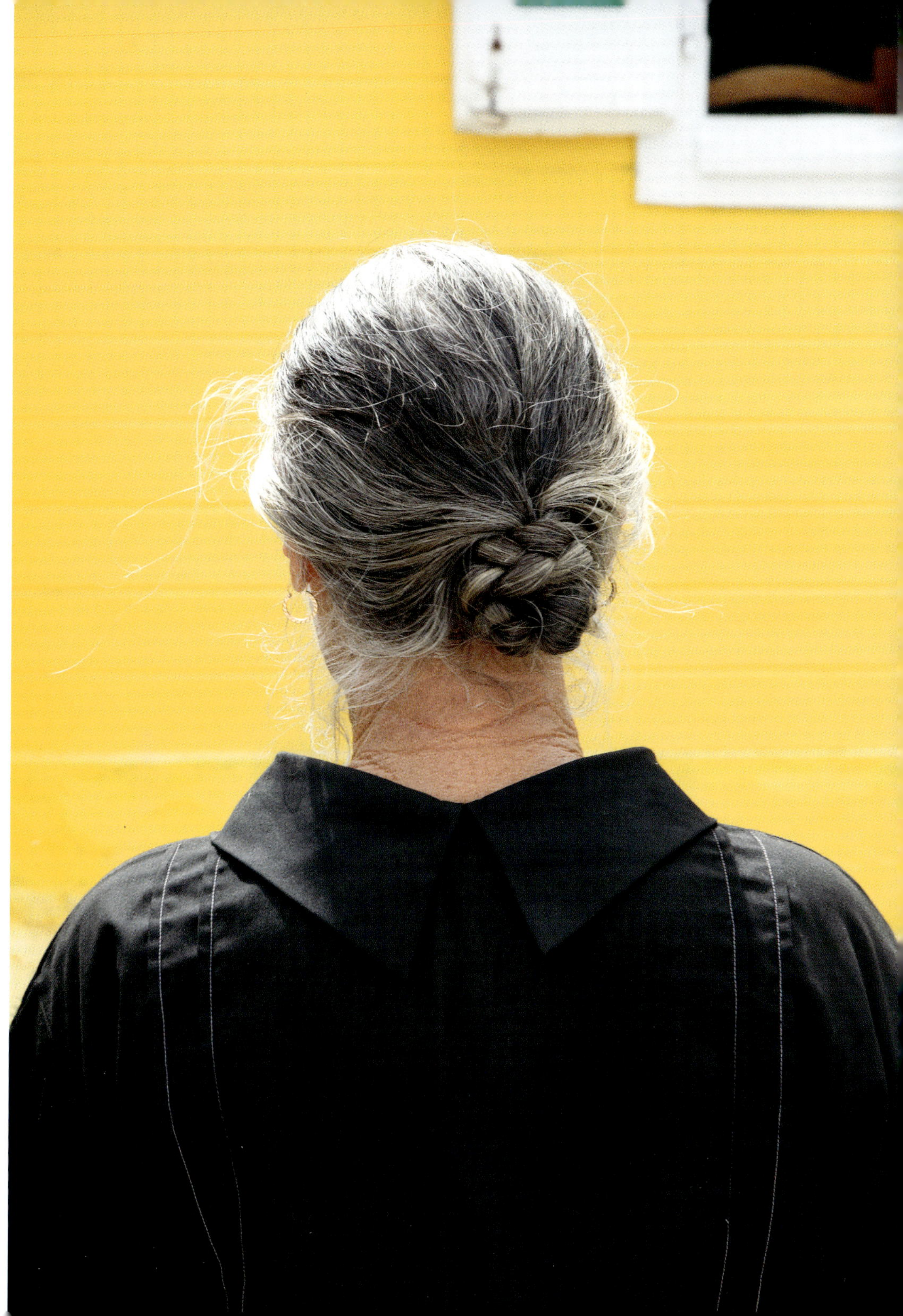

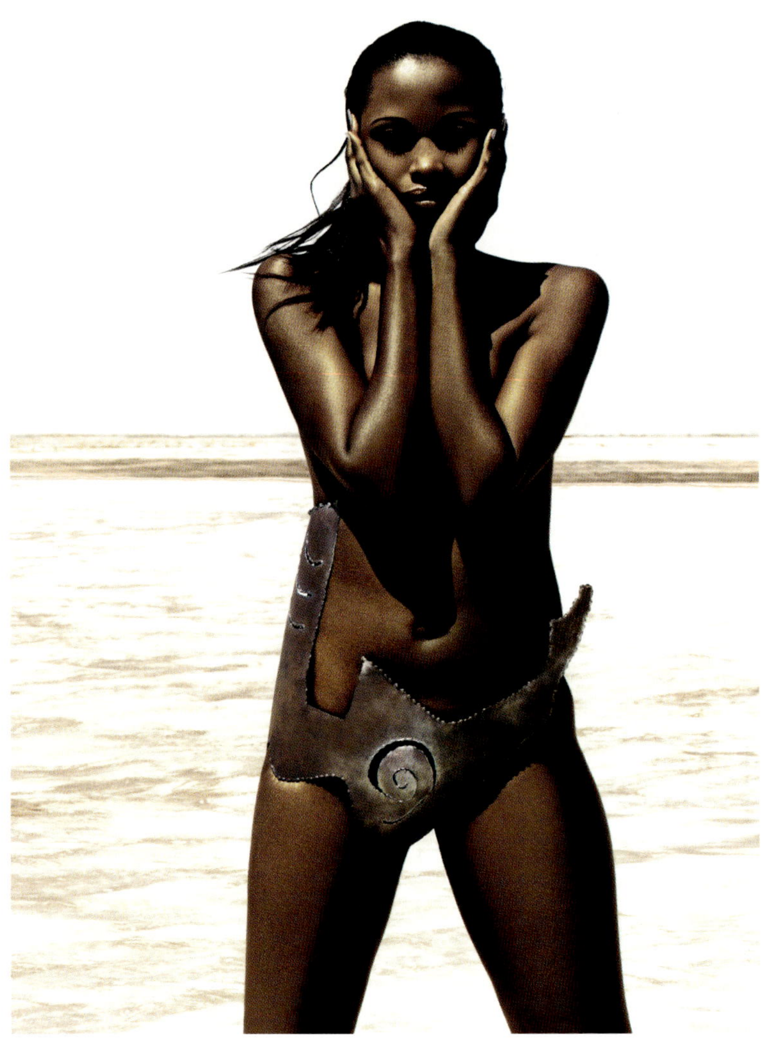

Roger Corona
Les Femmes de la Lune - Lune #1, 2018
EXPOWALL GALLERY

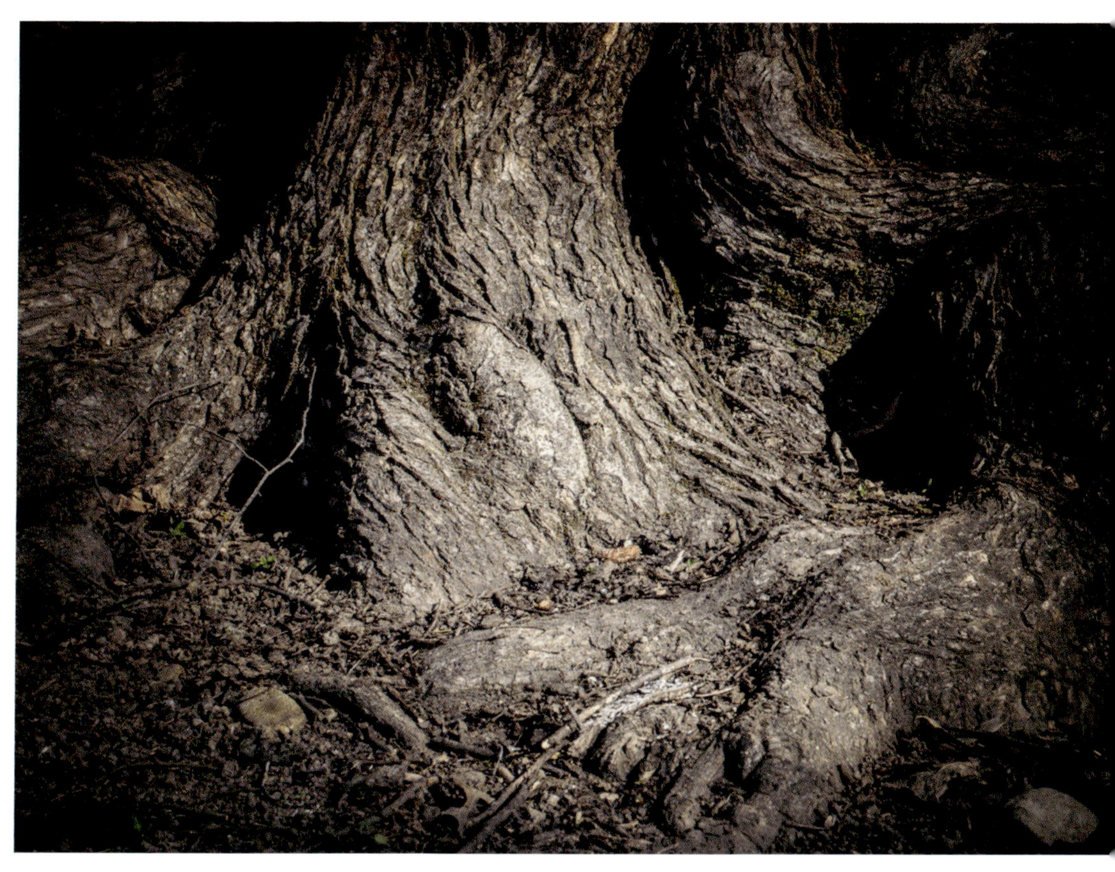

Loredana Celano
A Walk in the wood the Dark Matter #5, 2019
EXPOWALL GALLERY

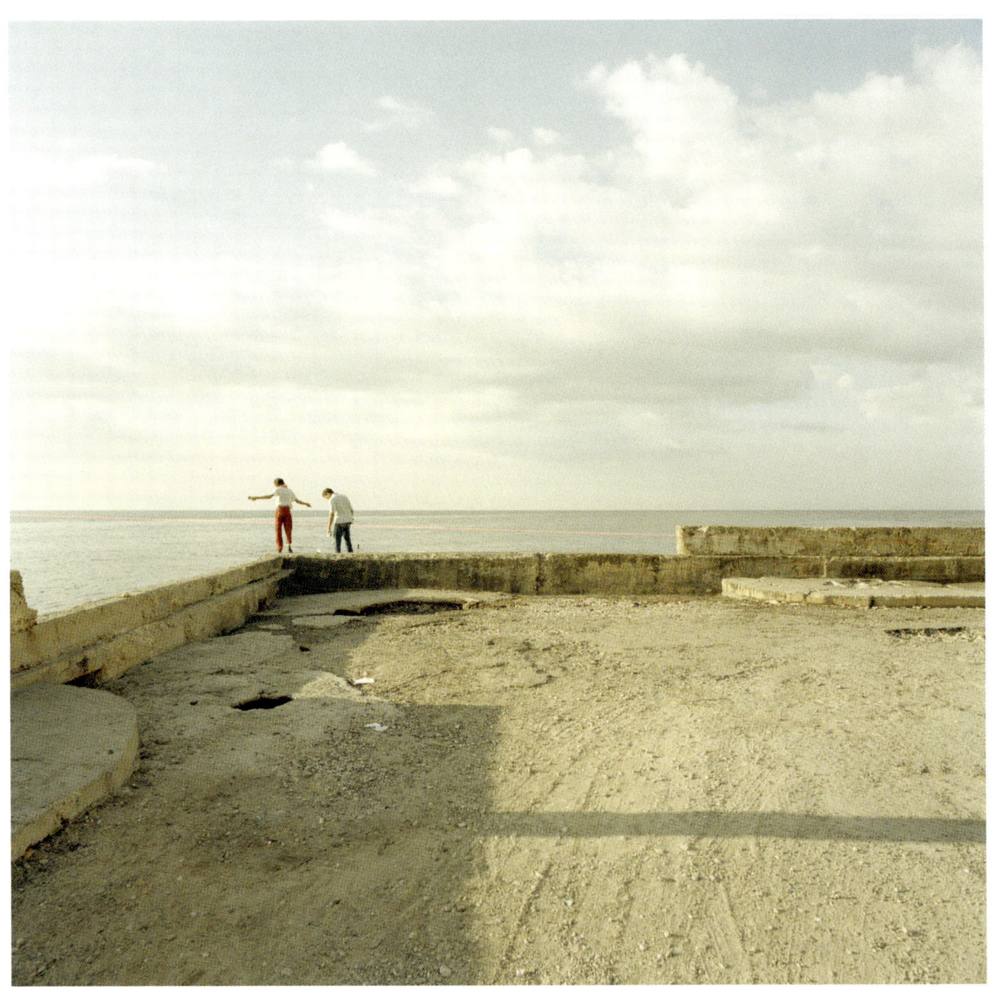

Giovanni Chiaramonte
L'Avana Cuba 1997 #110, 1997-2018
EXPOWALL GALLERY

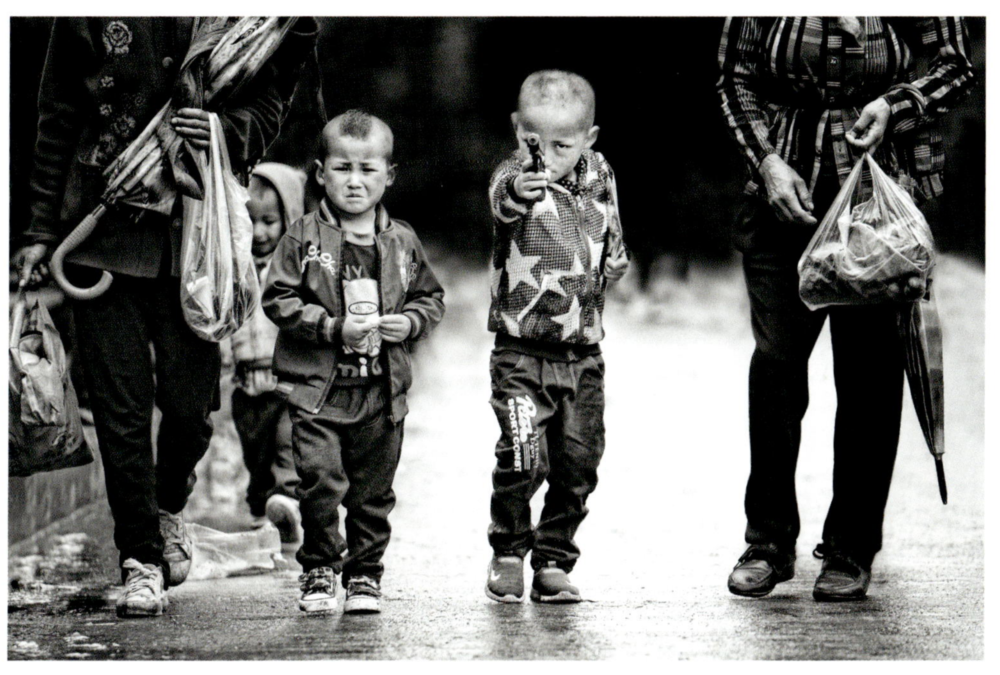

Oliver Klink
Boy with Toy Pistol, 2017
CULTURES IN TRANSITION

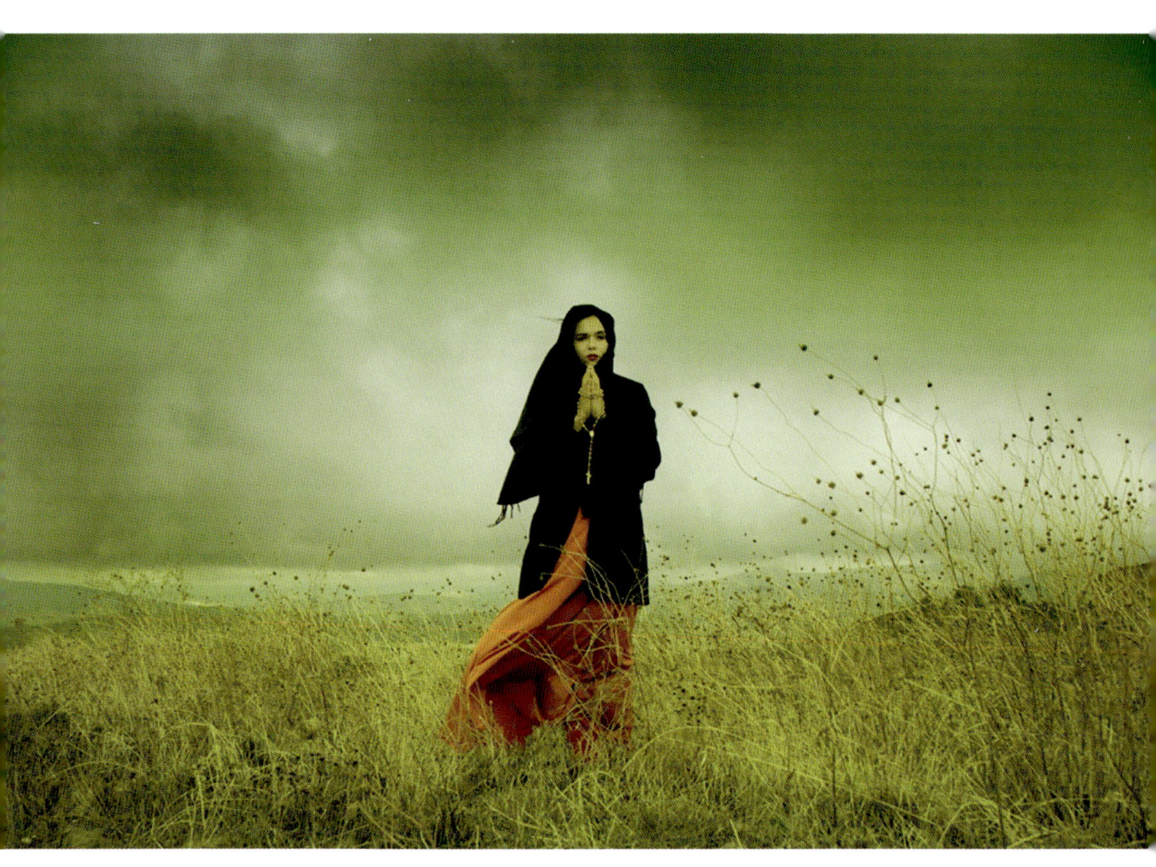

Gianluca Sodaro
Paulina, 2019
FABRIK PROJECTS

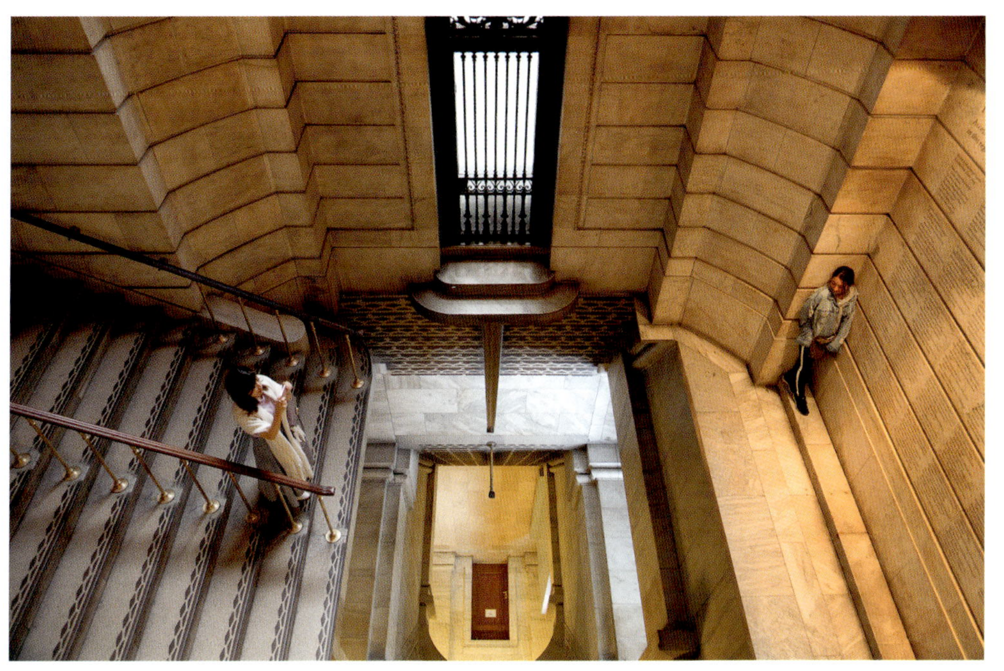

Christopher Sheils
Between the Years, 2018
FABRIK PROJECTS

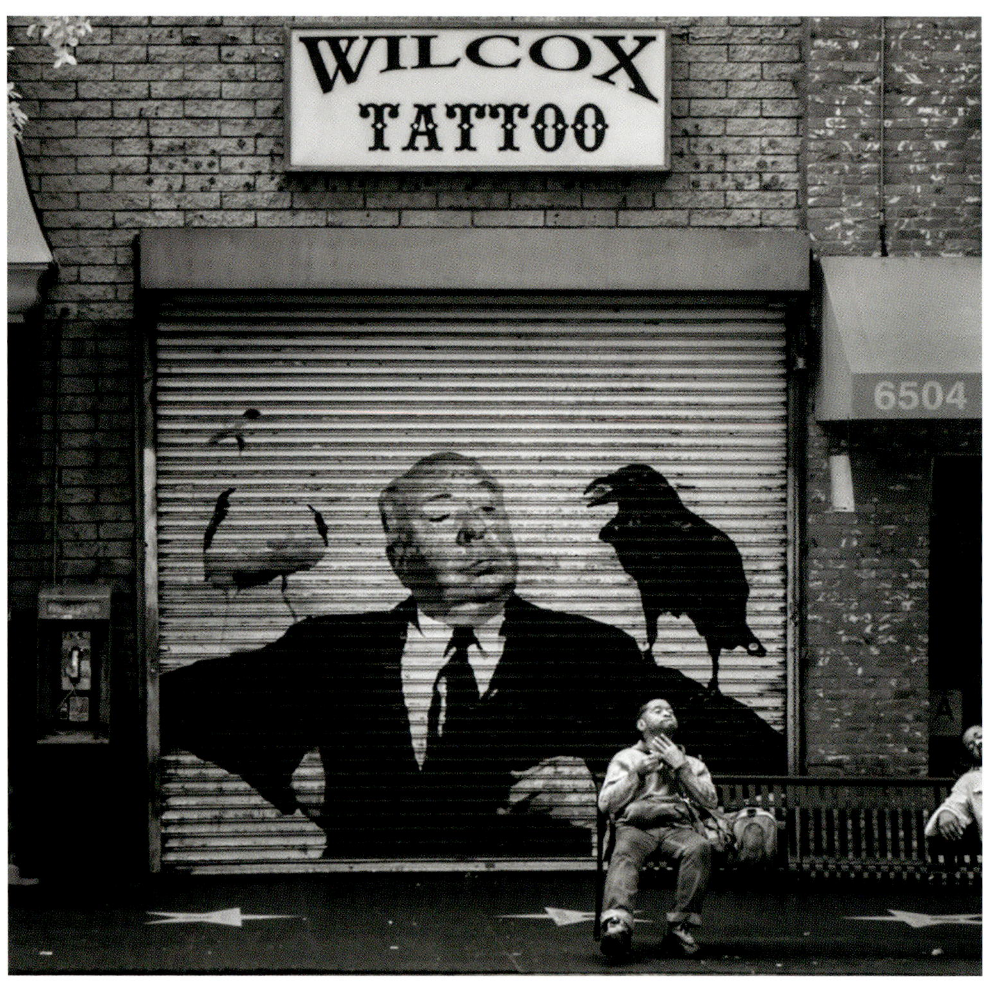

Erica Kelly Martin
Wilcox Tattoo, 2017
FABRIK PROJECTS

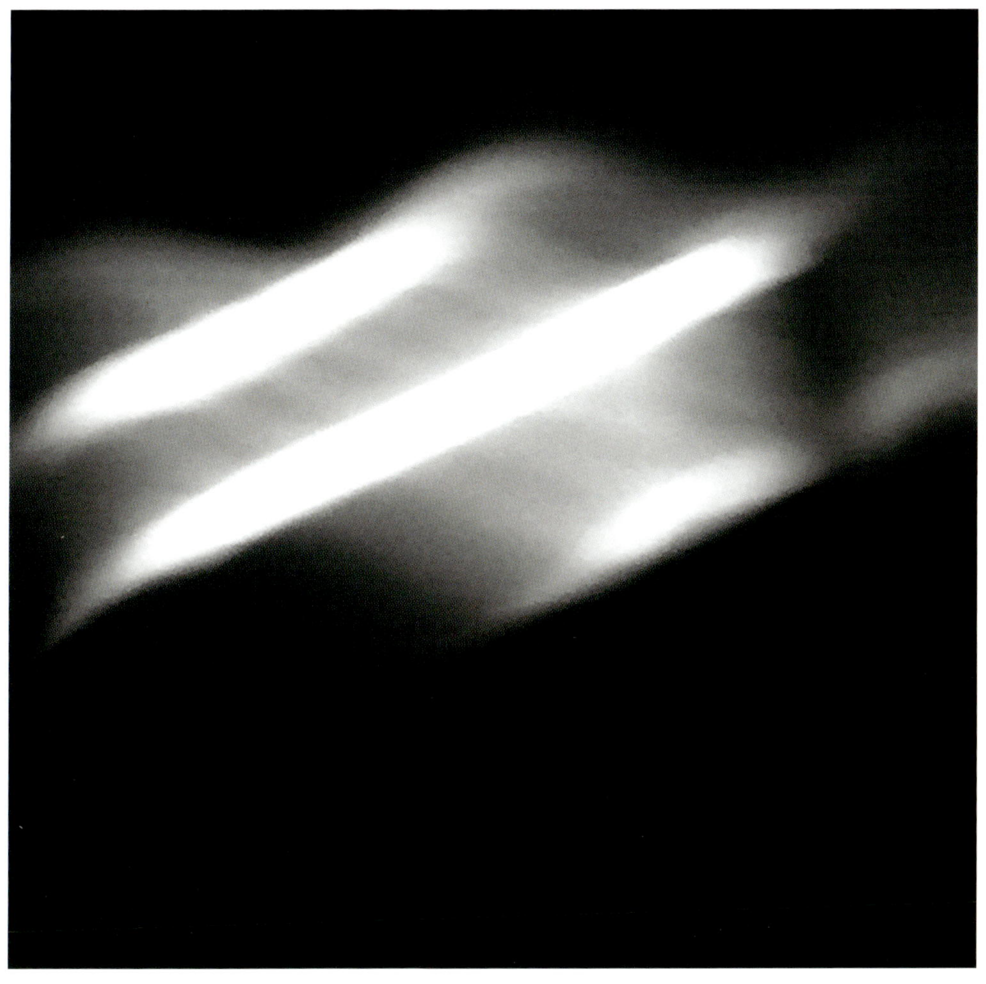

Maureen Haldeman
Shadow Secrets VII, 2018
FABRIK PROJECTS

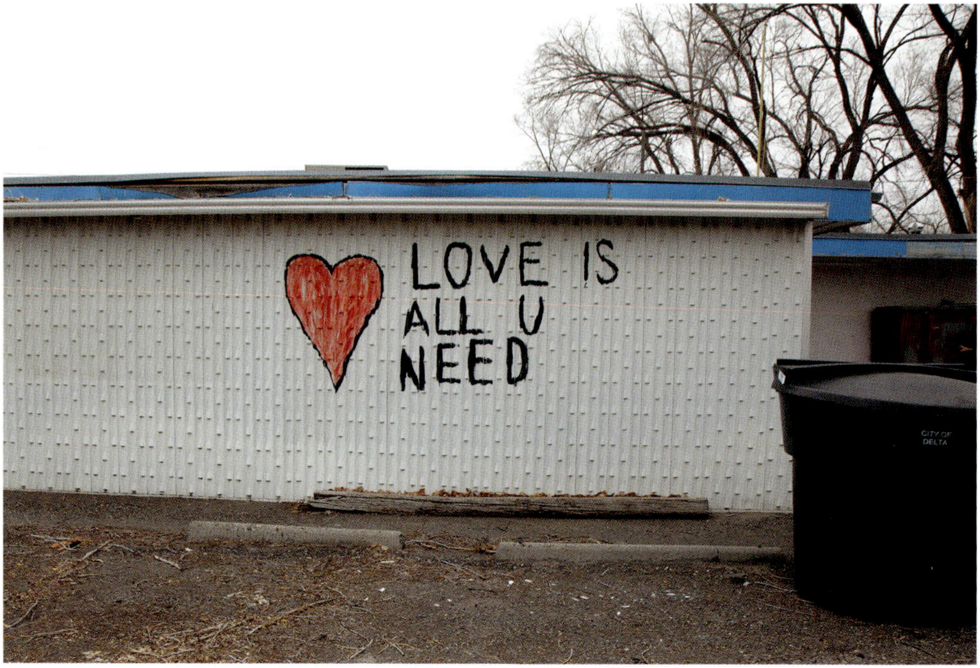

Jessie Chaney
Love is All U Need, 2019
FABRIK PROJECTS

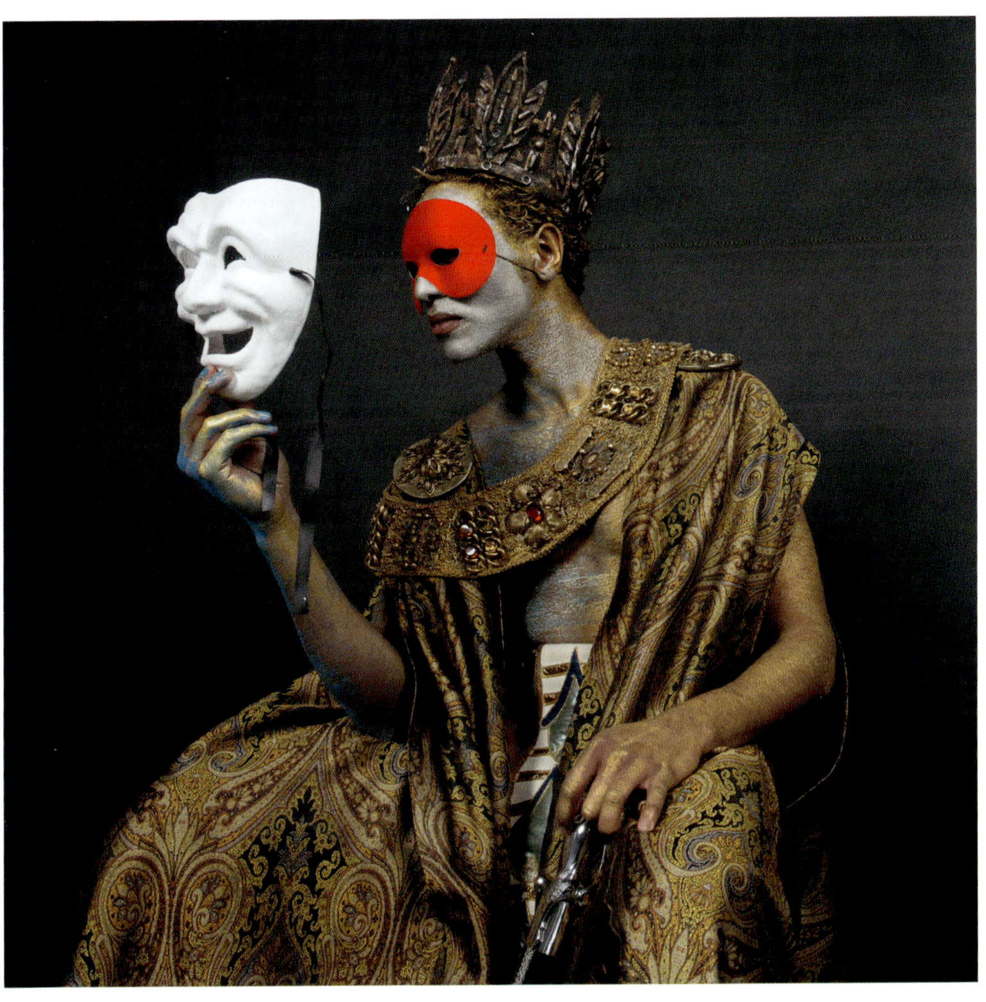

Yuri Boyko
The Persona, 2018
FABRIK PROJECTS

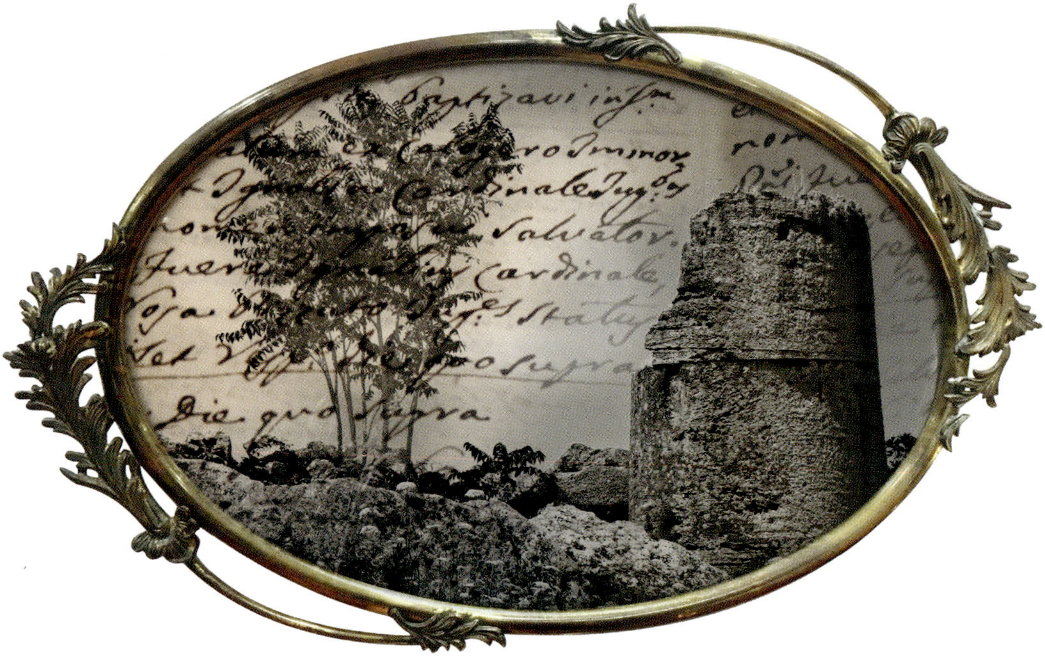

Cathy Immordino
The Ruins, 2019
FABRIK PROJECTS

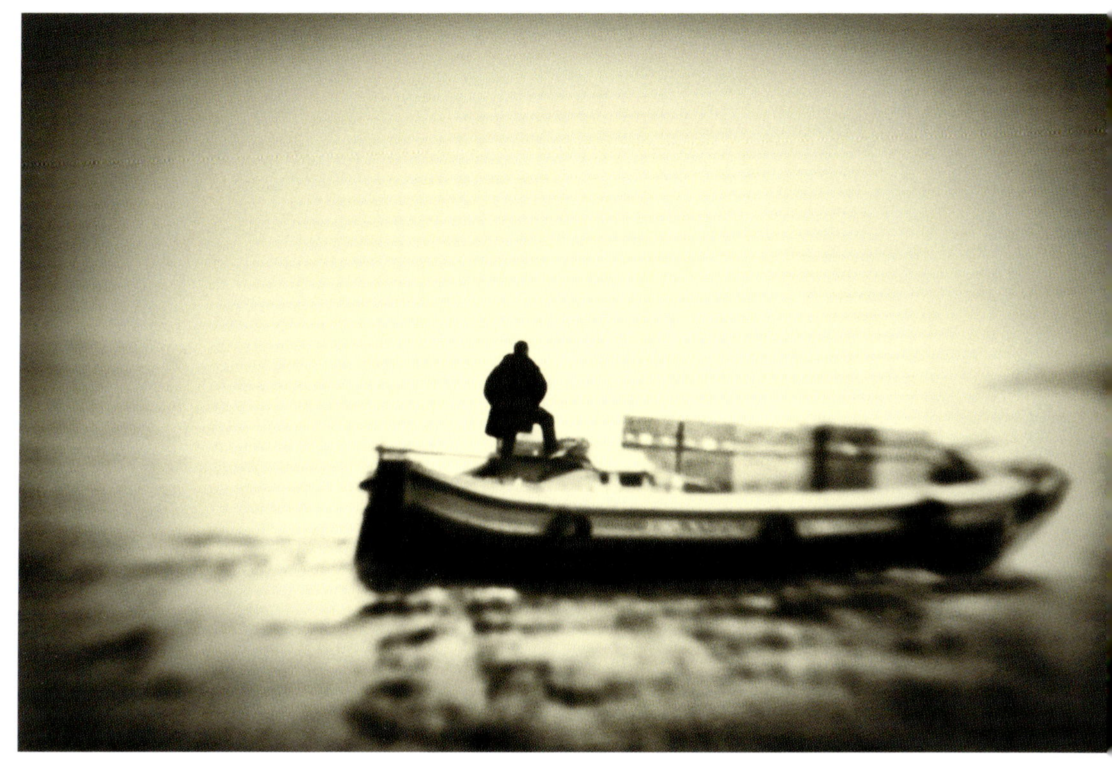

Sarah Hadley
On The Lagoon, 2006-2019
FABRIK PROJECTS

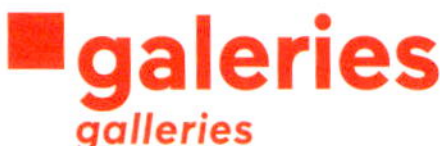

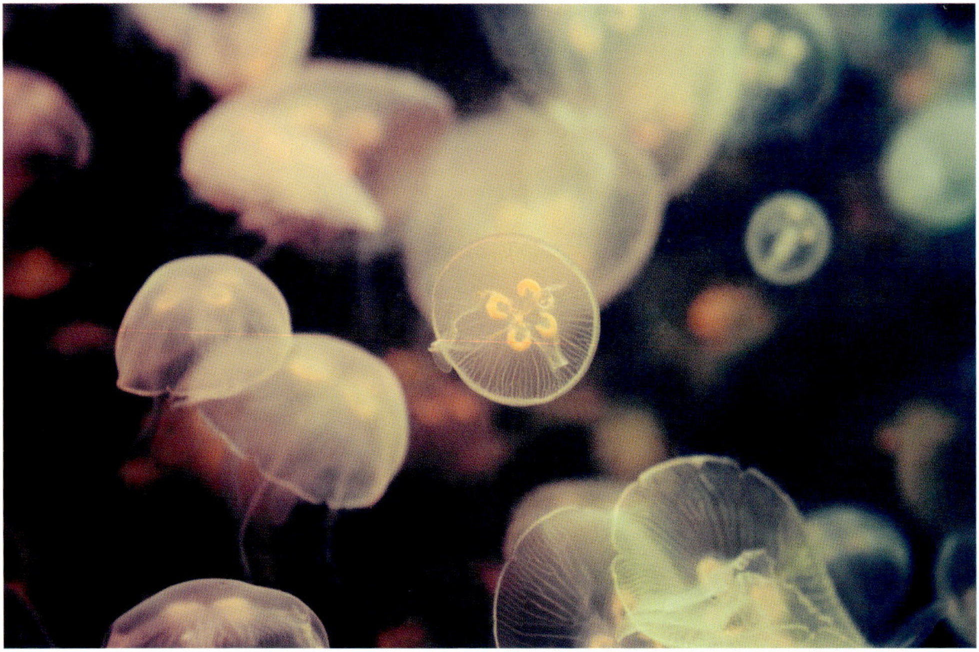

Dani García Sarabia
Contemplum #001, 2018
FIFTY DOTS GALLERY

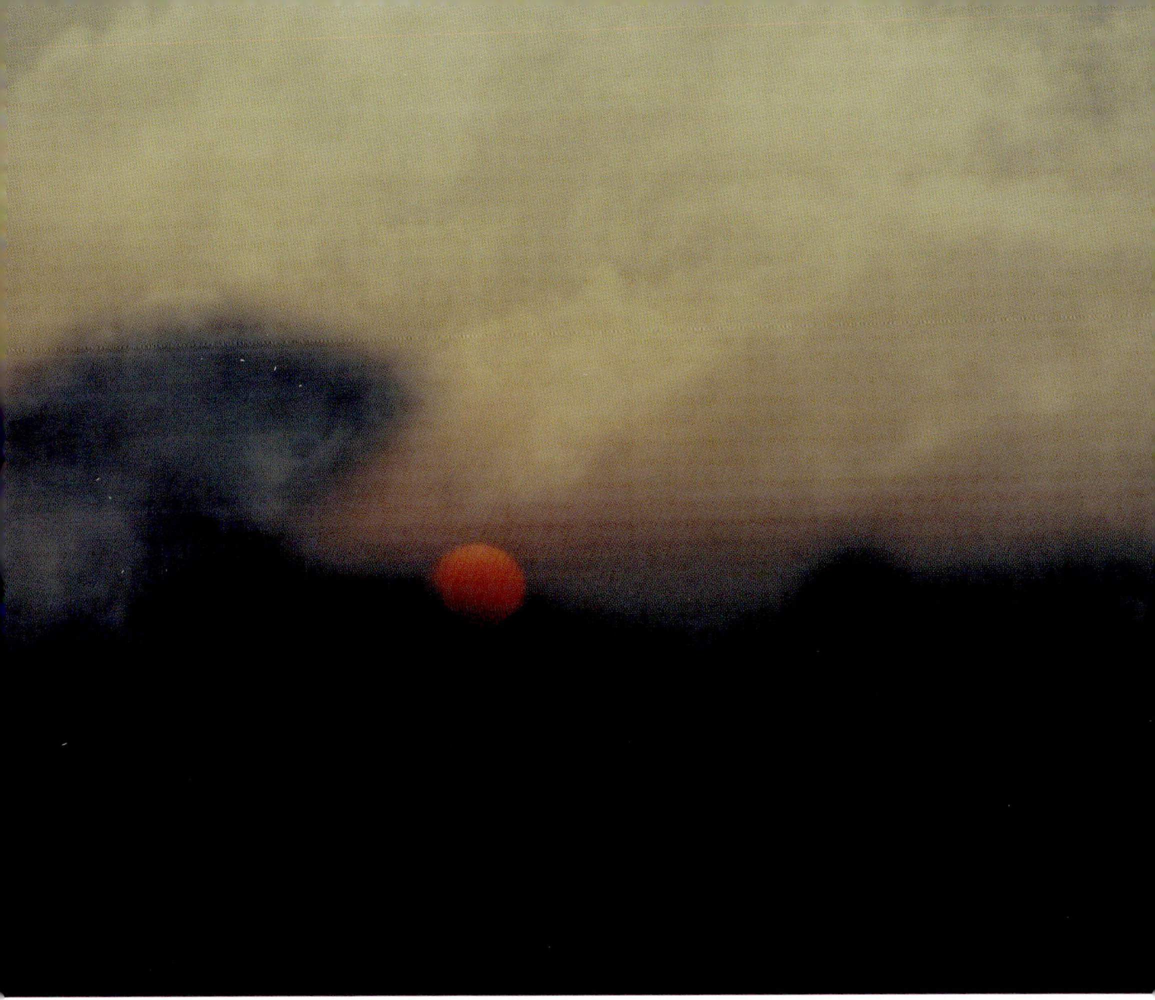

Nicholas Hughes
Field, Verse I, Untitled #1, 2009
FIFTY DOTS GALLERY

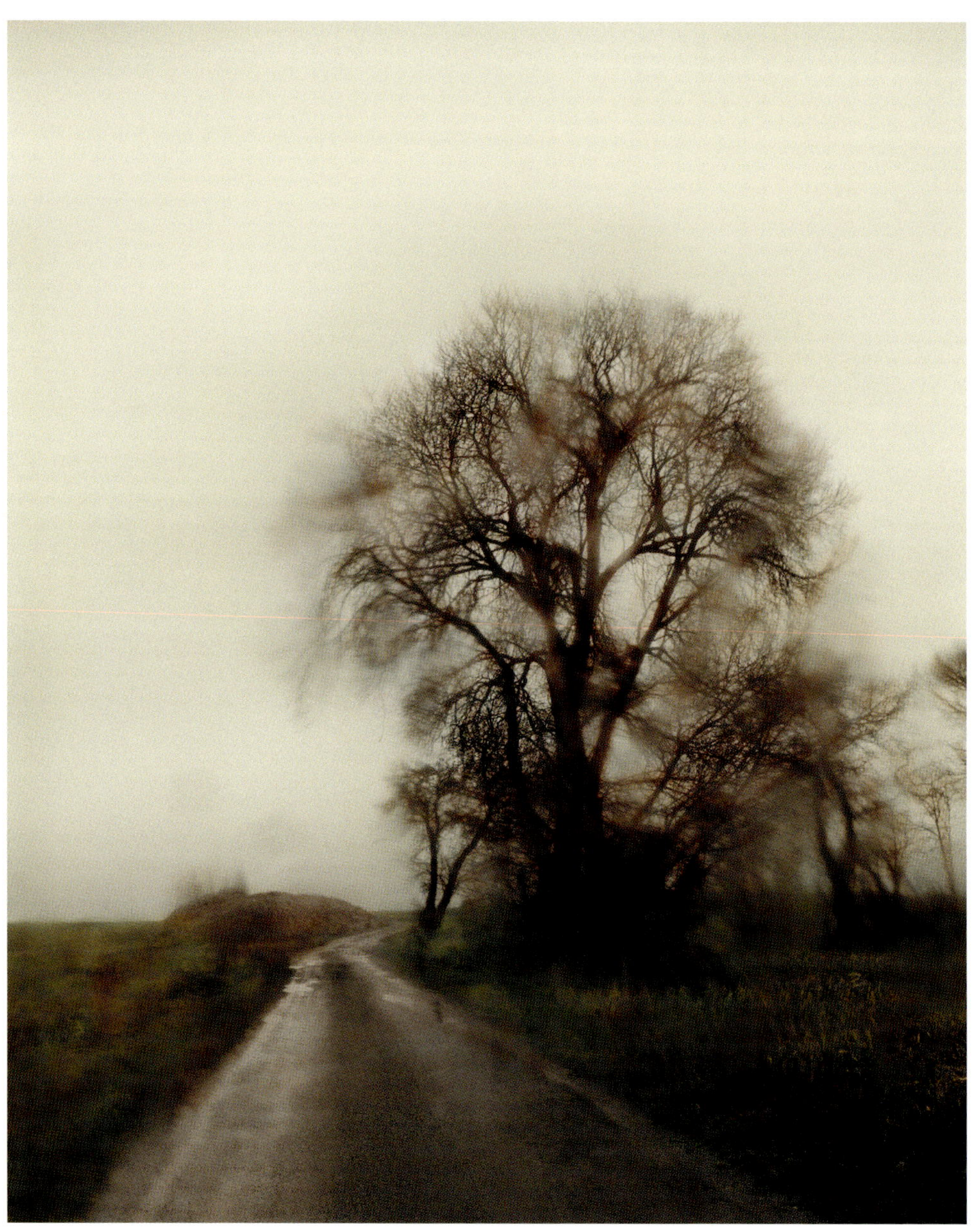

Israel Ariño
Voyage en pays du Clermontois 01, 2019
FIFTY DOTS GALLERY

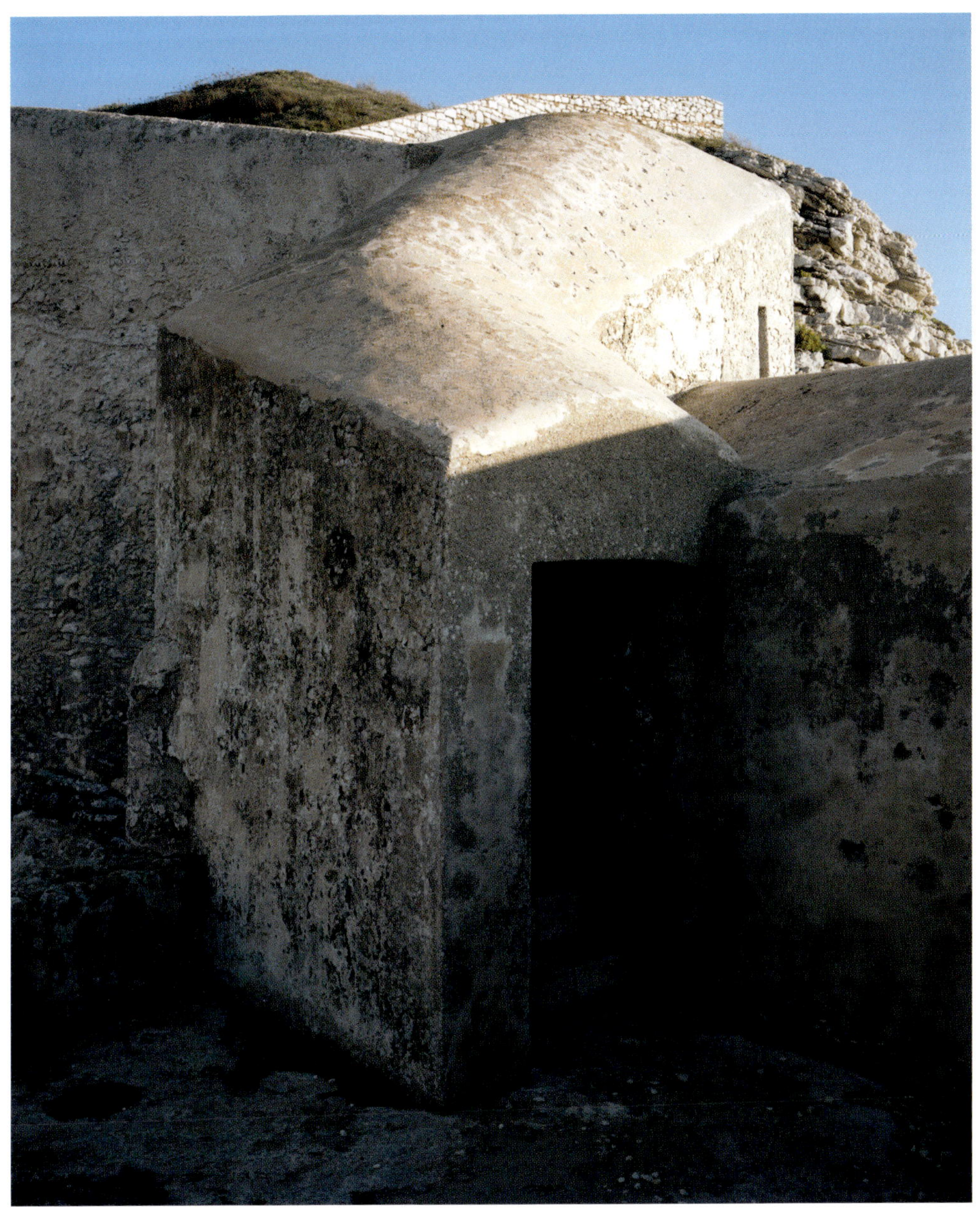

Sébastien Arrighi
Citadelle, 2019
GALERIE SINTITULO

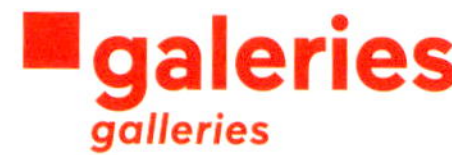

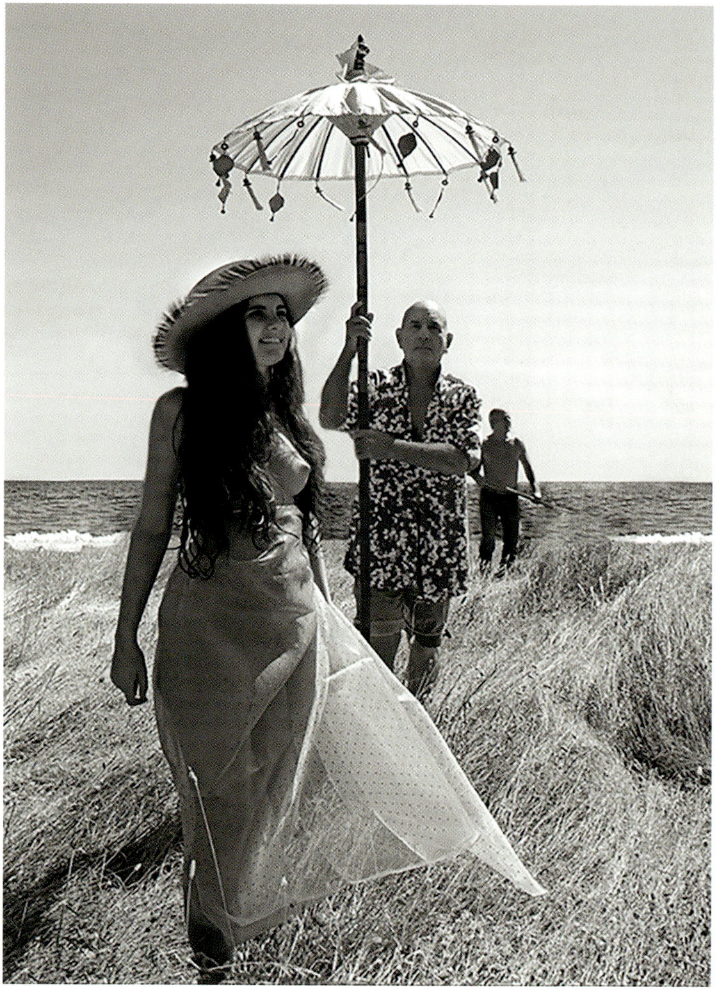

Miguel Soler-Roig
Pablo, Françoise y Jaime, 2018
FLUX ZONE

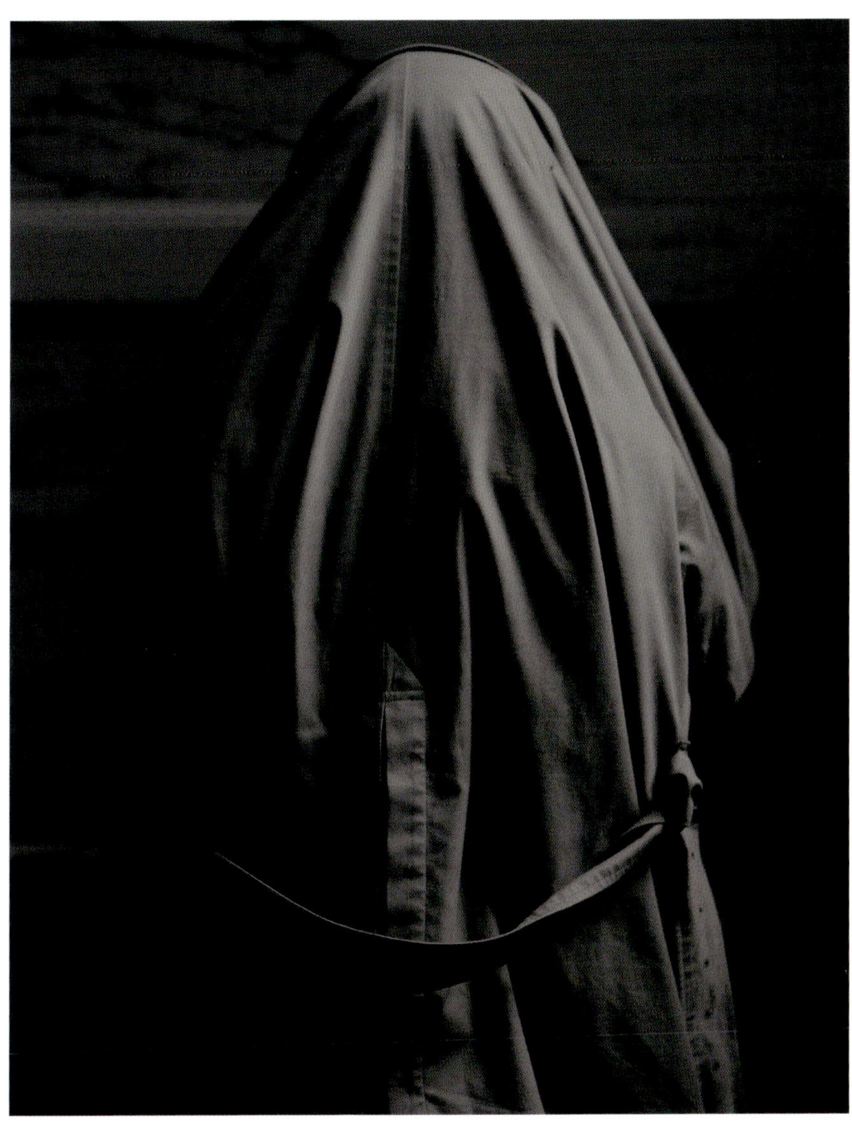

Isabel Miquel Arqués
Après l'Averse, 2018
FLUX ZONE

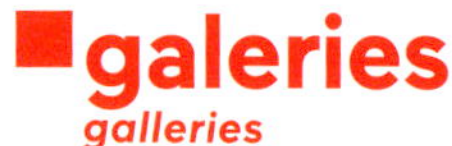

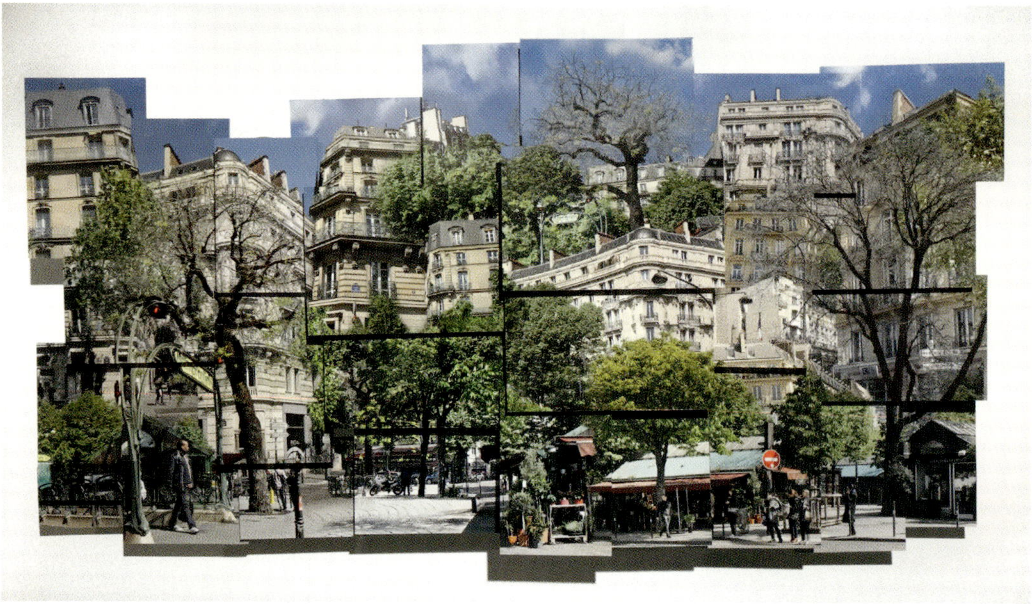

Brno Del Zou
Places des Ternes, 2019
GALERIE BARROU PLANQUART

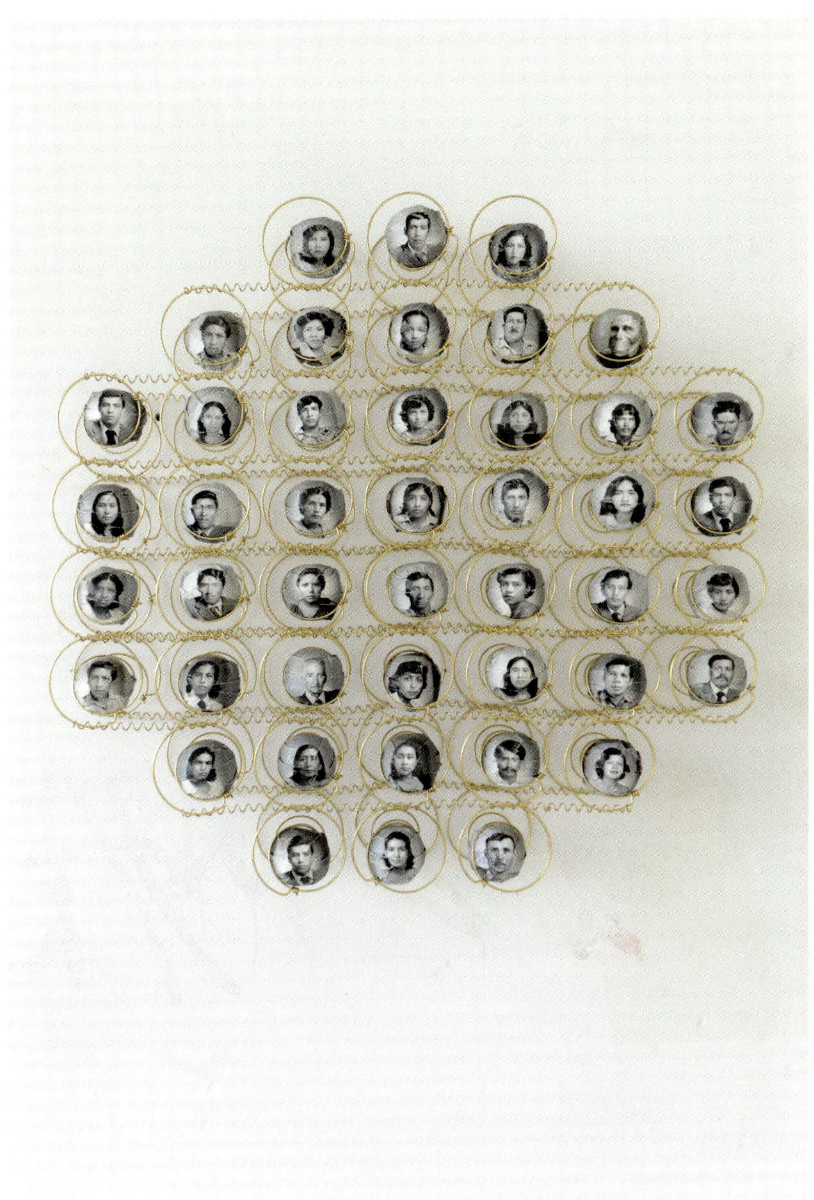

Double You
Sans Titre, 2019
GALERIE BARROU PLANQUART

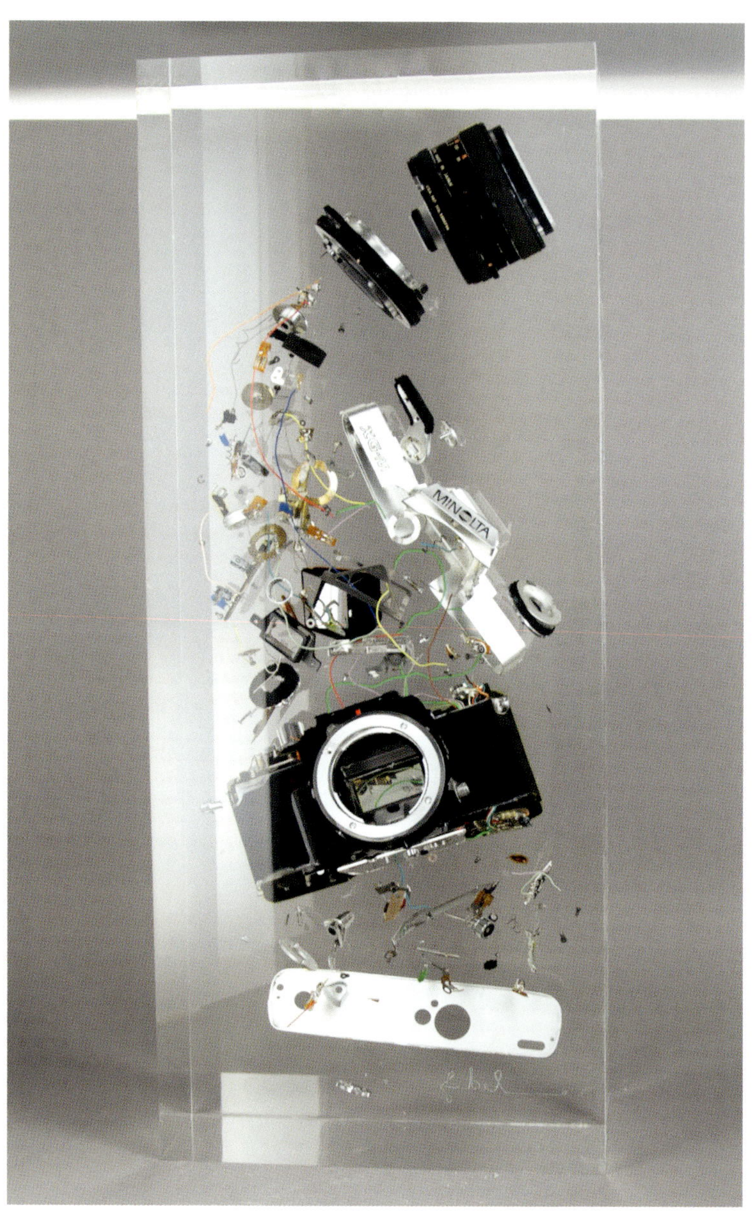

François Bel
Cliché Minolta, 2019
GALERIE BARROU PLANQUART

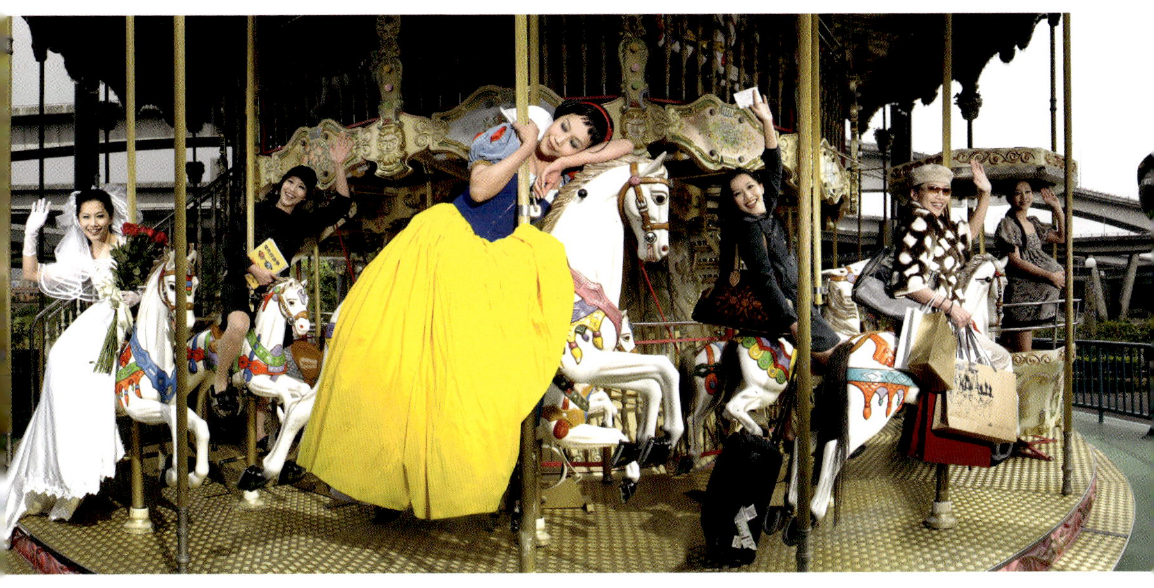

Isa Ho
Carousel, 2008
HO'S ART

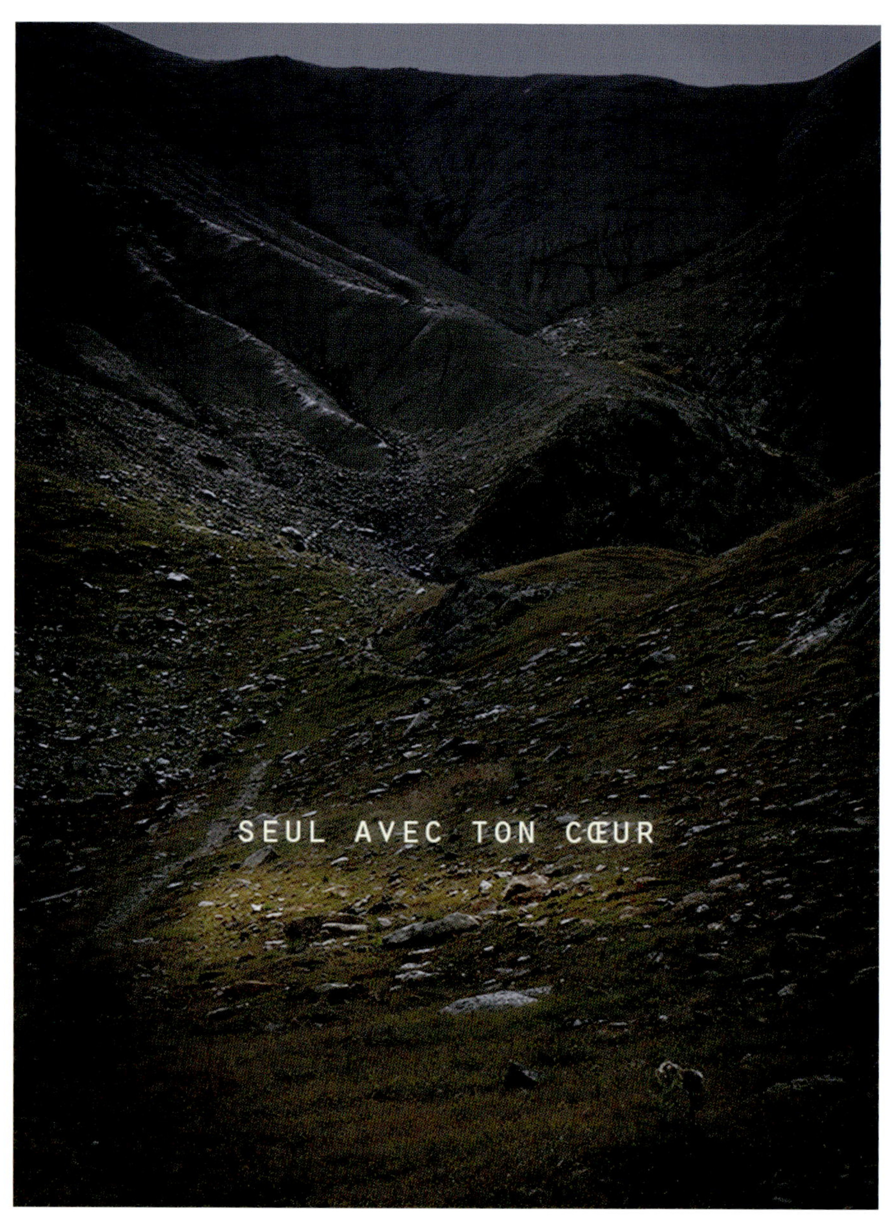

Sandrine Cnudde
Seul avec ton cœur, 2018
GALERIE INSULA

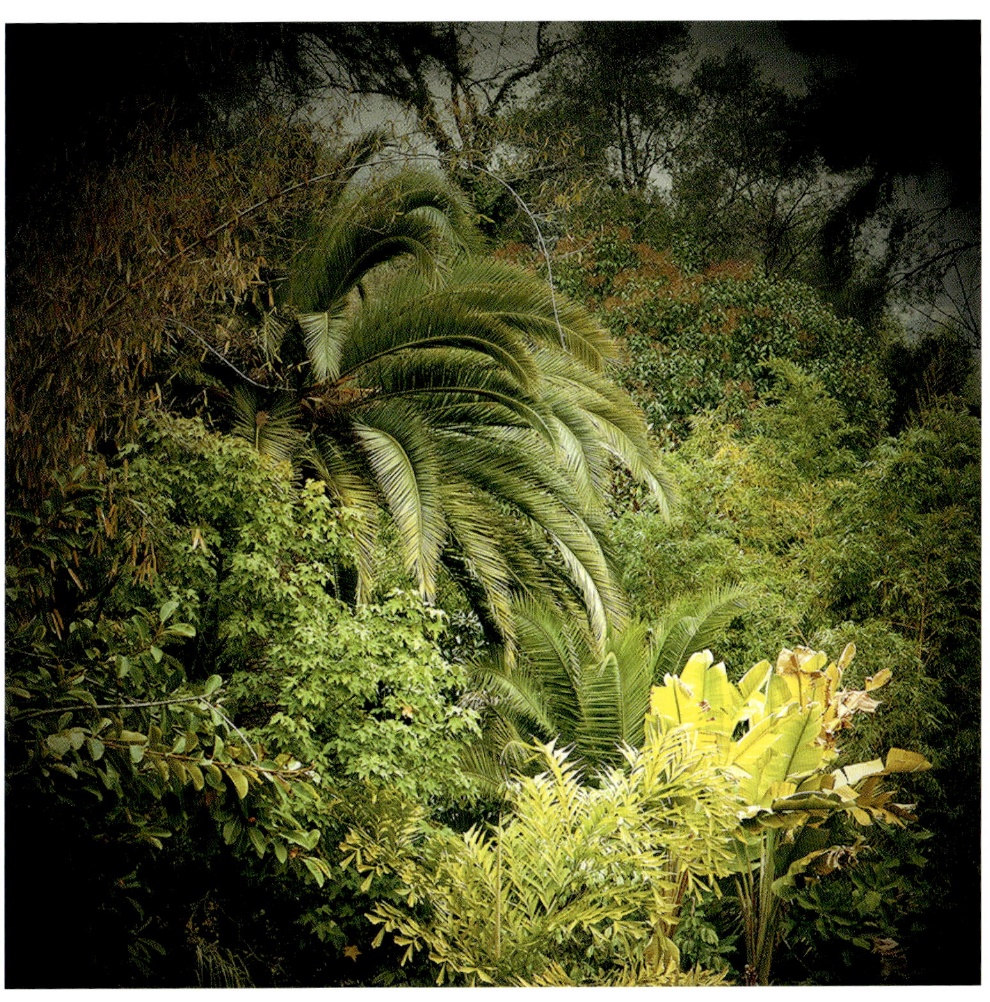

Olivia Lavergne
Jungles I, 2013
GALERIE INSULA

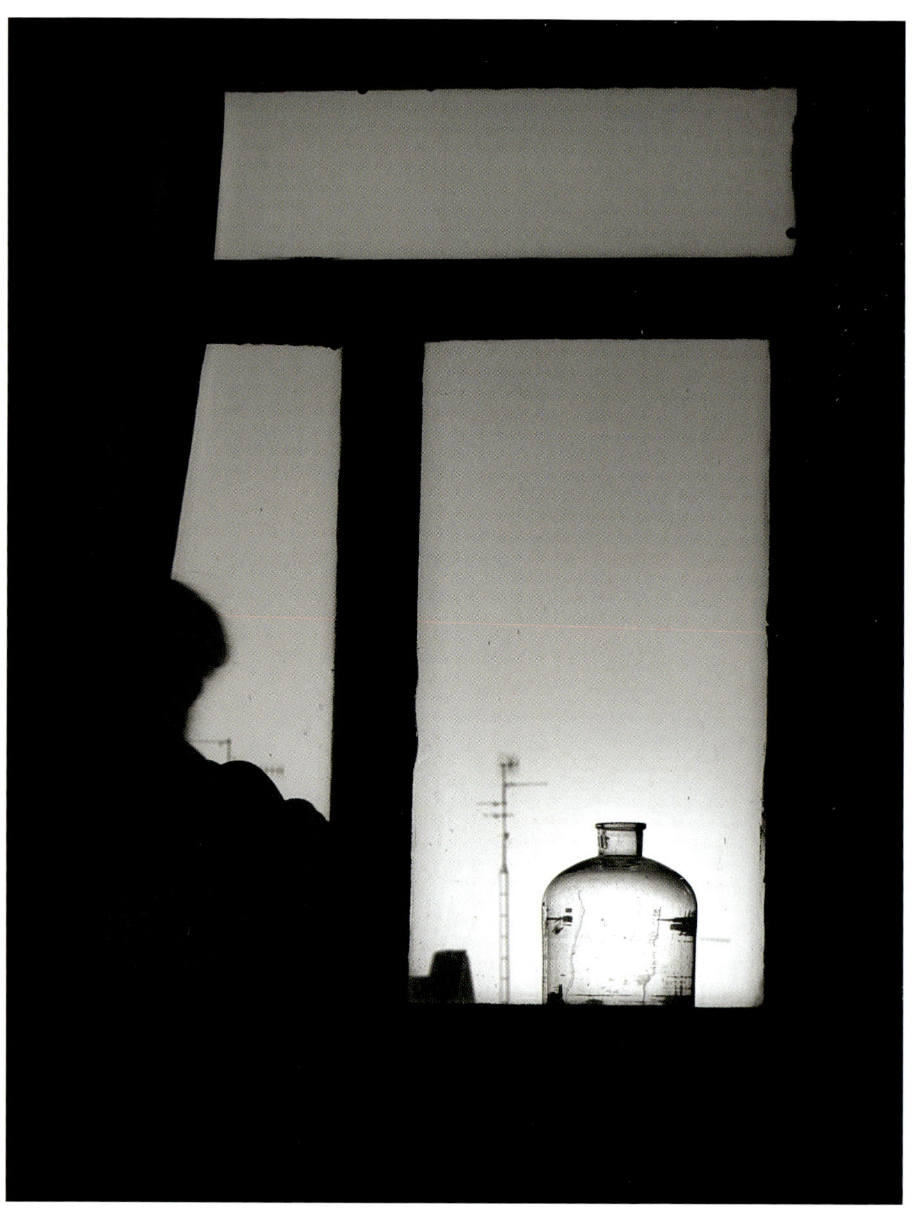

Caroline Polikar
Heure Exquise, 2018
GALERIE INSULA

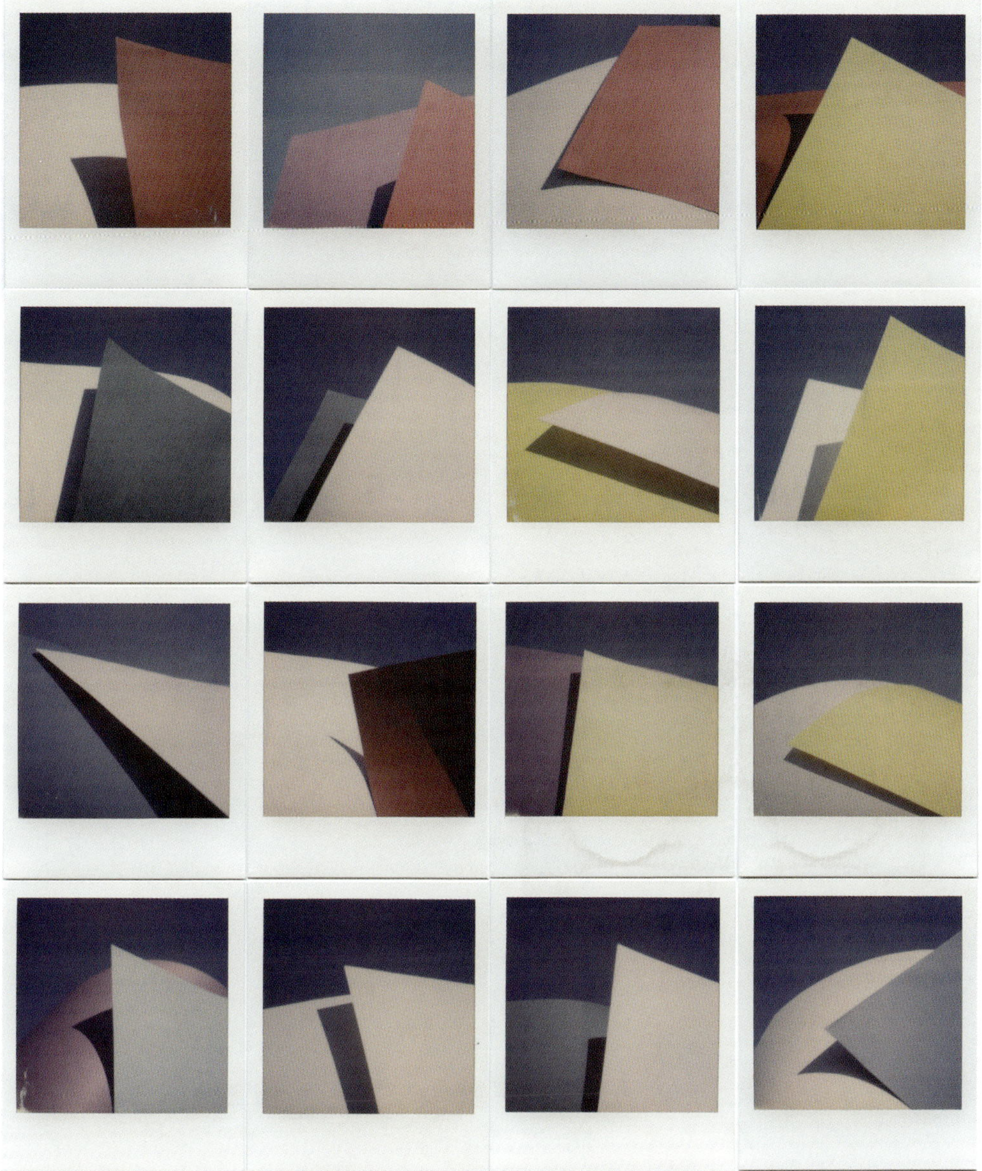

Andrea Tonellotto
Paper & Sky, 2017
HEILLANDI GALLERY

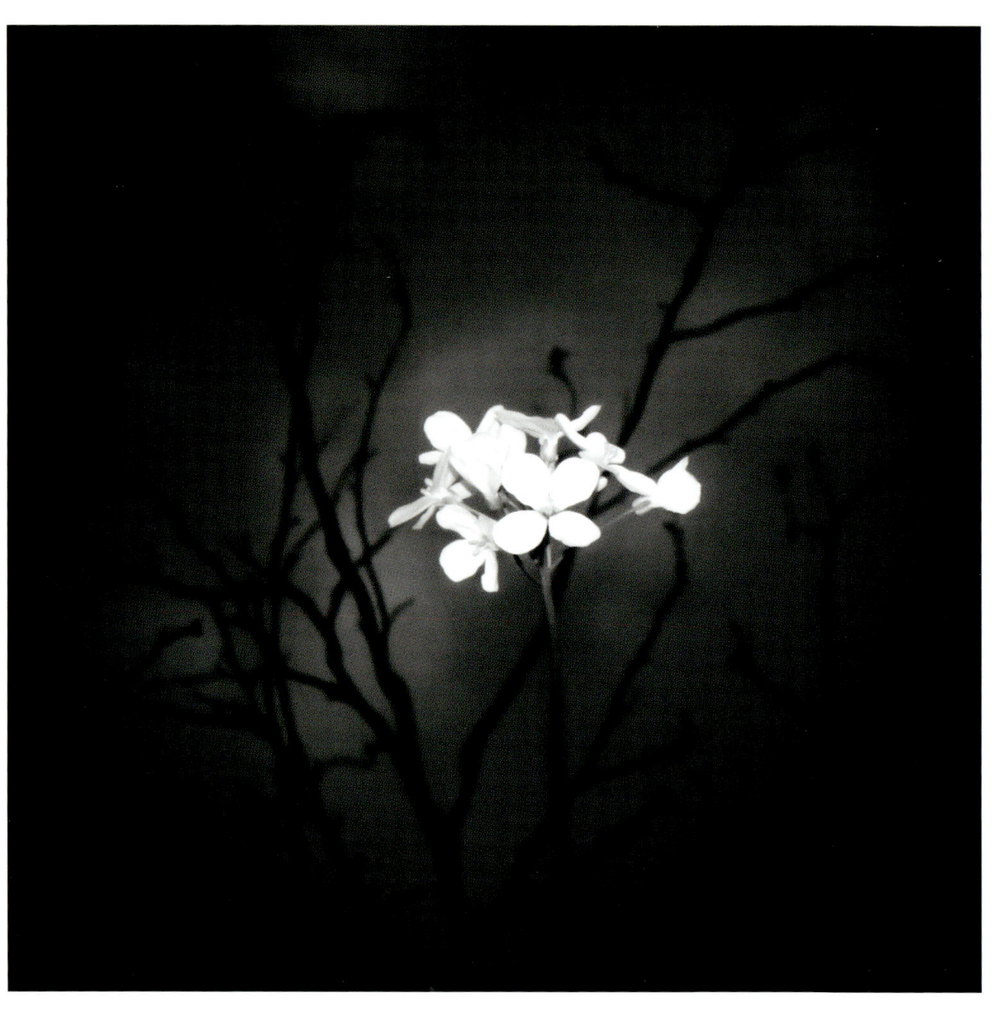

Daniel Karila-Cohen
L'unique, 2018
GALERIE RASTOLL

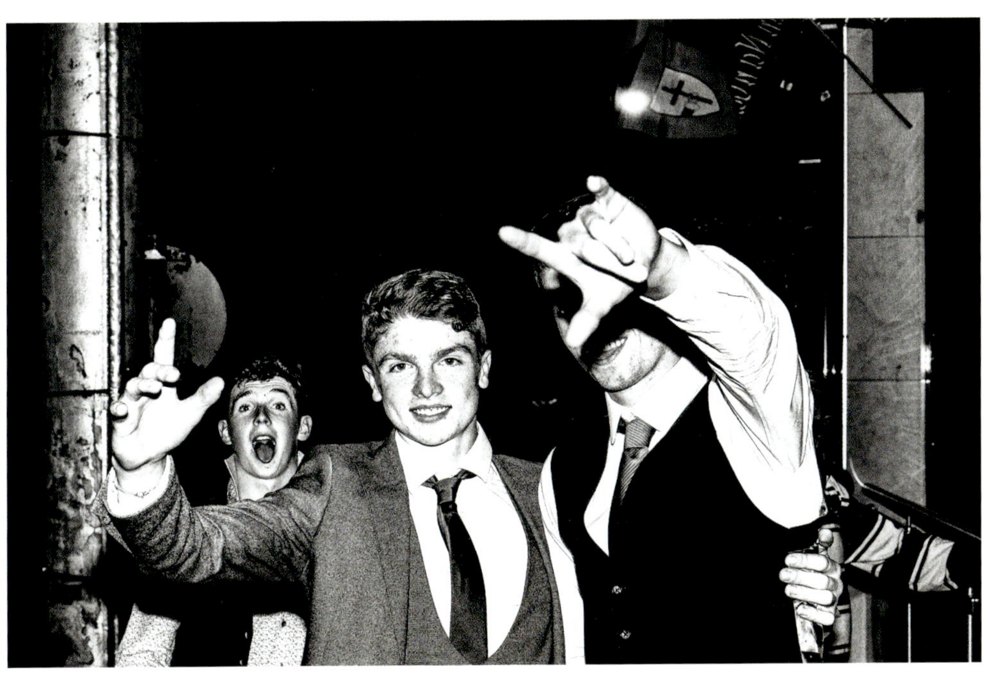

CarCam
Temeritas atis, 2018
GALERIE RASTOLL

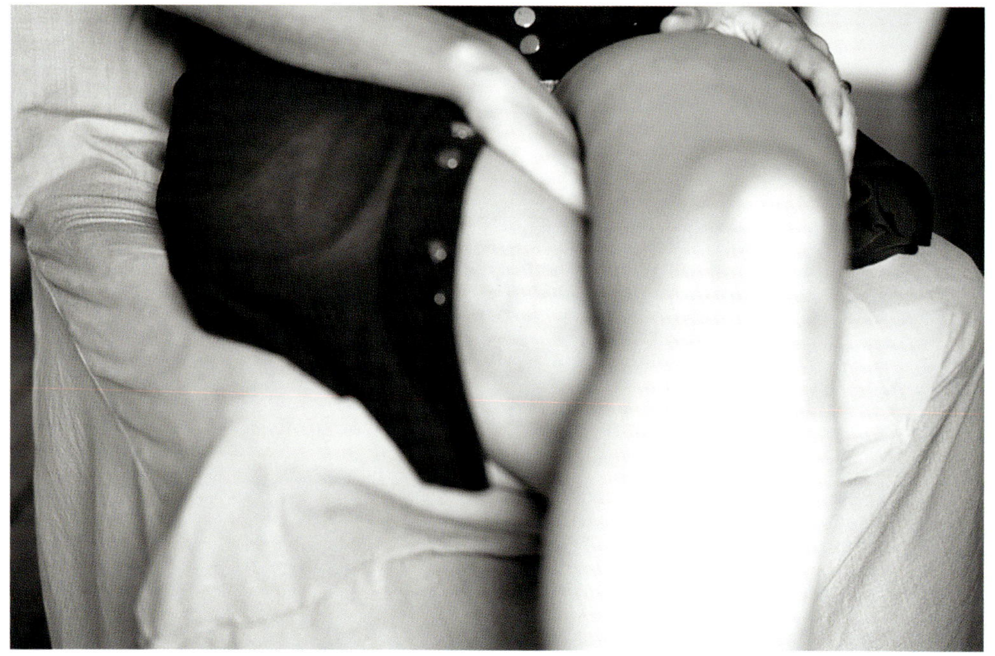

Willy Vynck
Intimacy, 2018
GALERIE S&H DE BUCK

Peter Bracke →
Mornington Bay, 2018
GALERIE S&H DE BUCK

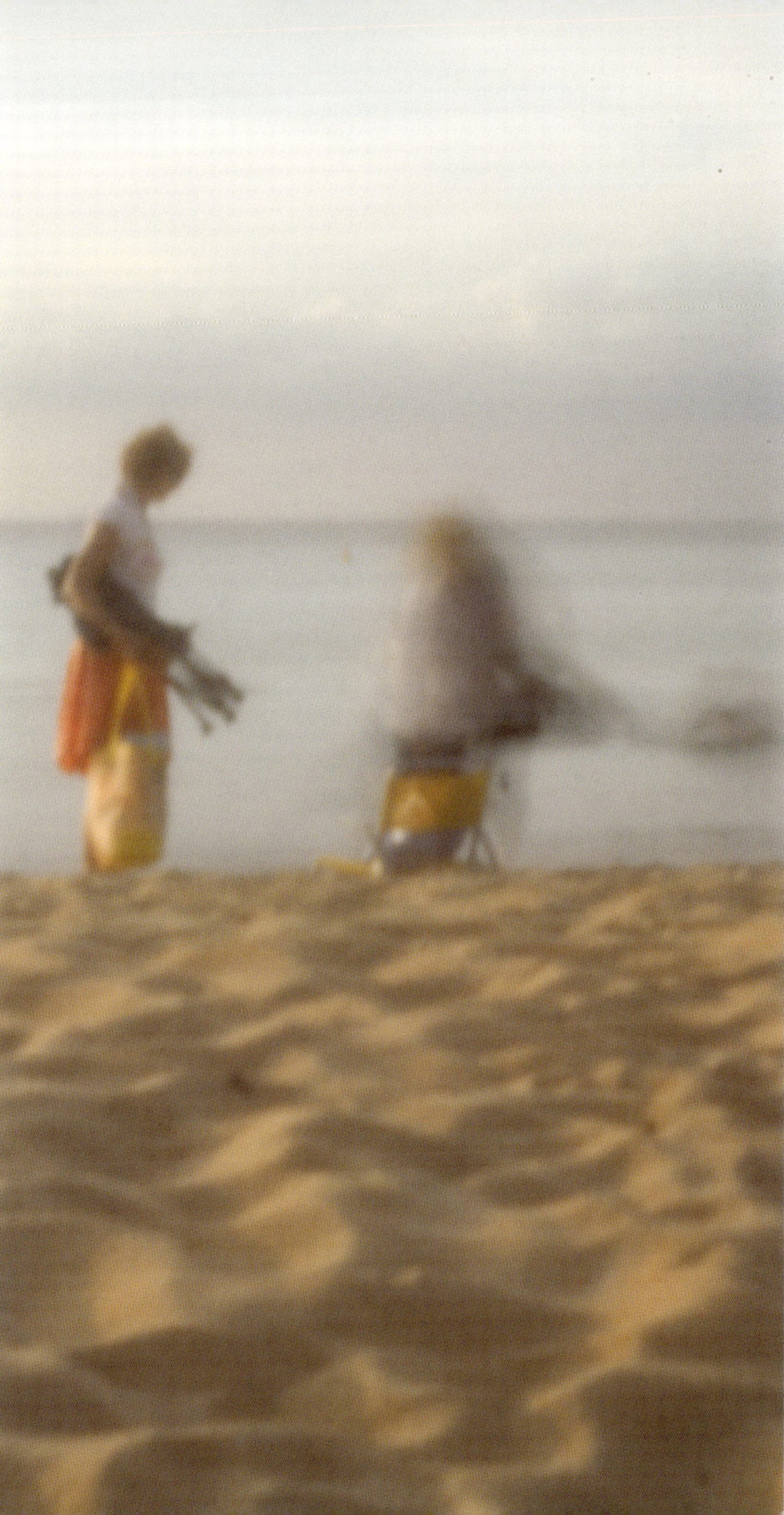

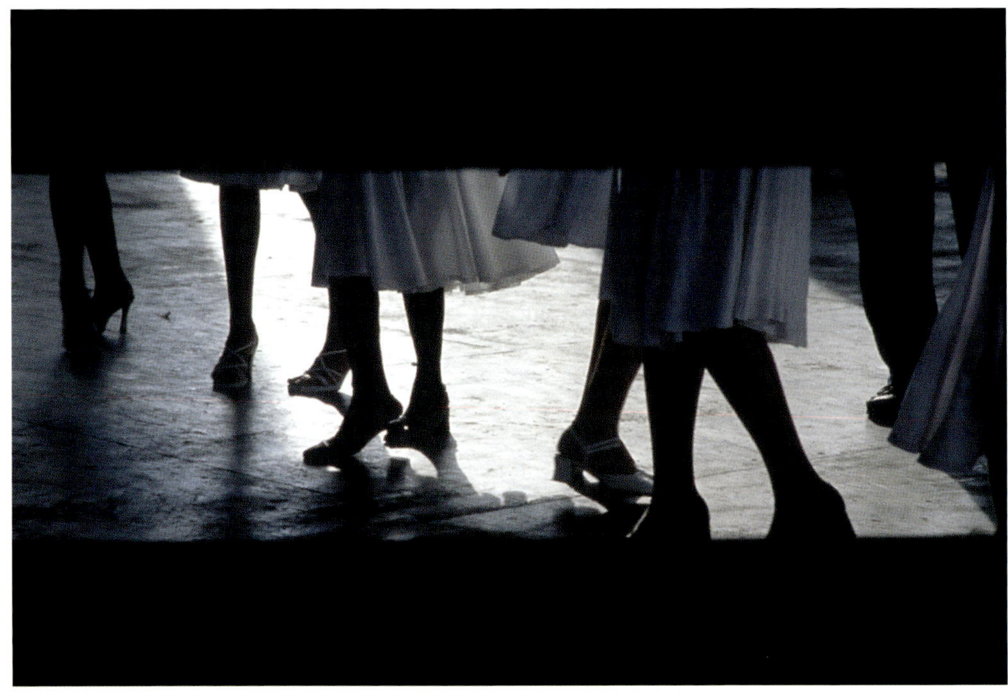

Elina Yamasaki
Saudade, 2001
GALERIE MONA LISA

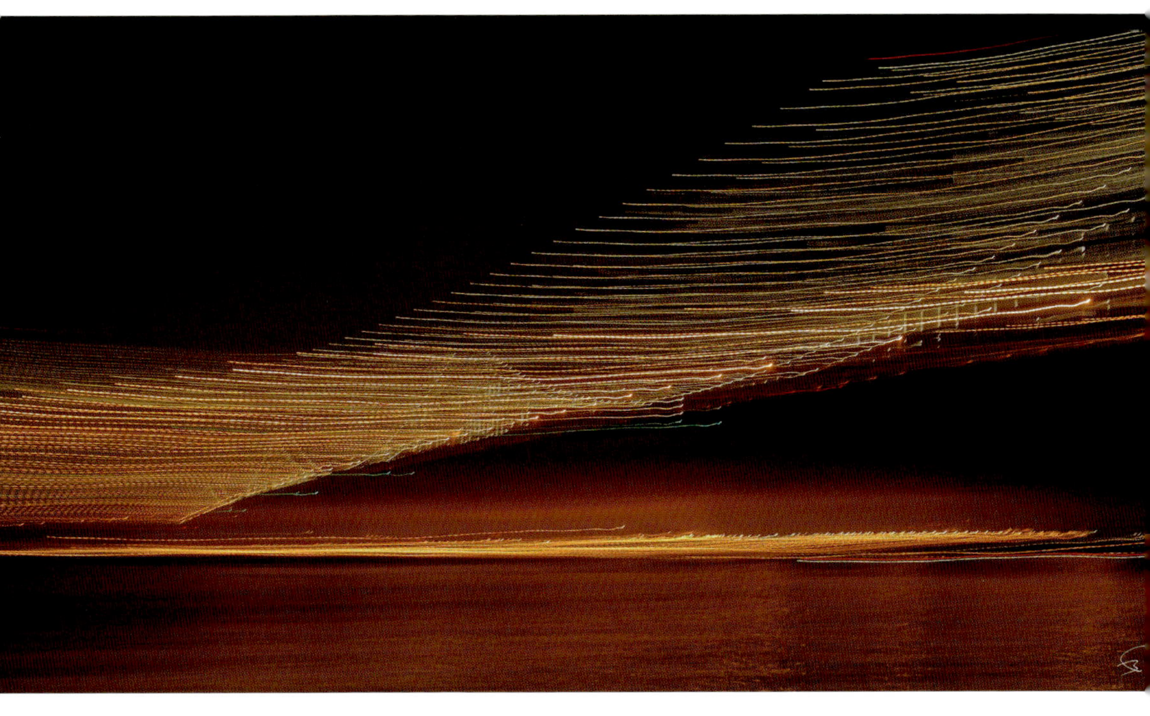

Bruno Paget
Gardens by the Bay, 2013
GALERIE MONA LISA

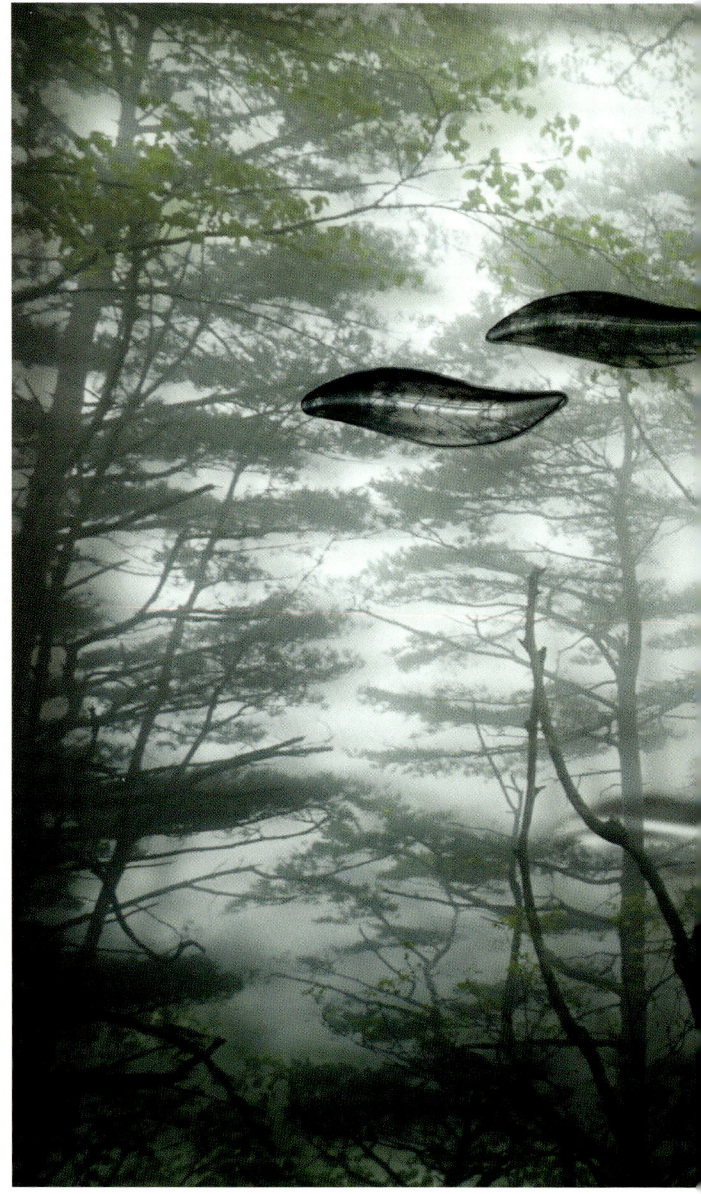

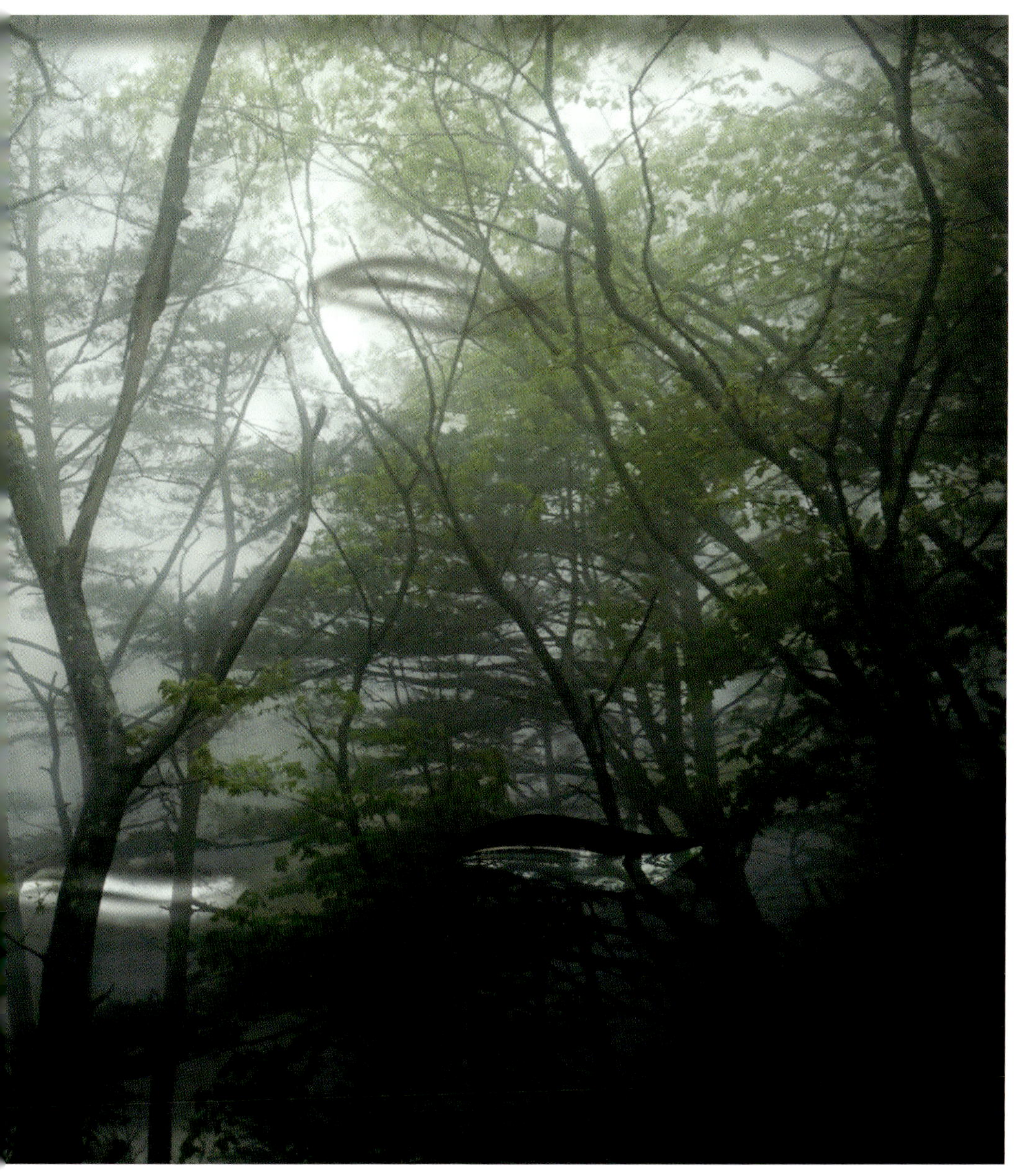

Soha Jeong Kyoung-Mee
Forest I , 2018
GALERIE MONA LISA

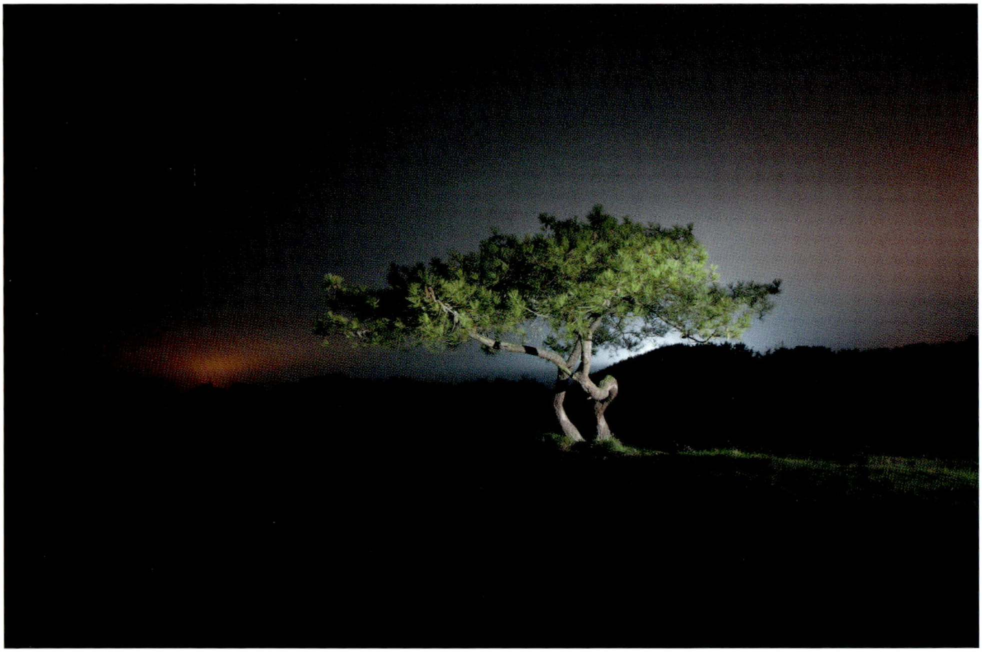

François Delebecque
Belil Bonsai265, 2011
GALERIE STP

Peter Mathis →
Aiguille de la Brenva, 2012
GALERIE STP

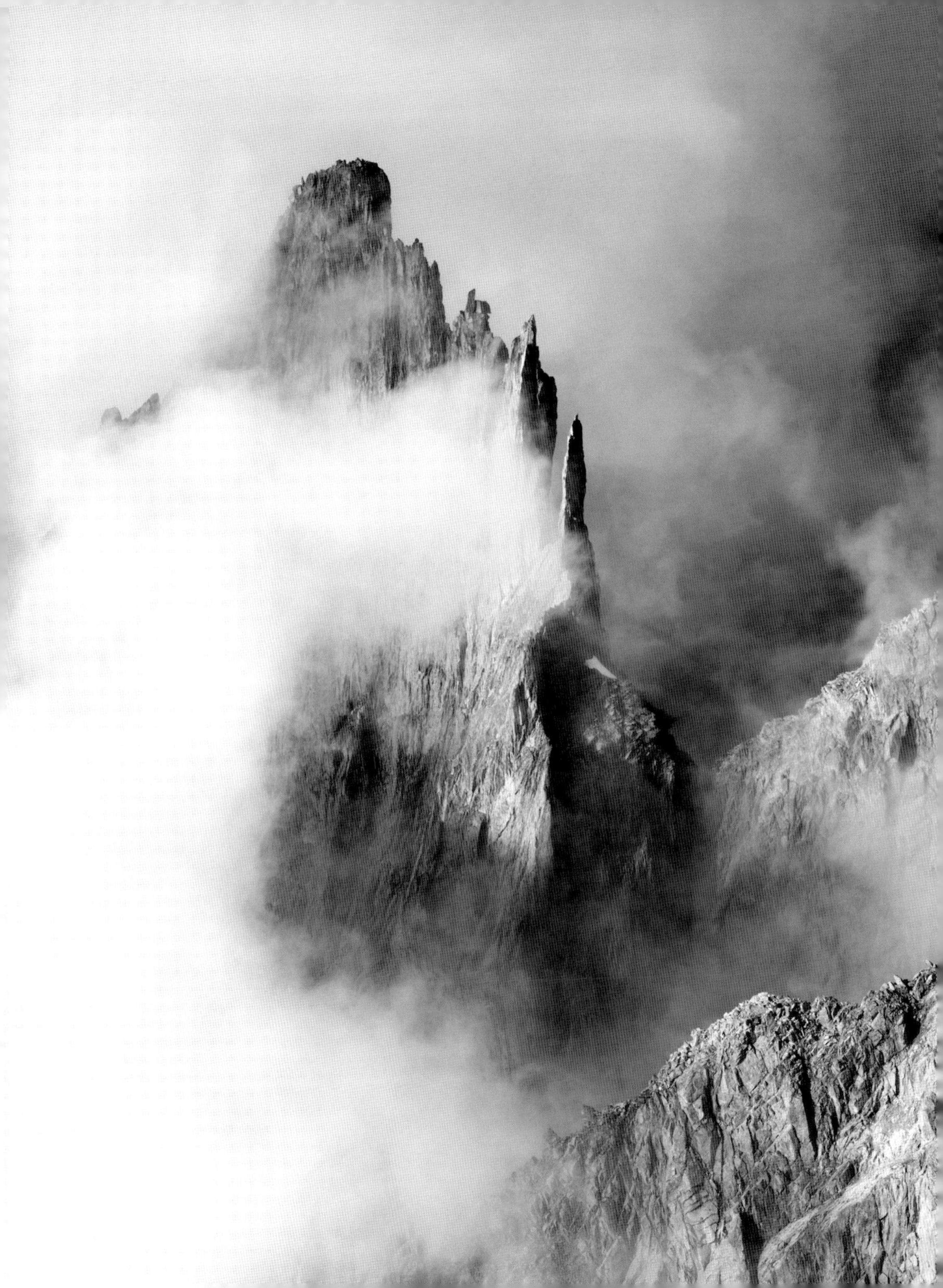

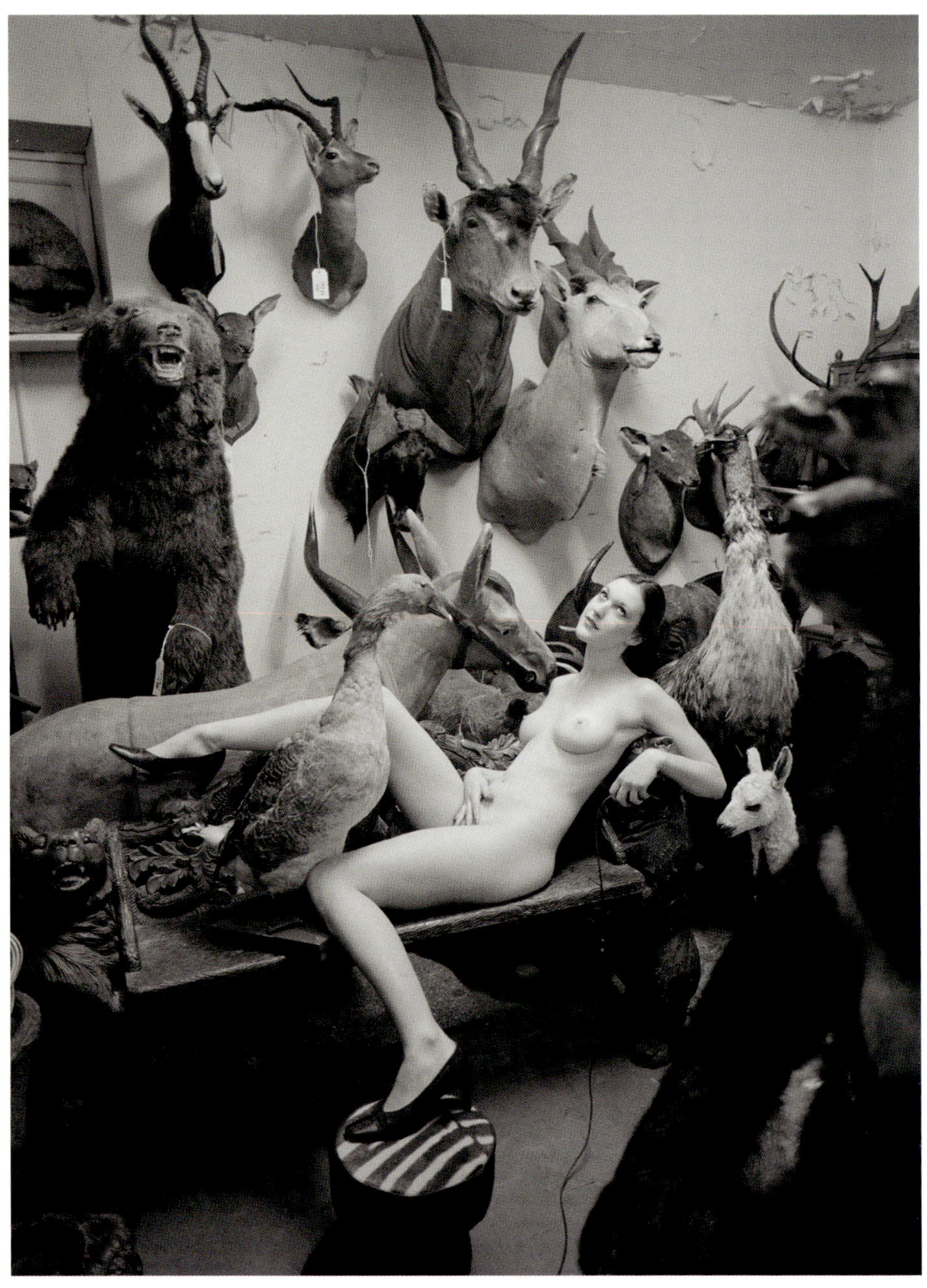

Uwe Ommer
Leda and the Swan, 2003
GALERIE STP

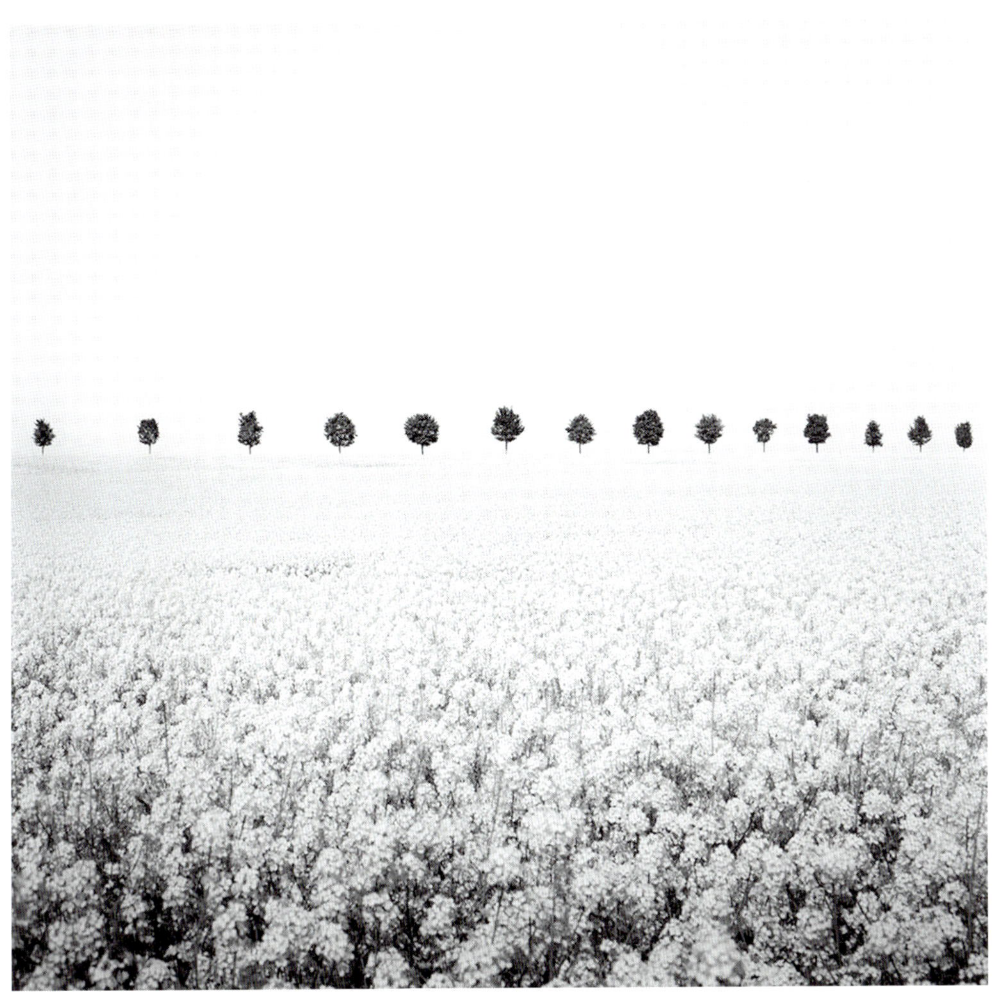

Silverfineart
Brassica Napus Study 1, 2018
GALERIE STP

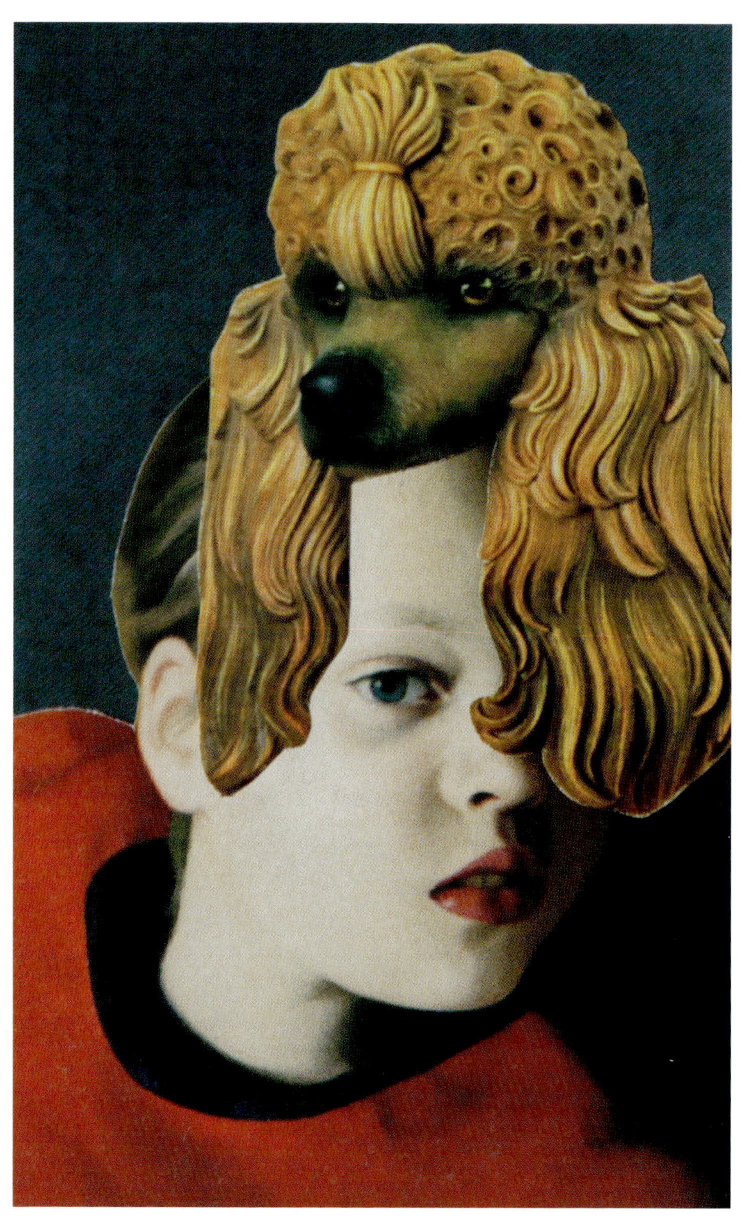

Anna Muller
Friends, 2012
GALERIE STP

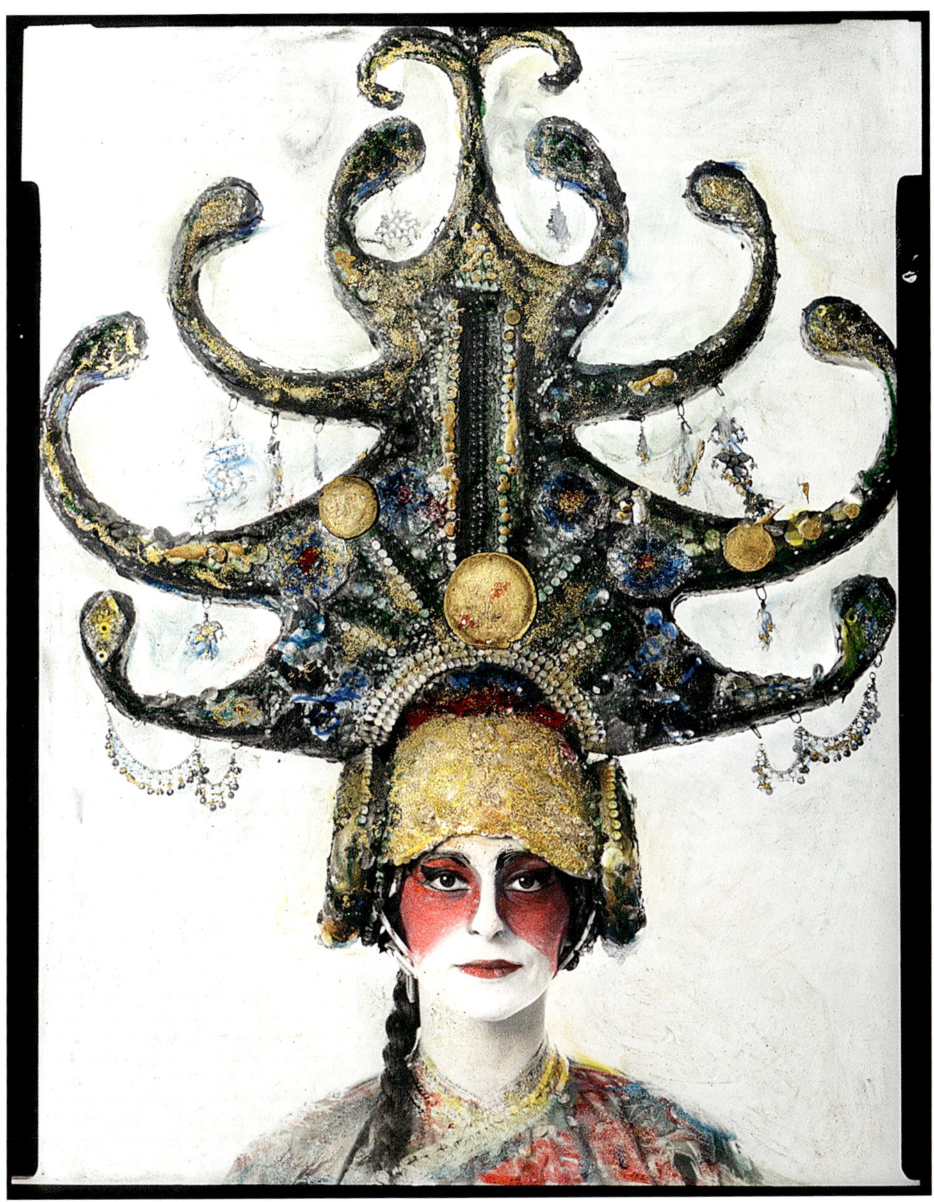

Walter Schels
Chinese Princess, 1981
GALERIE STP

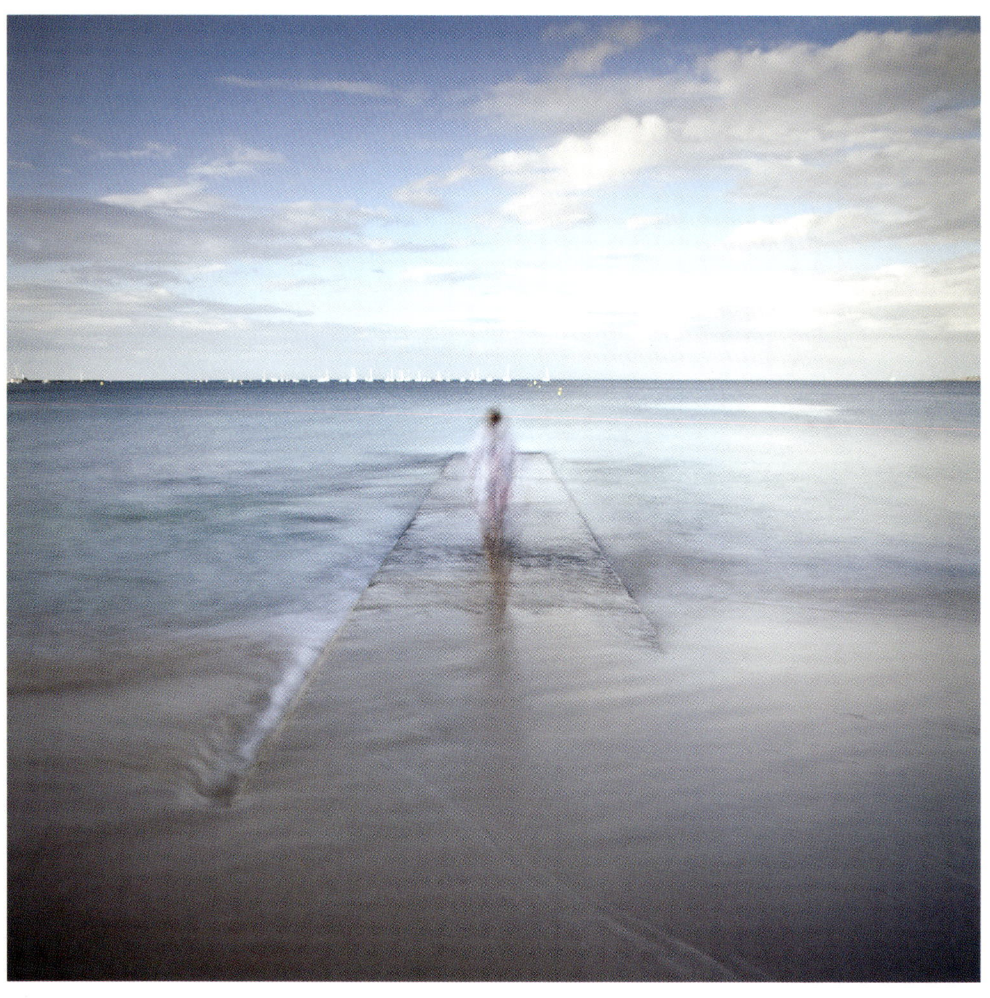

Marc Josse
La Dame Blanche, 2012
GALERIE WALLPEPPER

Yuna Yagi →
Kaze-no-Oka, 2016
MEETING ART POINT

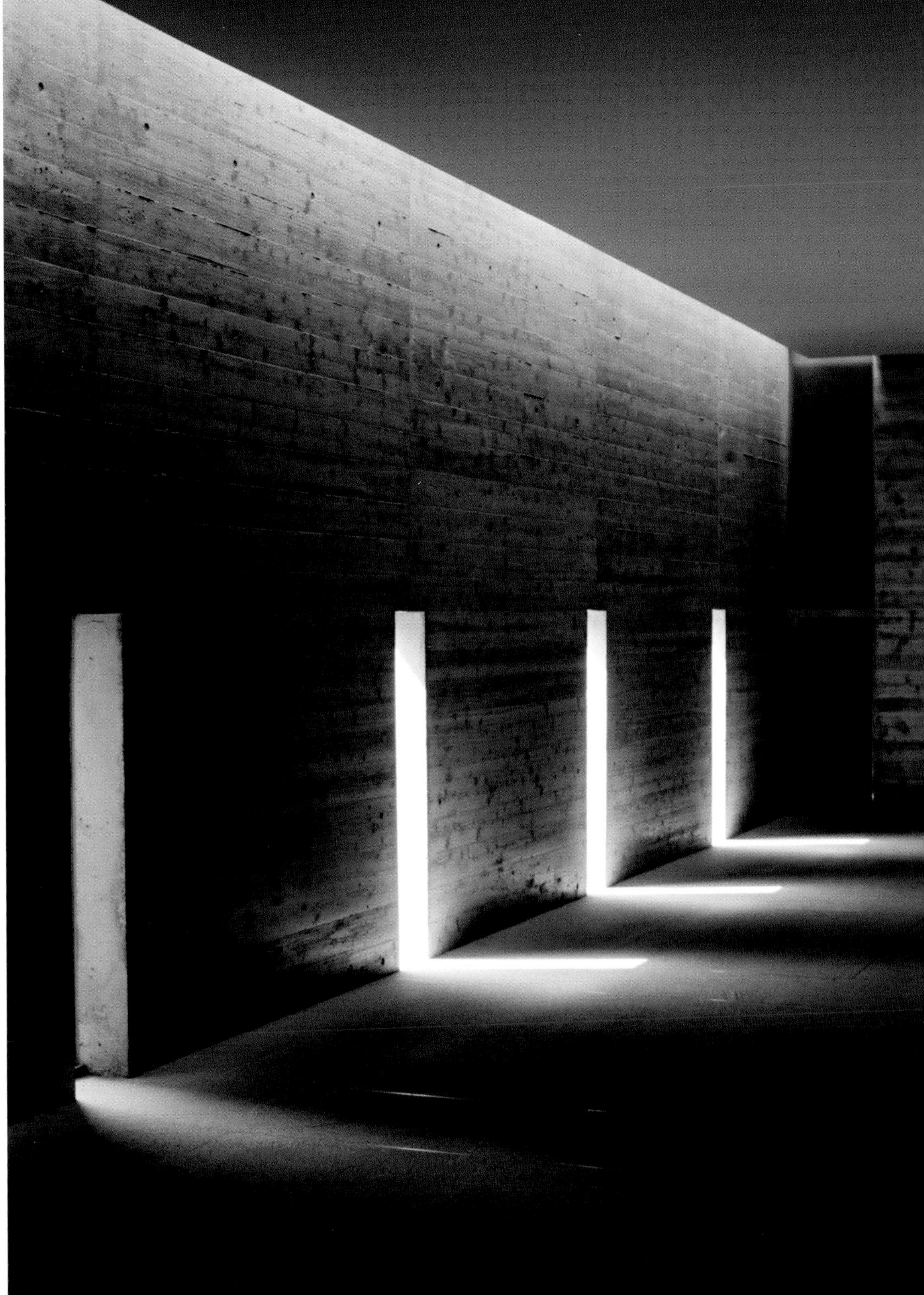

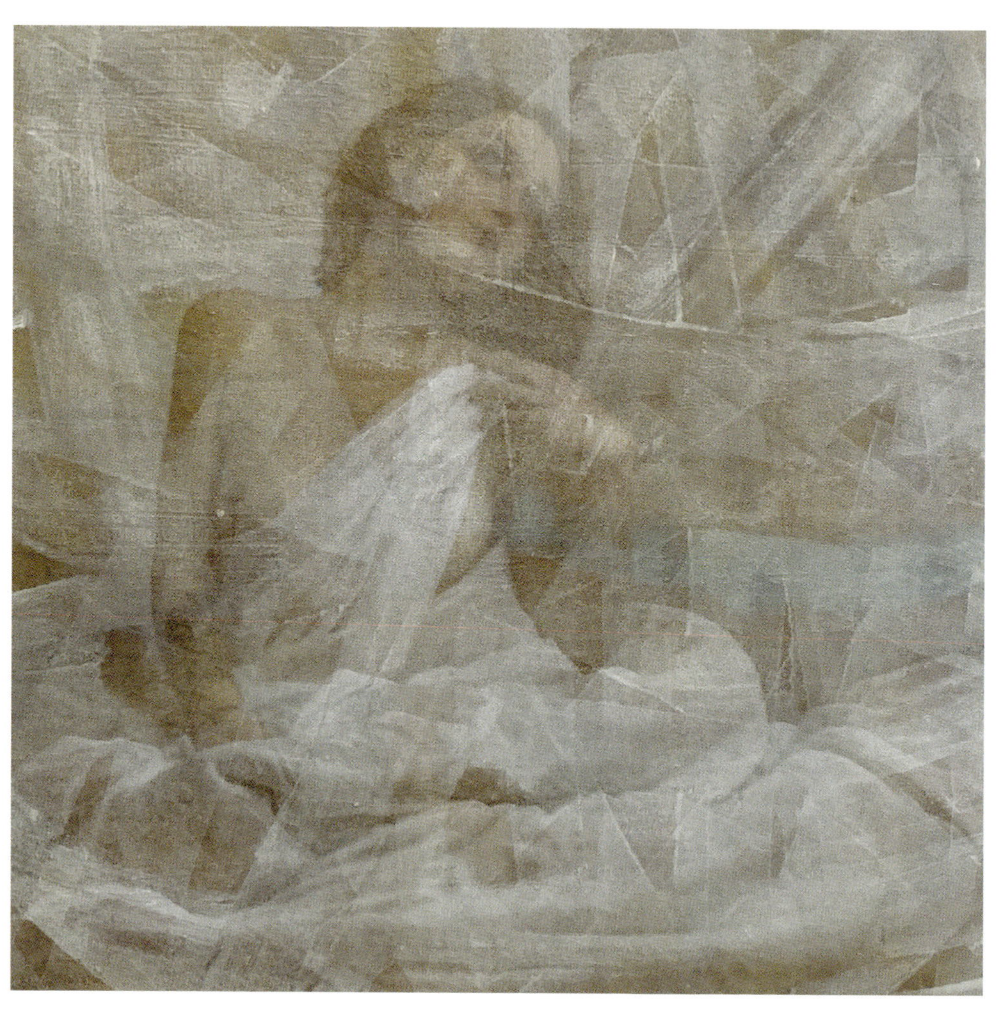

Nicolas Baghir
PP#3370, 2018
GALERIE XII

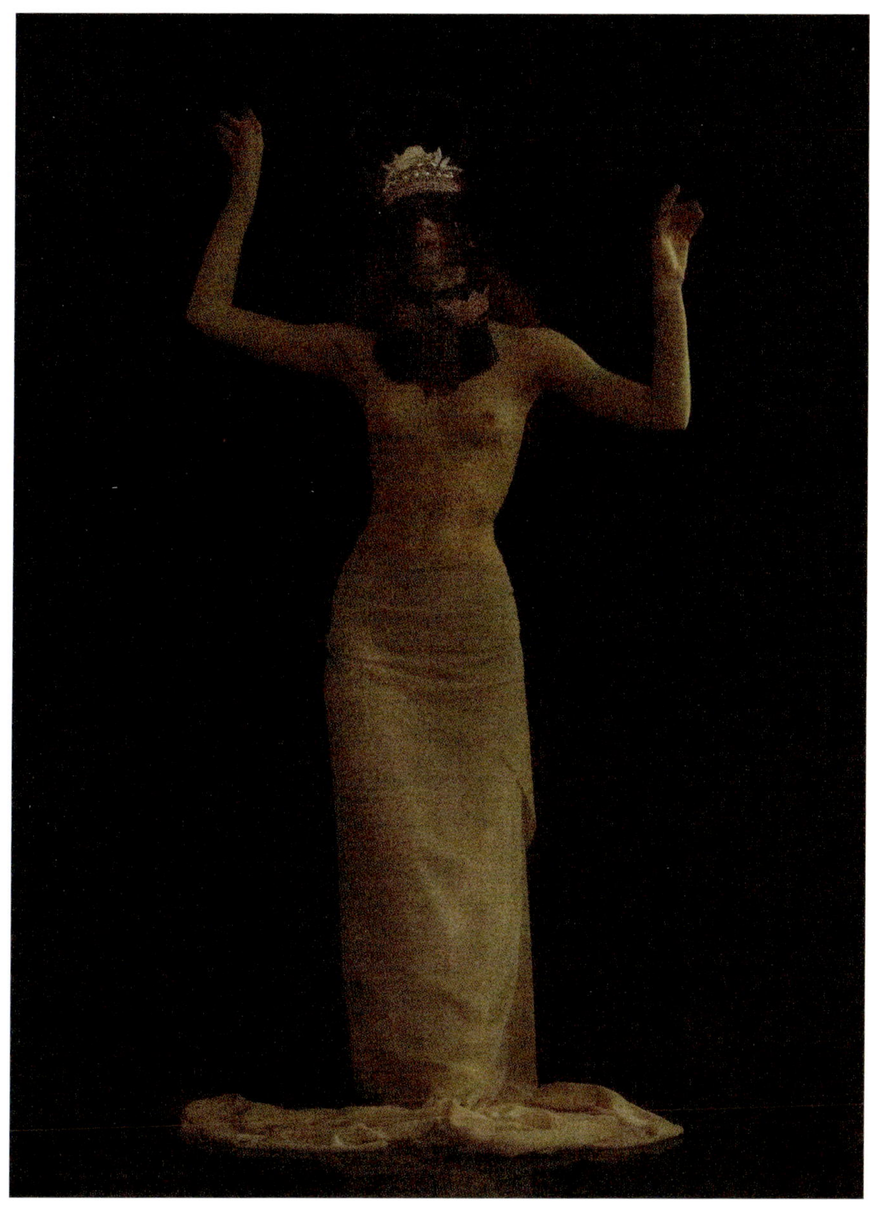

Charlotte Mano
Muse I, 2017
GALERIE XII

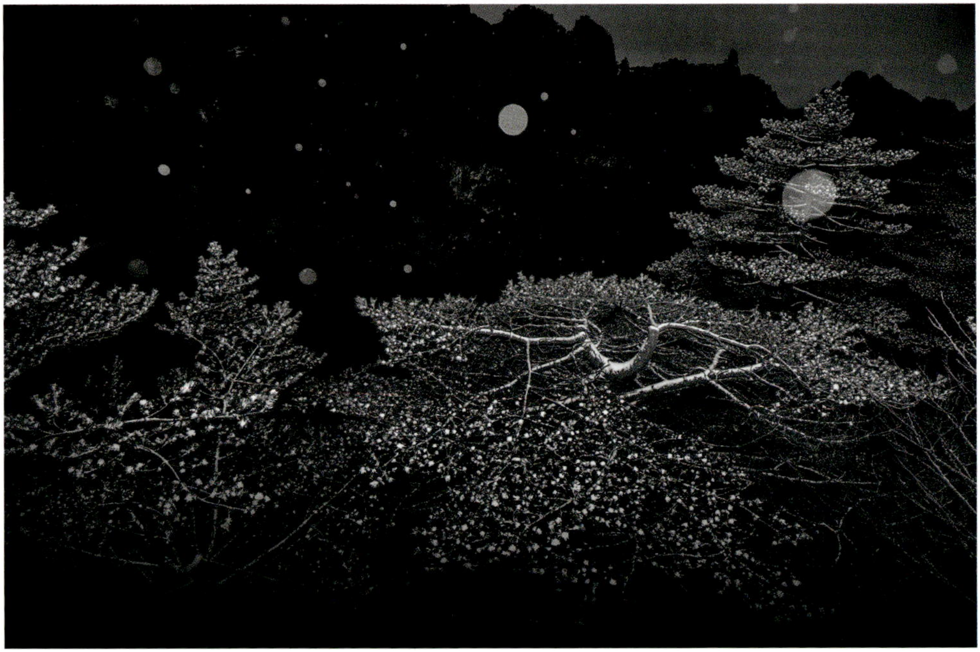

Wenlong Ye
Winter Snow #4, 2018
GALERIE XII

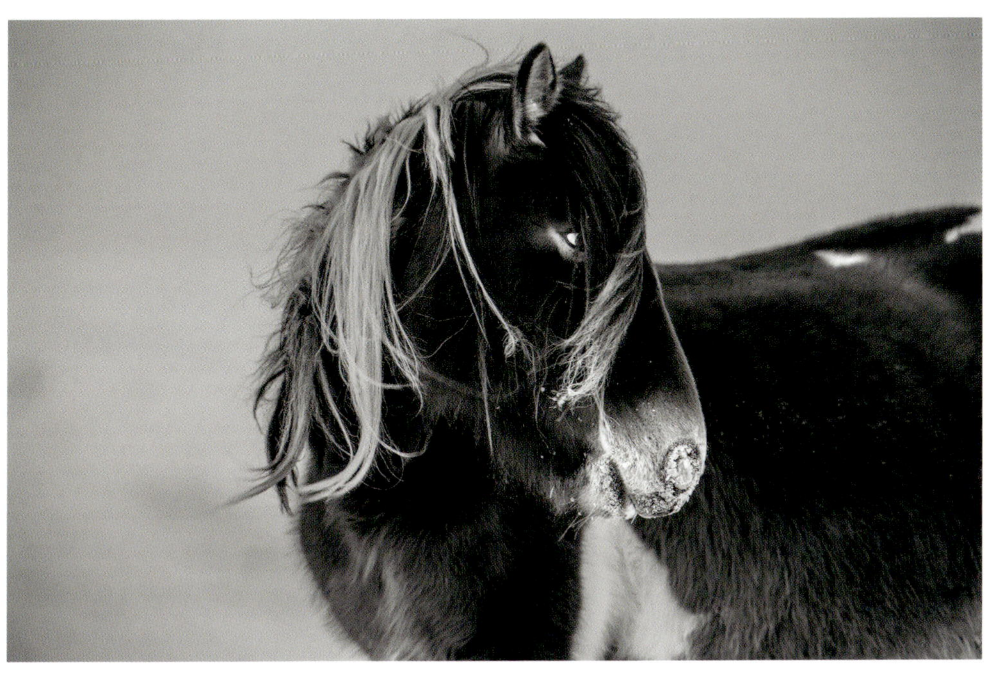

A Yin
Spirit of Mongolian Horses, 2015
GALERIE YI

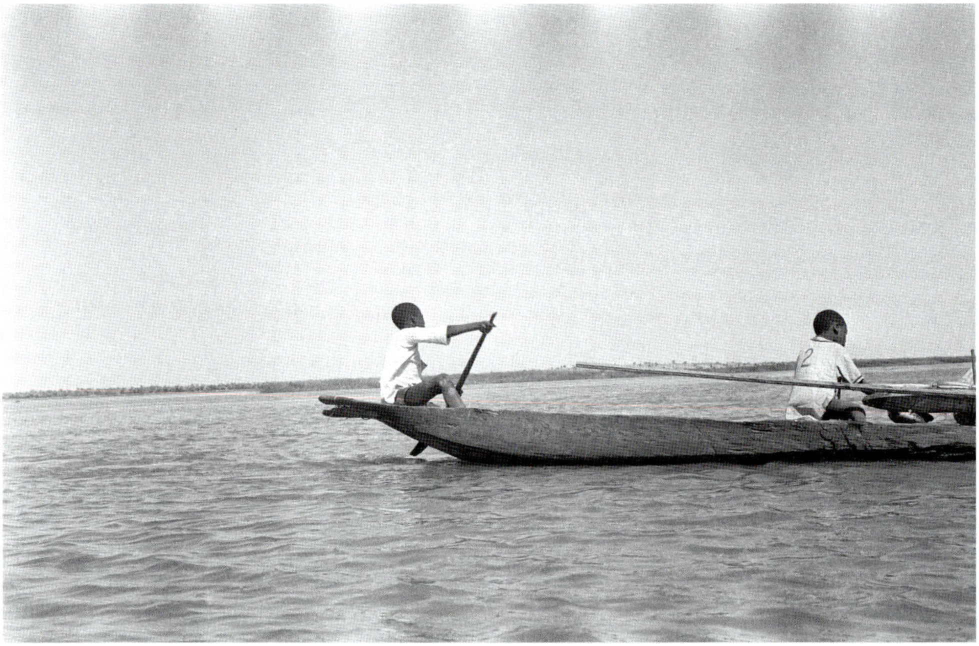

Mario Dondero
Sul fiume Niger, 1966
GALLERIA CERIBELLI

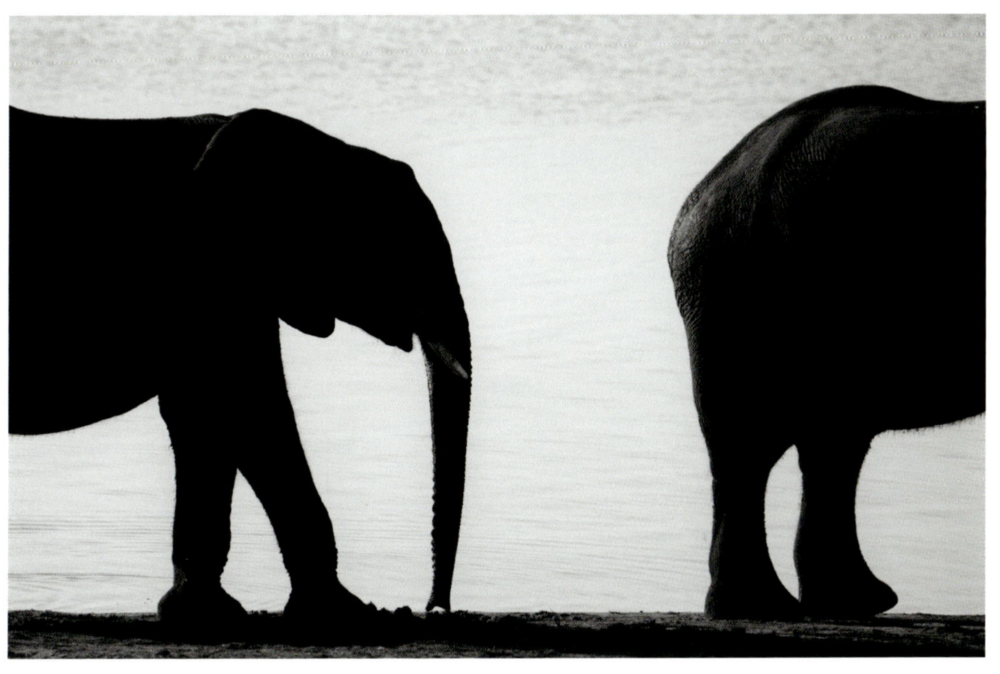

Andrea Micheli
Elefante Botswana, 2006
GALLERIA CERIBELLI

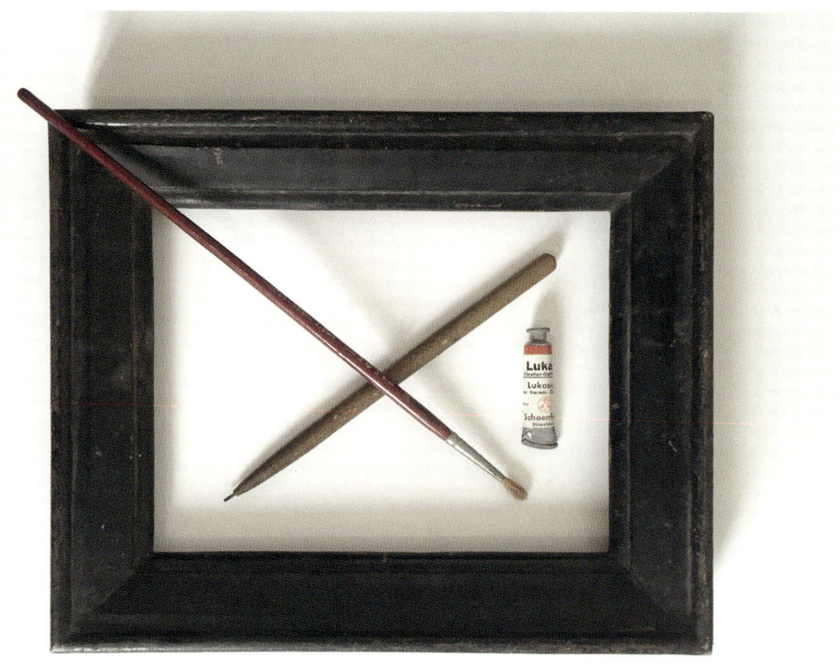

Giancarlo Fabbi
Natura morta, 2014
GALLERIA CERIBELLI

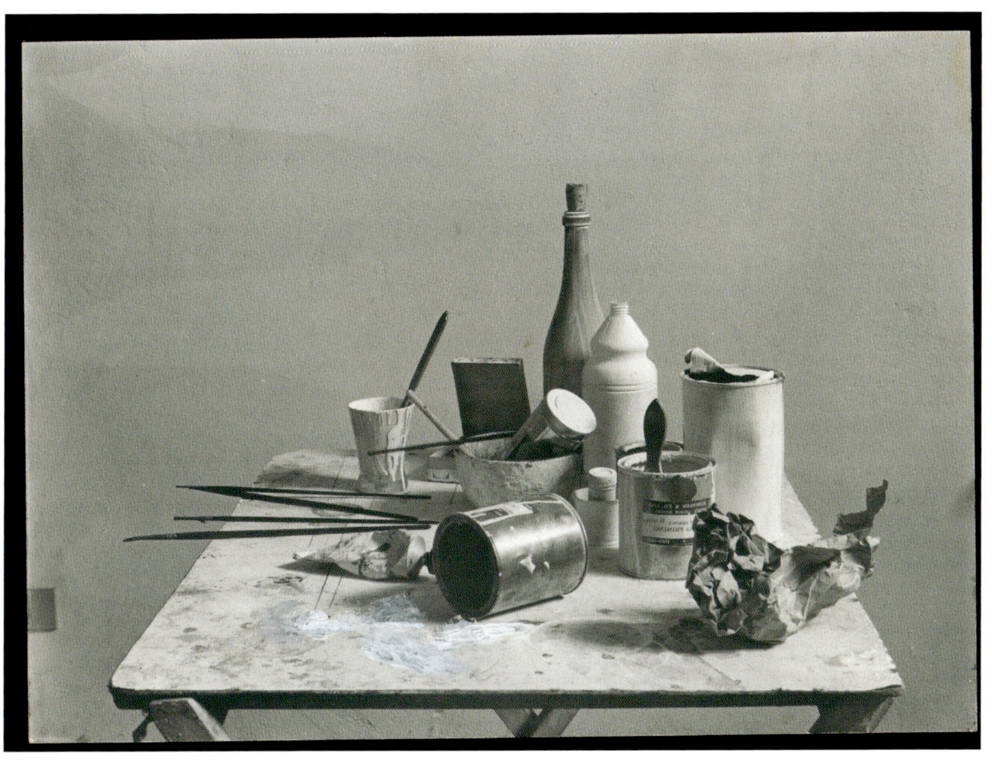

Gianfranco Ferroni
Oggettti, ca.1986
GALLERIA CERIBELLI

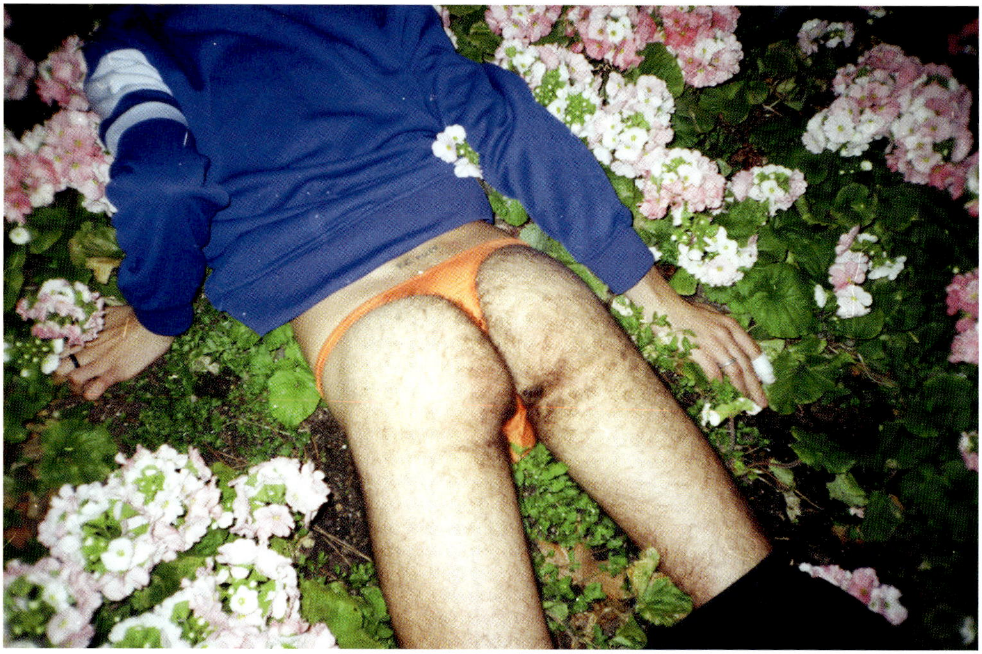

Simone Coitiño
Mejor que los colores de Peñarol, 2019
GRISART

David Molero Saura →
Los lobos nunca aullaron a la luna, 2018
GRISART

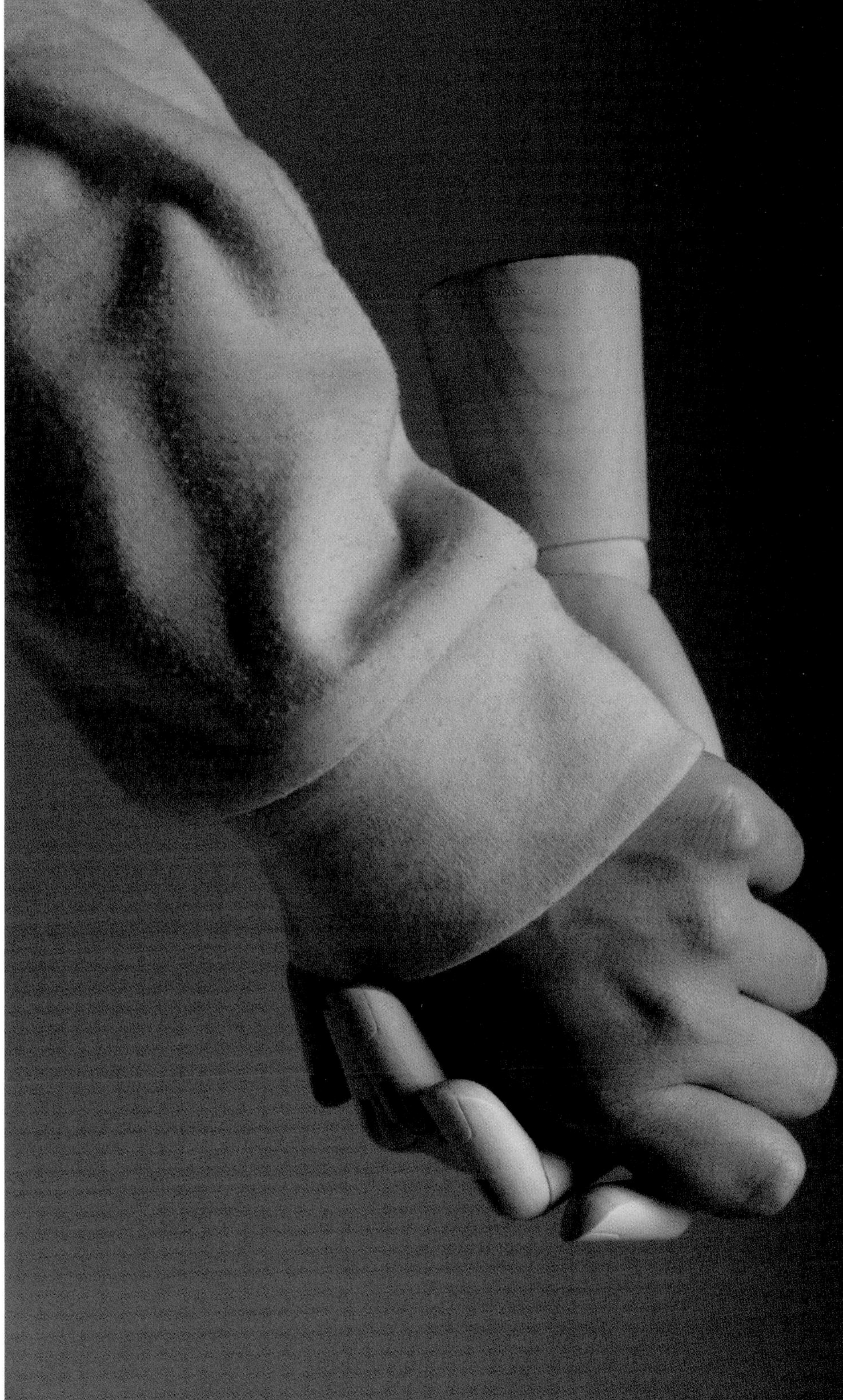

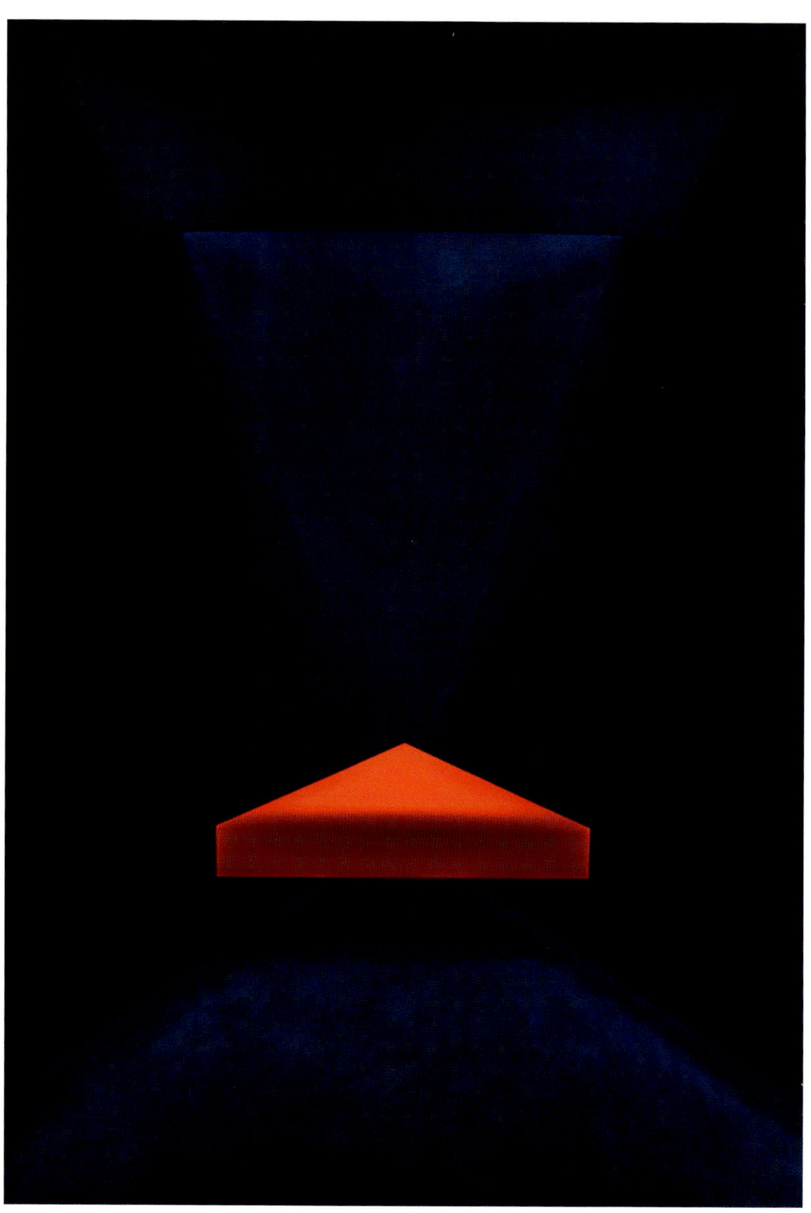

Lia Stein
Forme Sospese # 1, 2018-2019
GLI EROICI FURORI

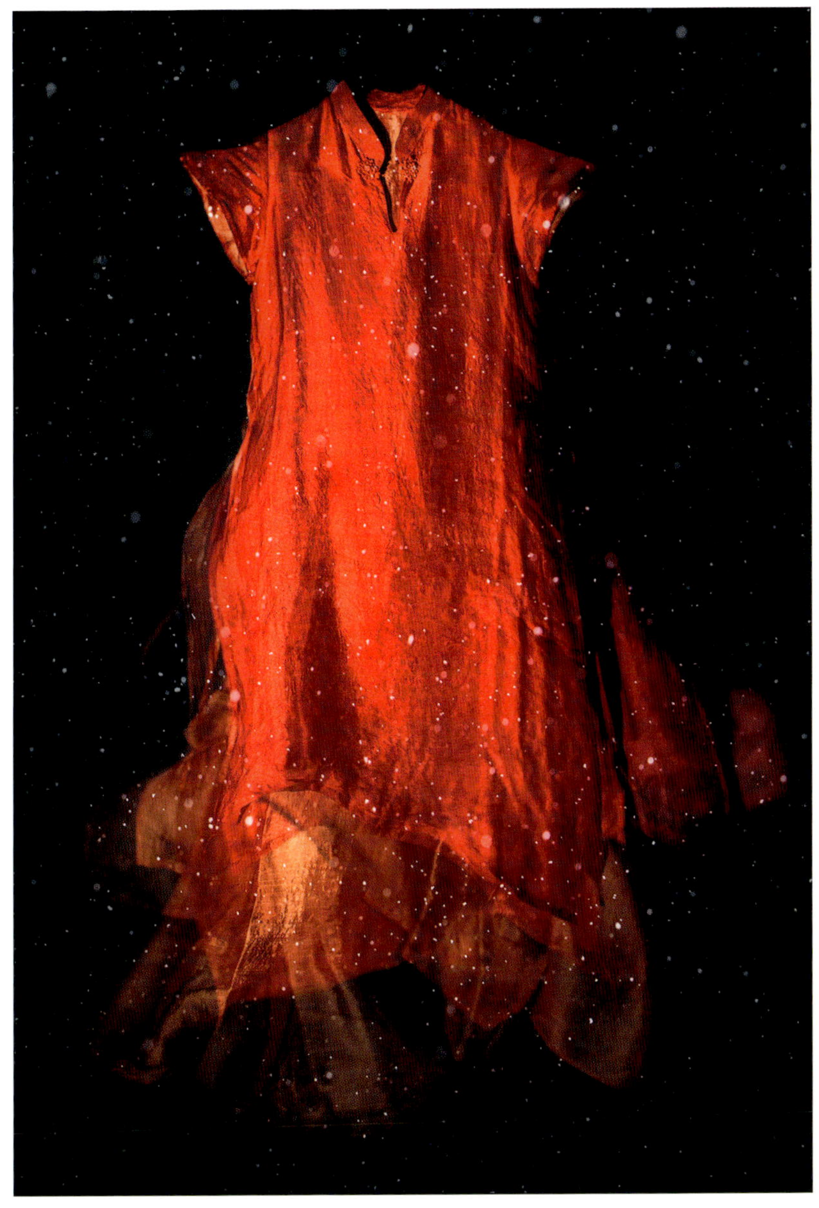

Margot Errante
Metamorphosis, 2017
HEILLANDI GALLERY

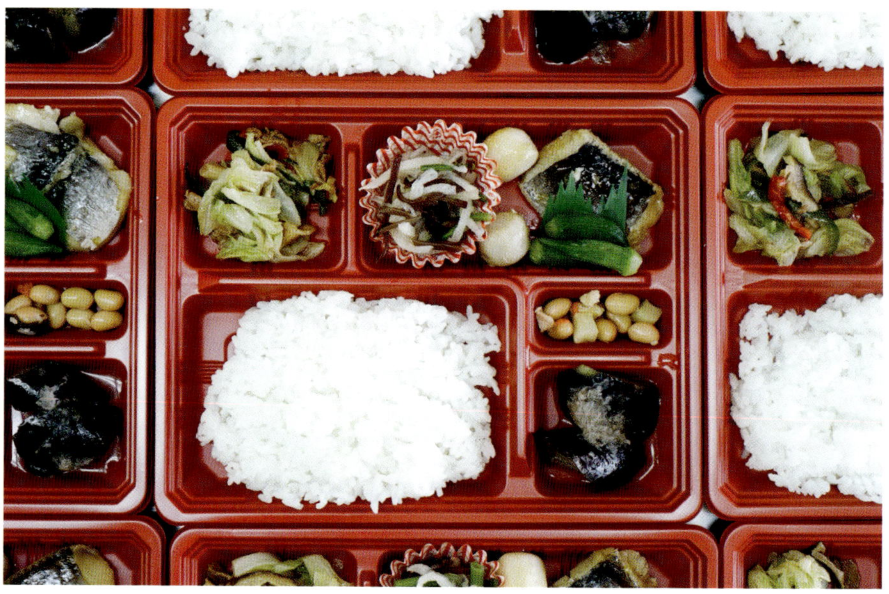

Atsushi Fukushima
#10, 2013
KG+

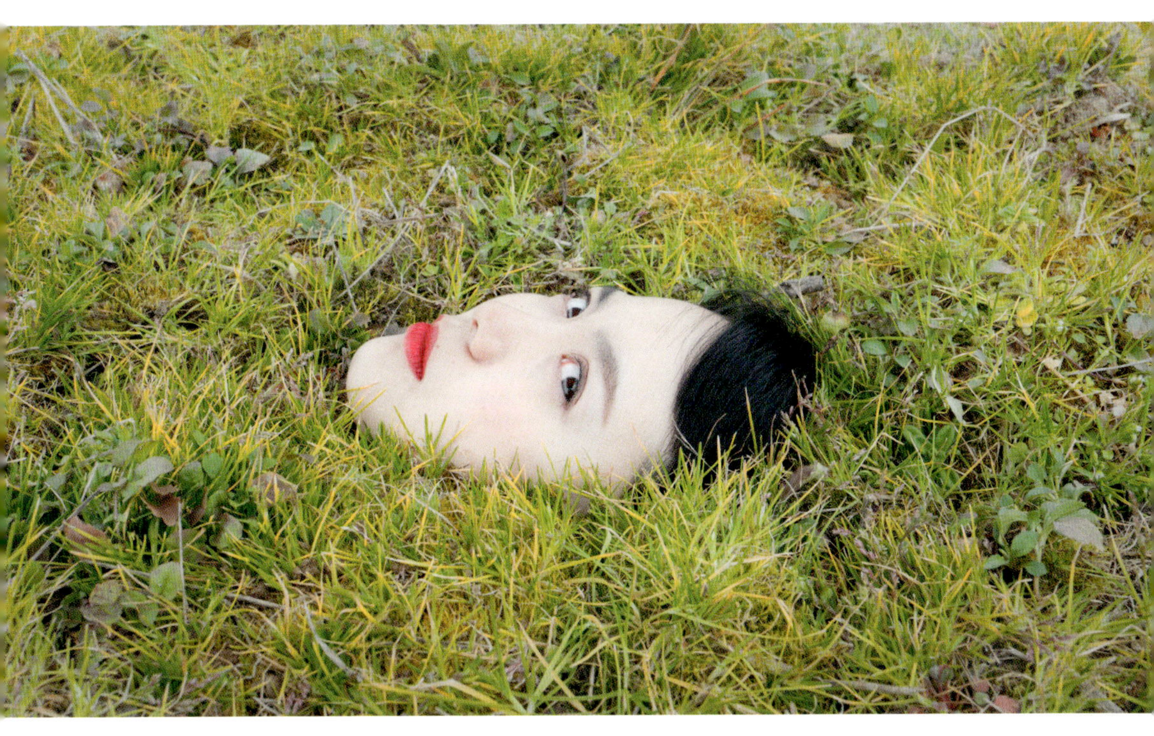

Chika & Ichio Usui
#9, 2017
KG+

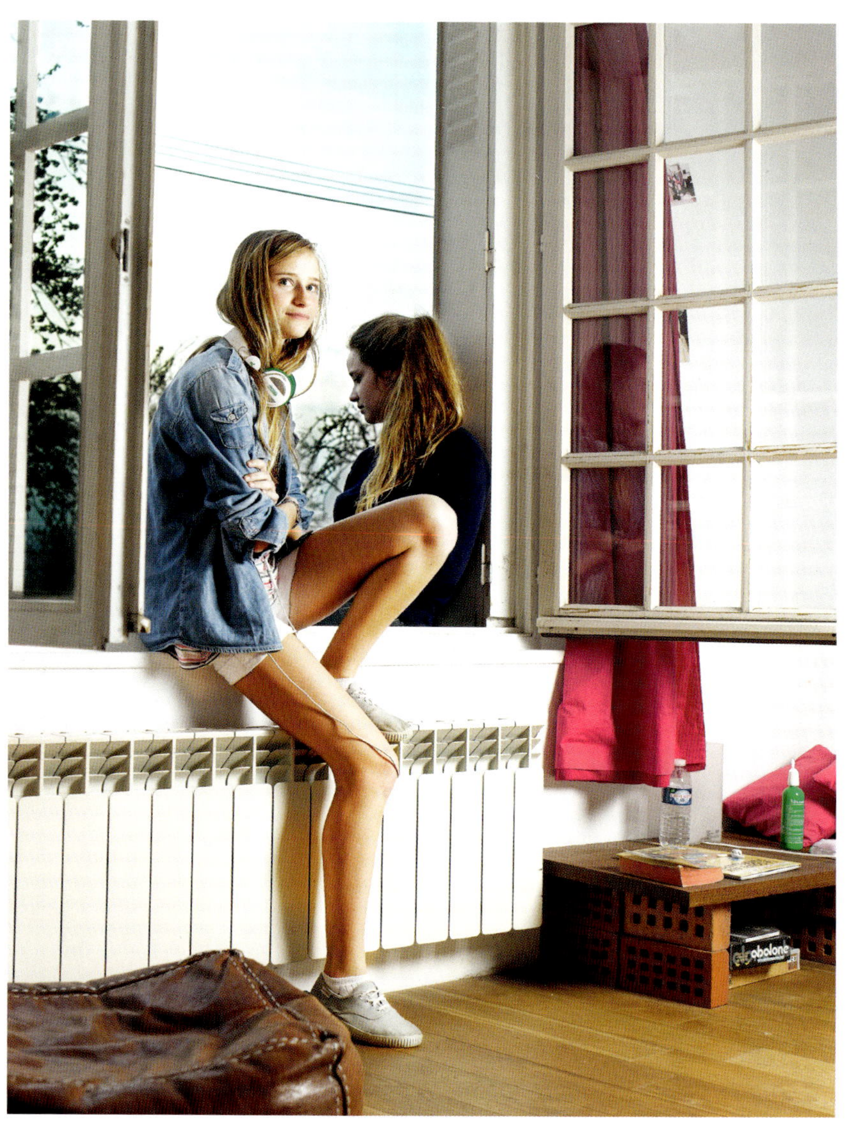

Armelle Kergall
Jeanne & Chloé, Chevrières, 2011
KG+

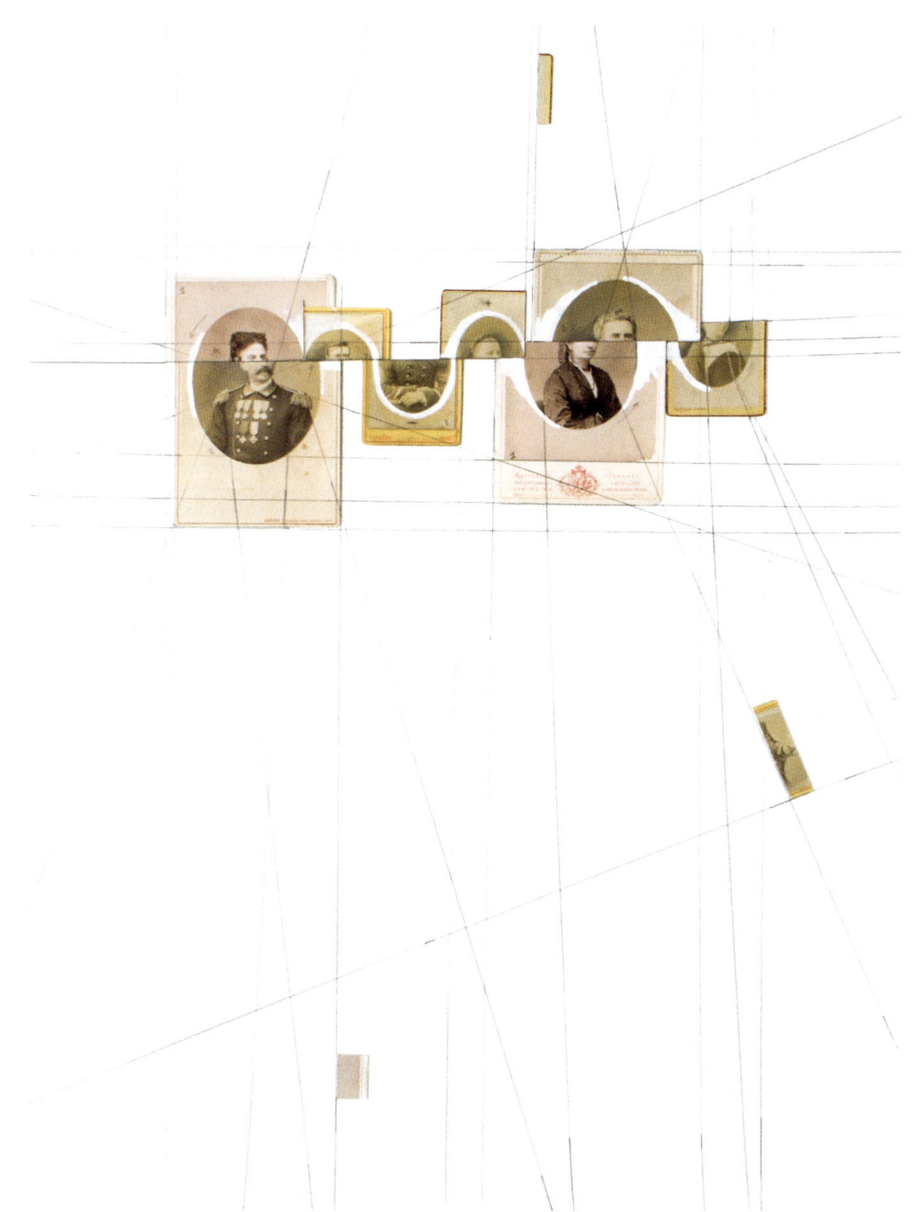

Alfred Drago Rens
L'altra metà della mela, 2018
GALLERIA L'AFFICHE

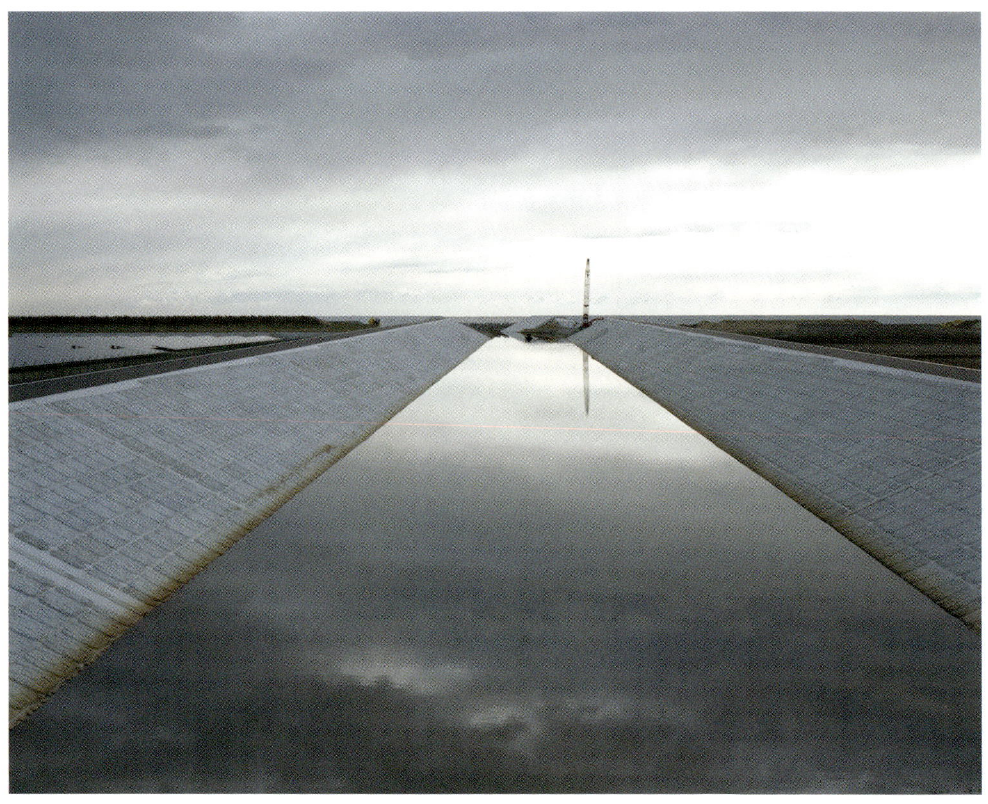

Tominaga Shin
Eight years after Fukushima, 2019
KICHIJOJI GALLERY

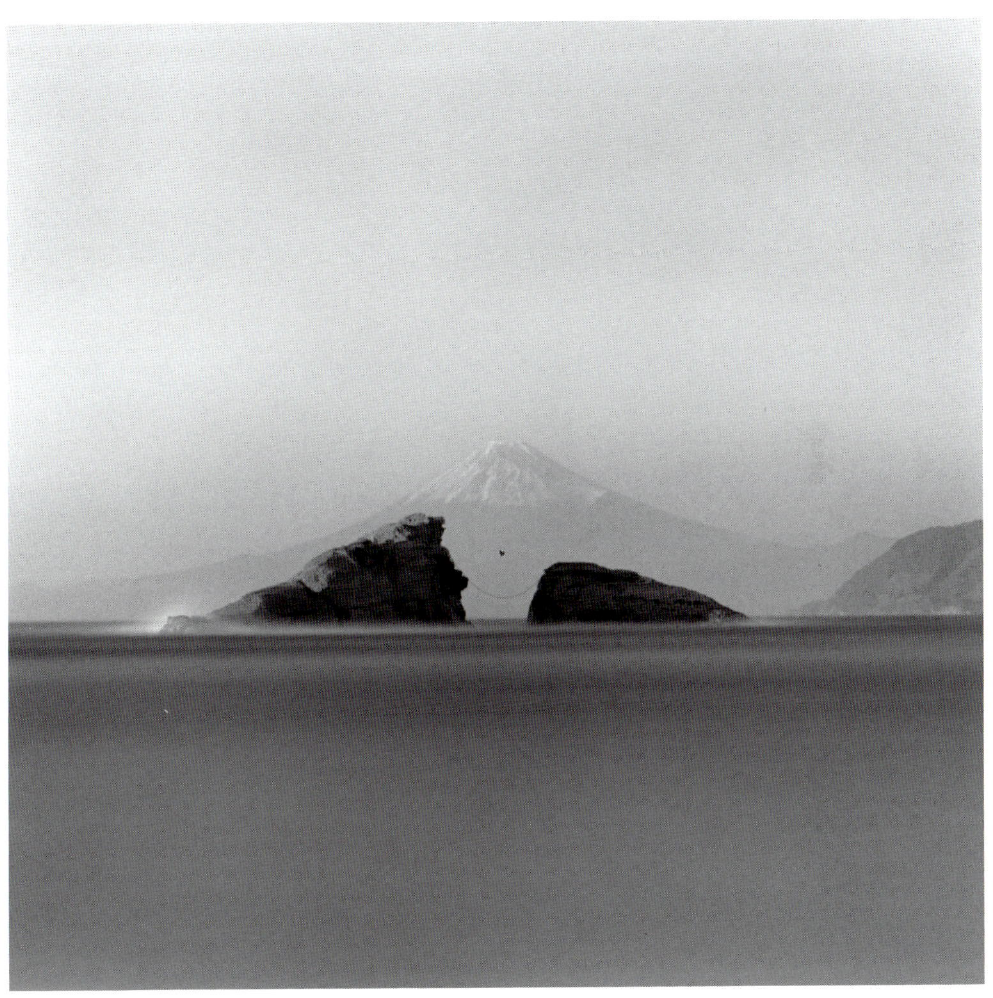

Ehira Tatsunori
Fuji#1, 2019
KICHIJOJI GALLERY

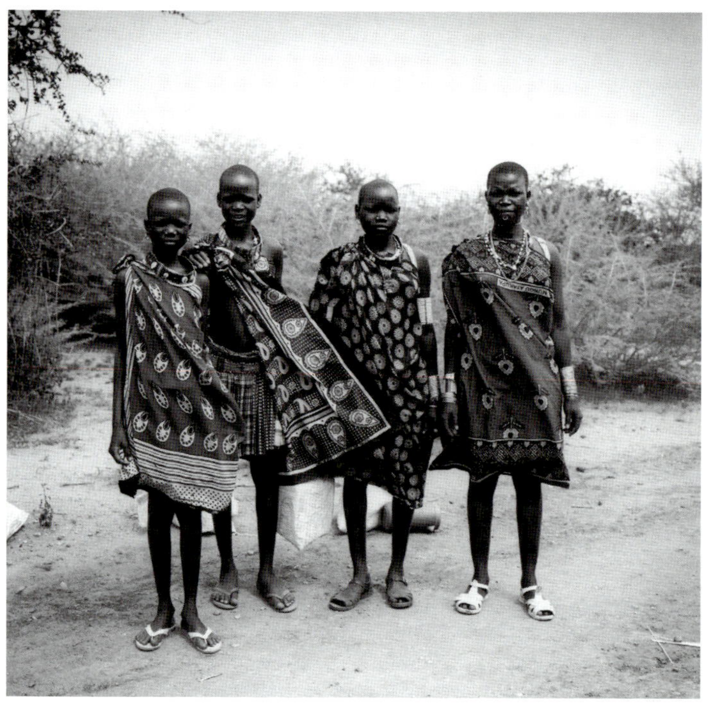

Maruyama Ko
Toposa, 2013
KICHIJOJI GALLERY

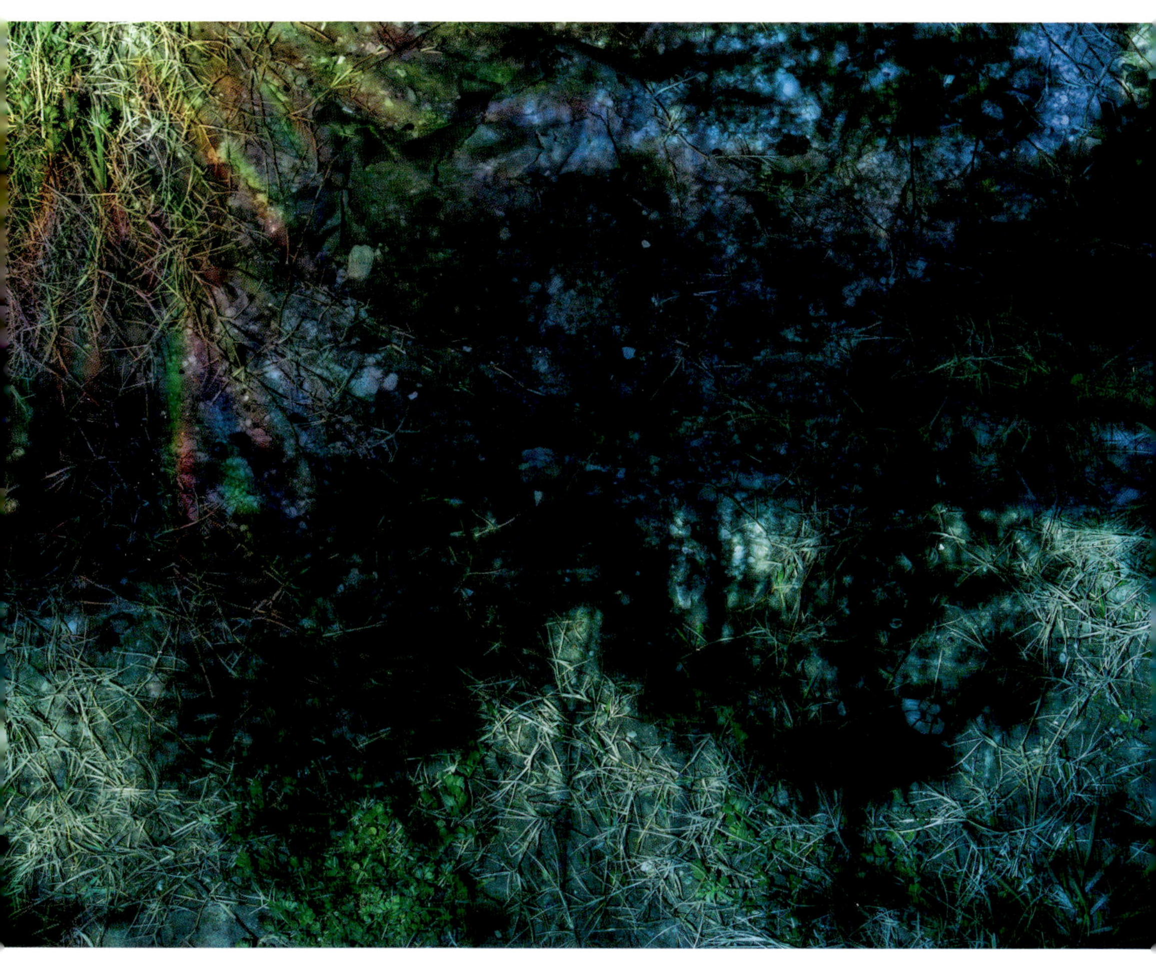

Saitoh Koyata
Gyoutoku Fuji 01, 2019
KICHIJOJI GALLERY

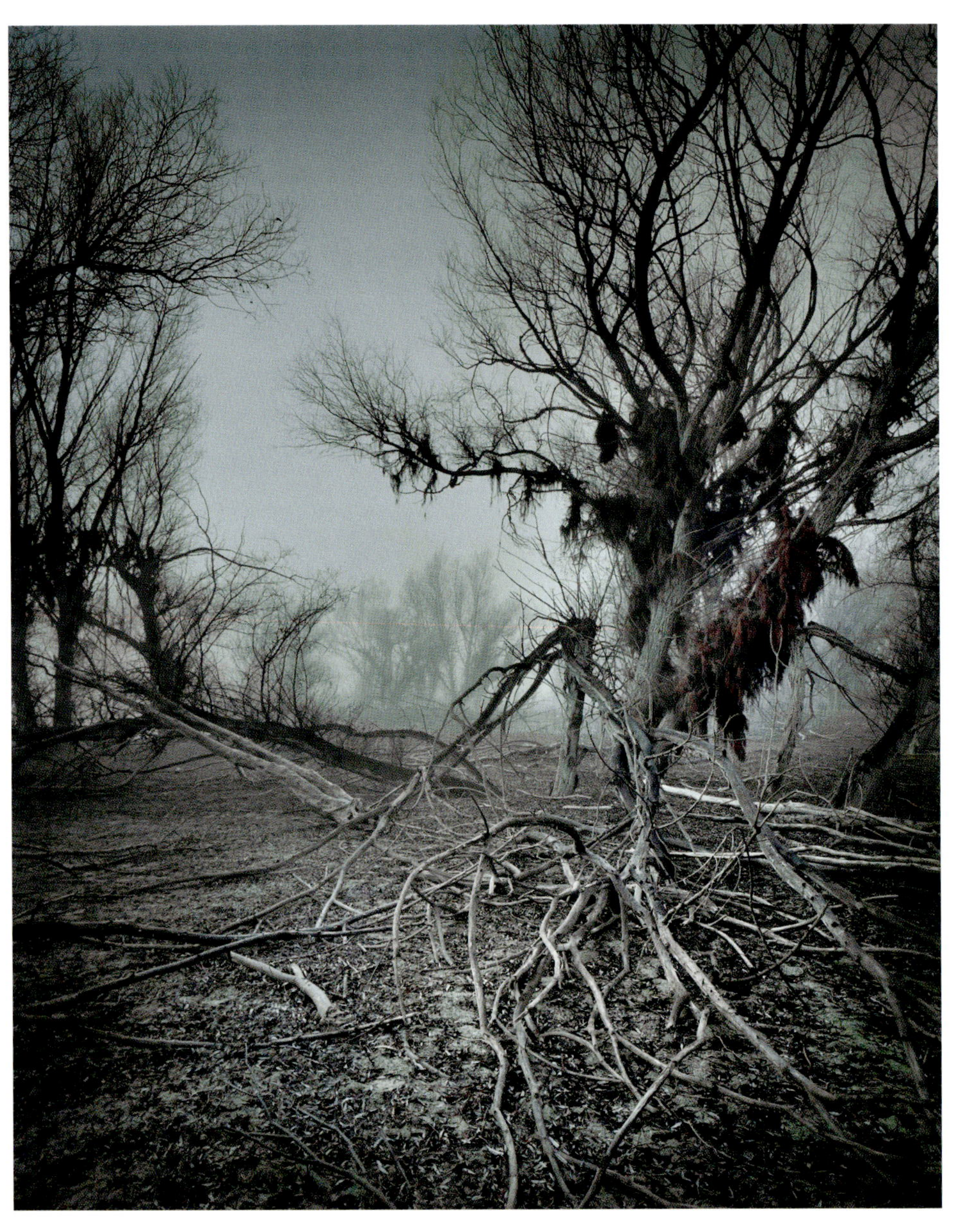

Abel Bourgeois
Sans Titre #1, 2019
L'ANGLE

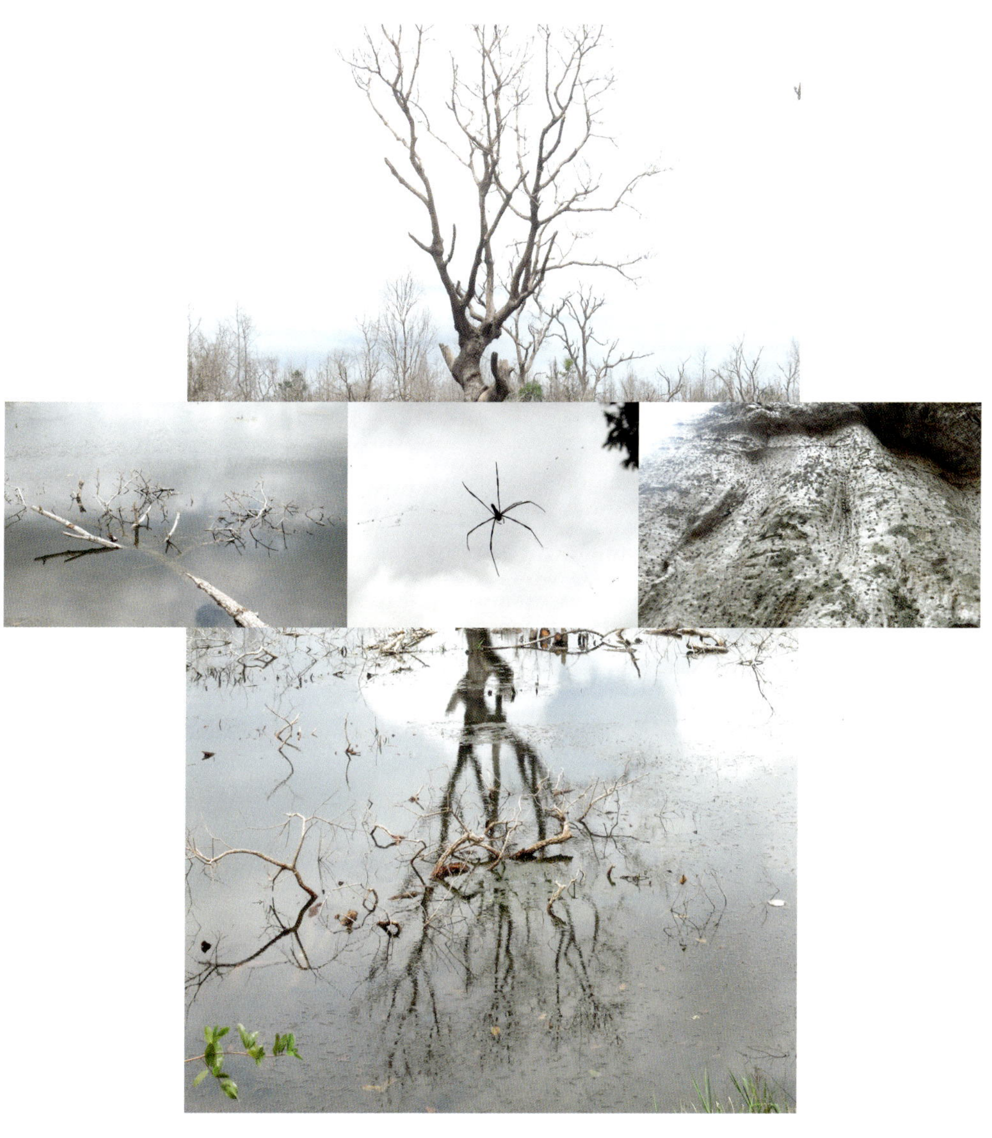

Francesca Di Bonito
Sans Titre #2, 2016
L'ANGLE

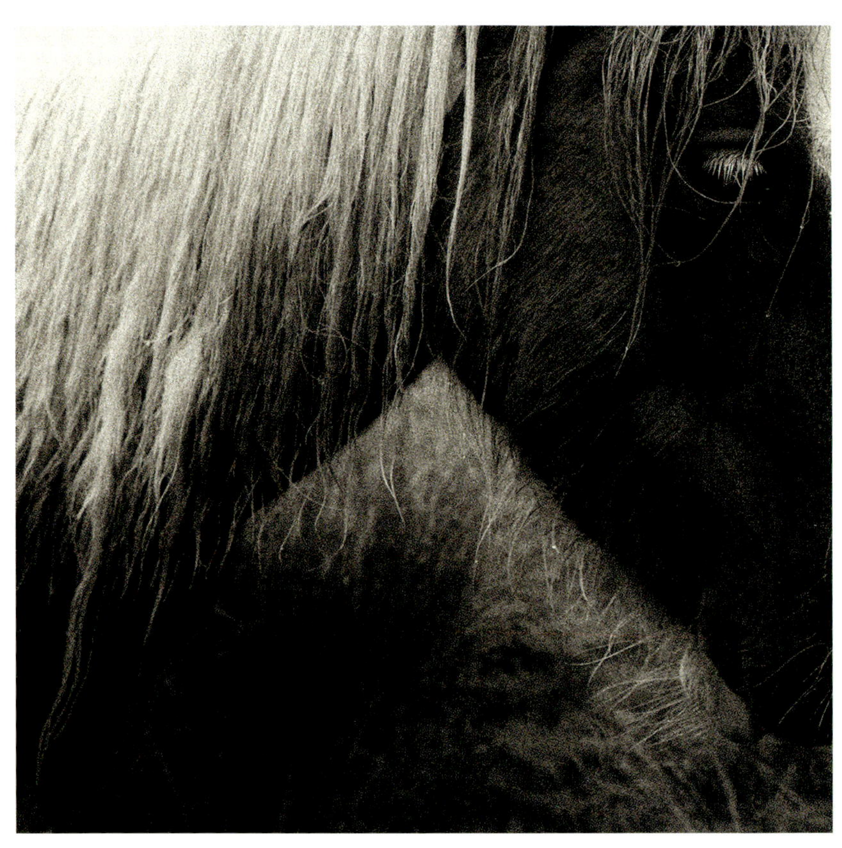

Fabrice Domenet
Voir les yeux fermés #12, 2019
L'ANGLE

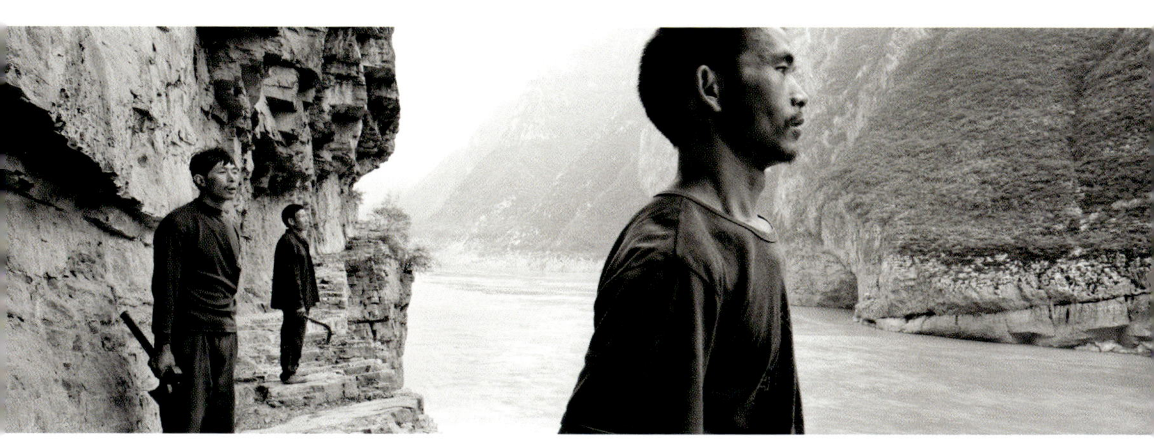

Nian Zeng
The entrance of Three Gorges: Qutang Gorge.
The three woodsmen on the Plank Road, with Sun Ligao in the front, 1996
LA GALERIE PARIS 1839

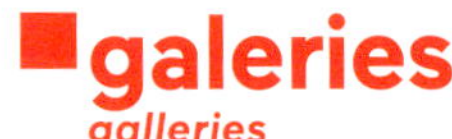

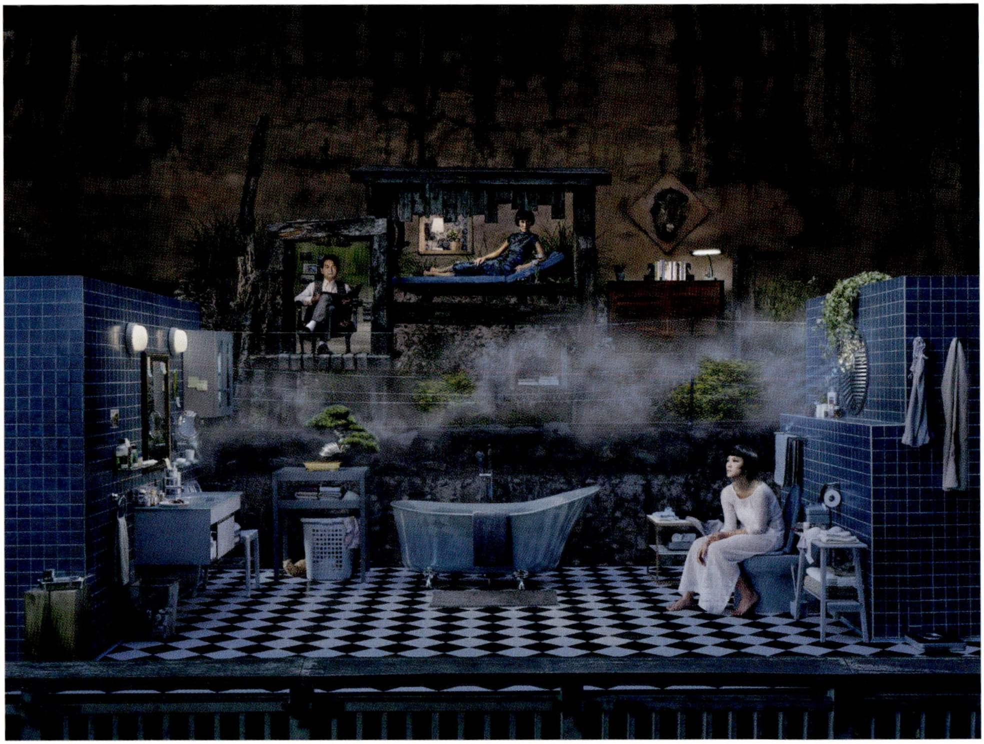

Ching-hui Chou
Animal Farm #6, 2014
LA GALERIE PARIS 1839

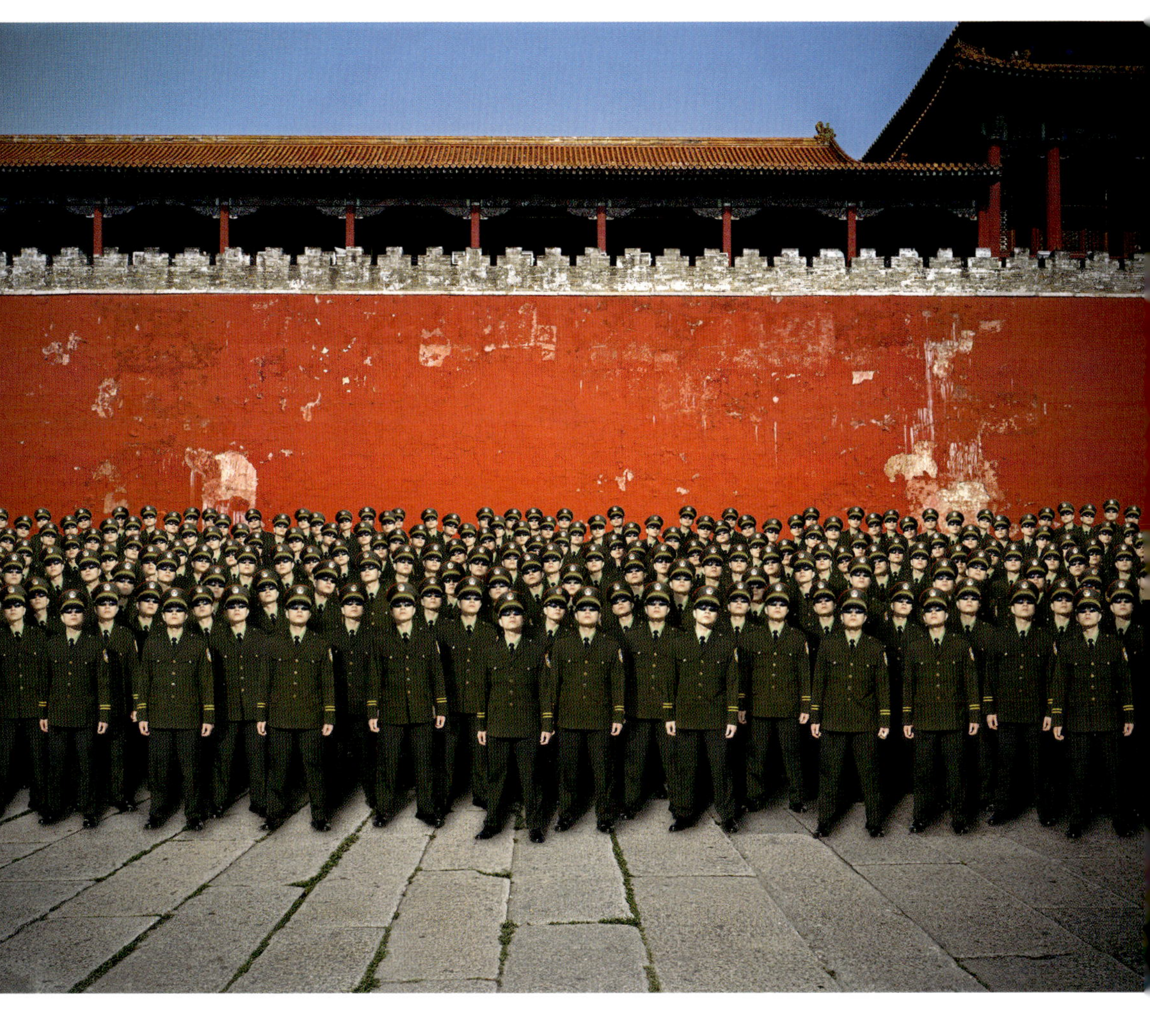

Almond Chu
Parade 9, 2012
LA GALERIE PARIS 1839

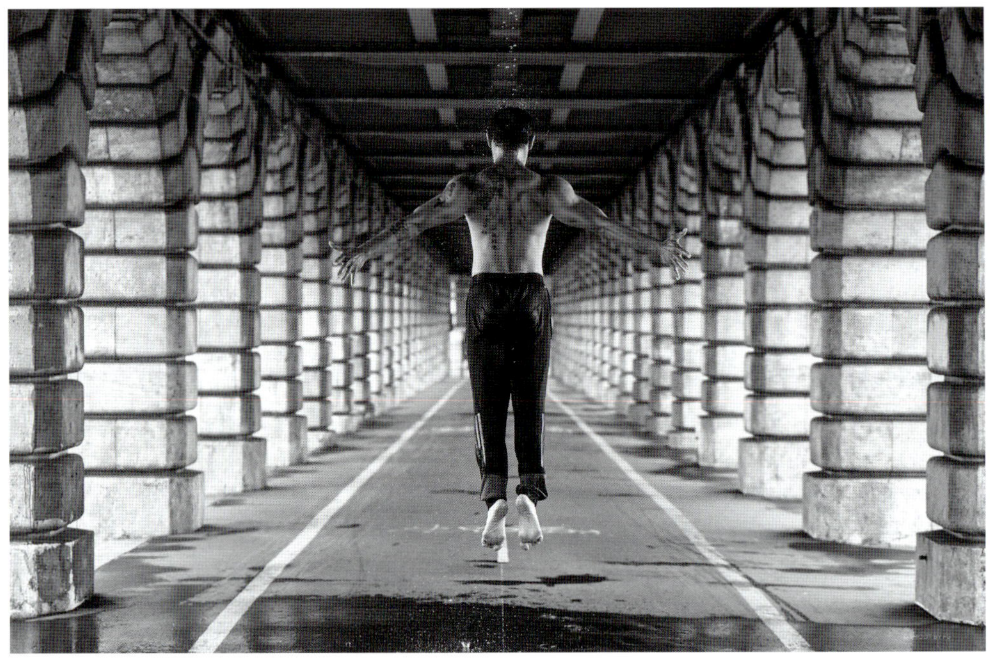

Franck Guedj
Impulse 1.0, 2019
LIMITED EDITIONS

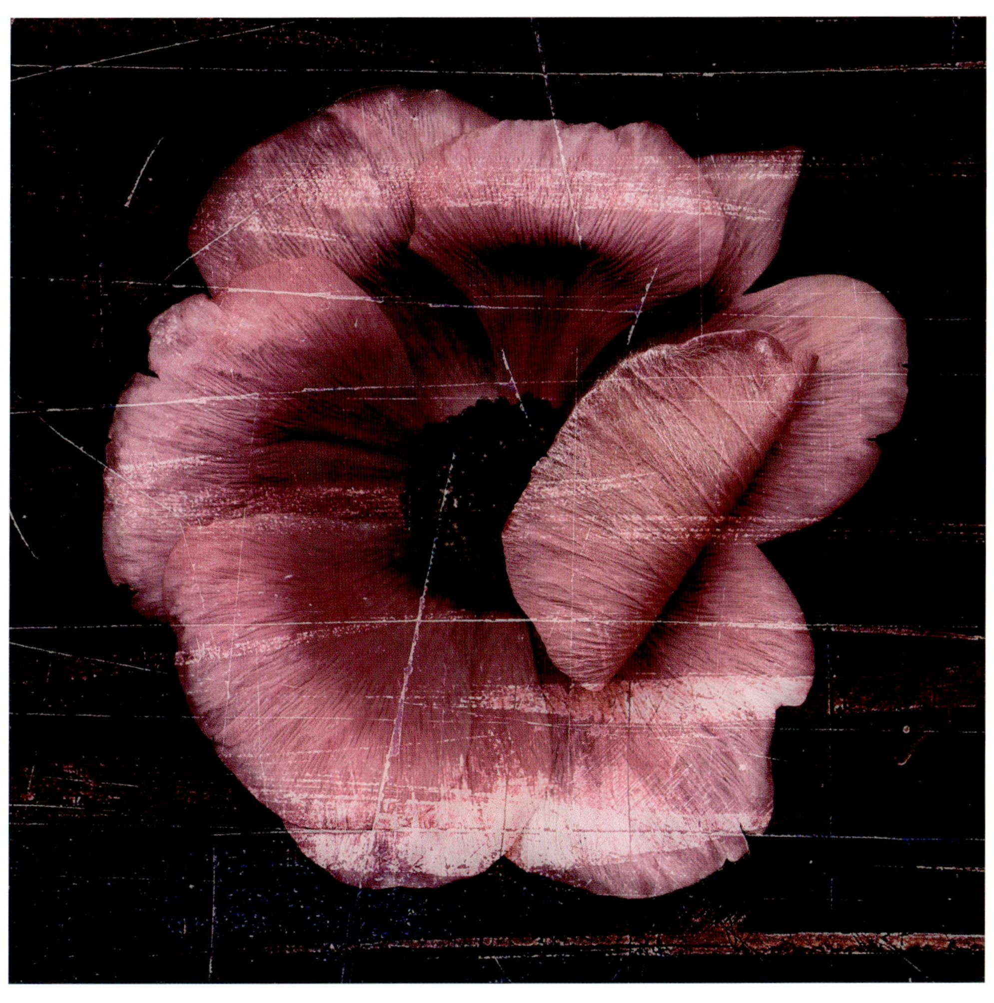

Marc Harrold
Vegetal Portrait 01, 2019
LIMITED EDITIONS

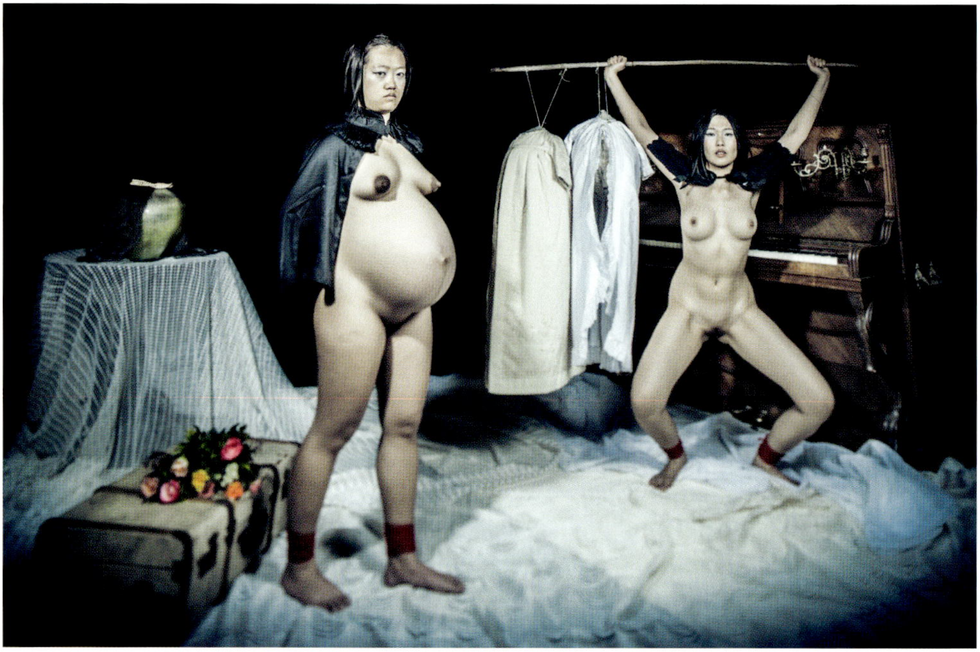

The Minotaur
Preparing Birth, 2018
LES SOEURS GRÉES

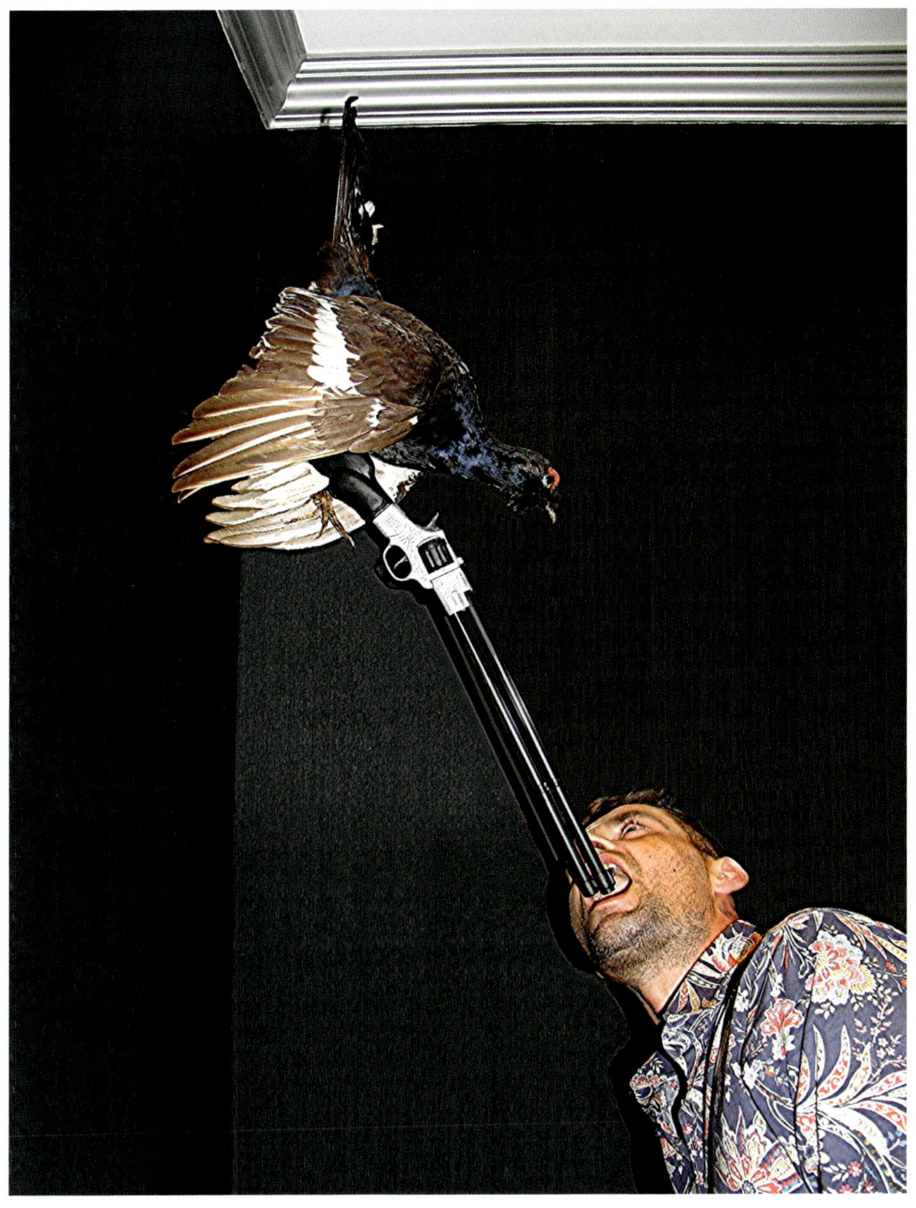

Alberto Magrin
Today I want embalm a man, 2015
MAGREEN GALLERY

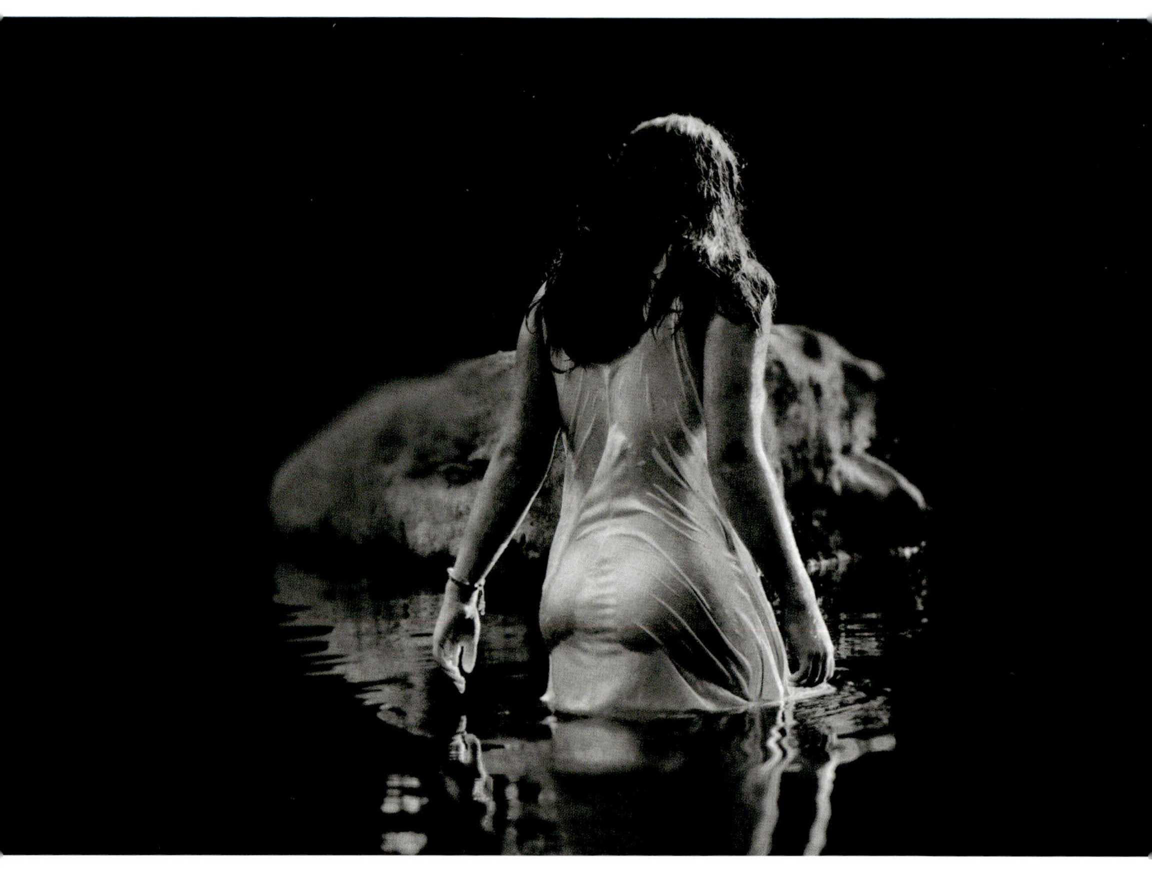

Vincent Descotils
Fleur passagère, 2017
MELTING ART GALLERY

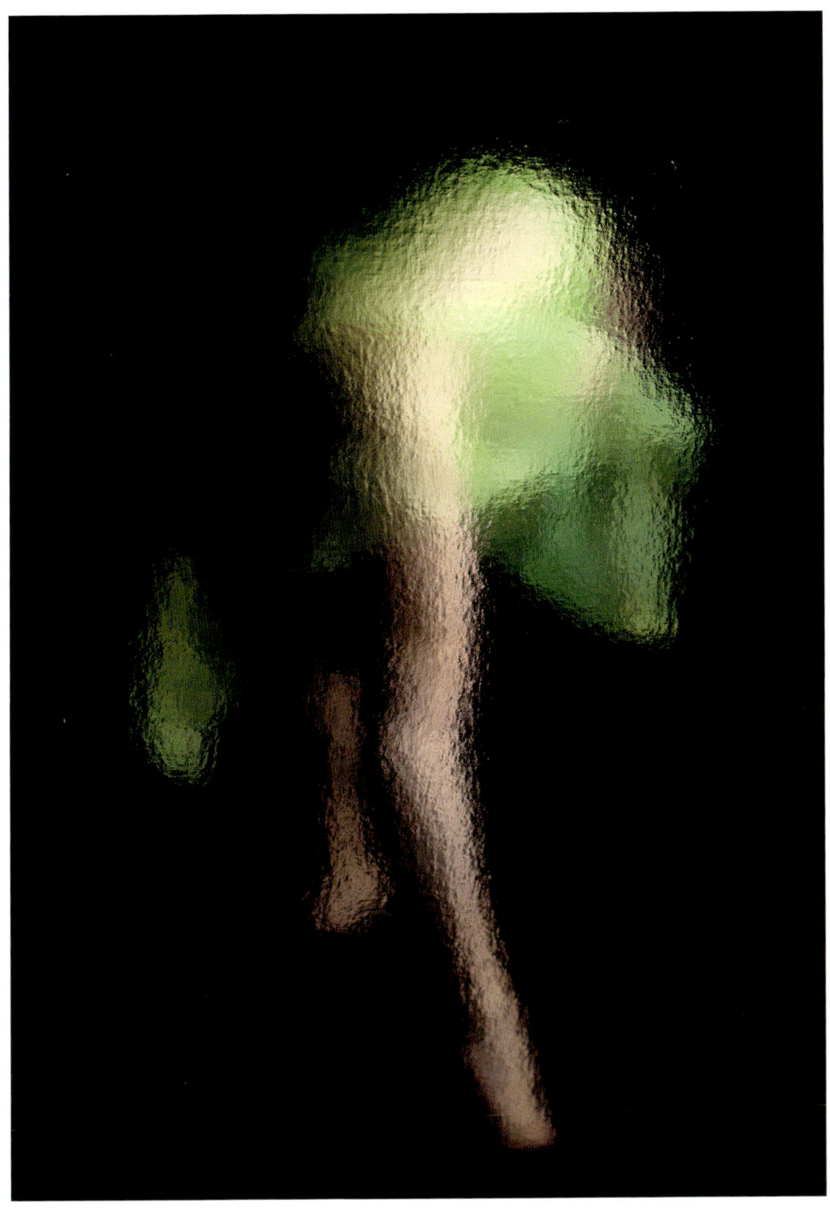

Laetitia Lesaffre
L'Insoutenable légèreté, 2015
MELTING ART GALLERY

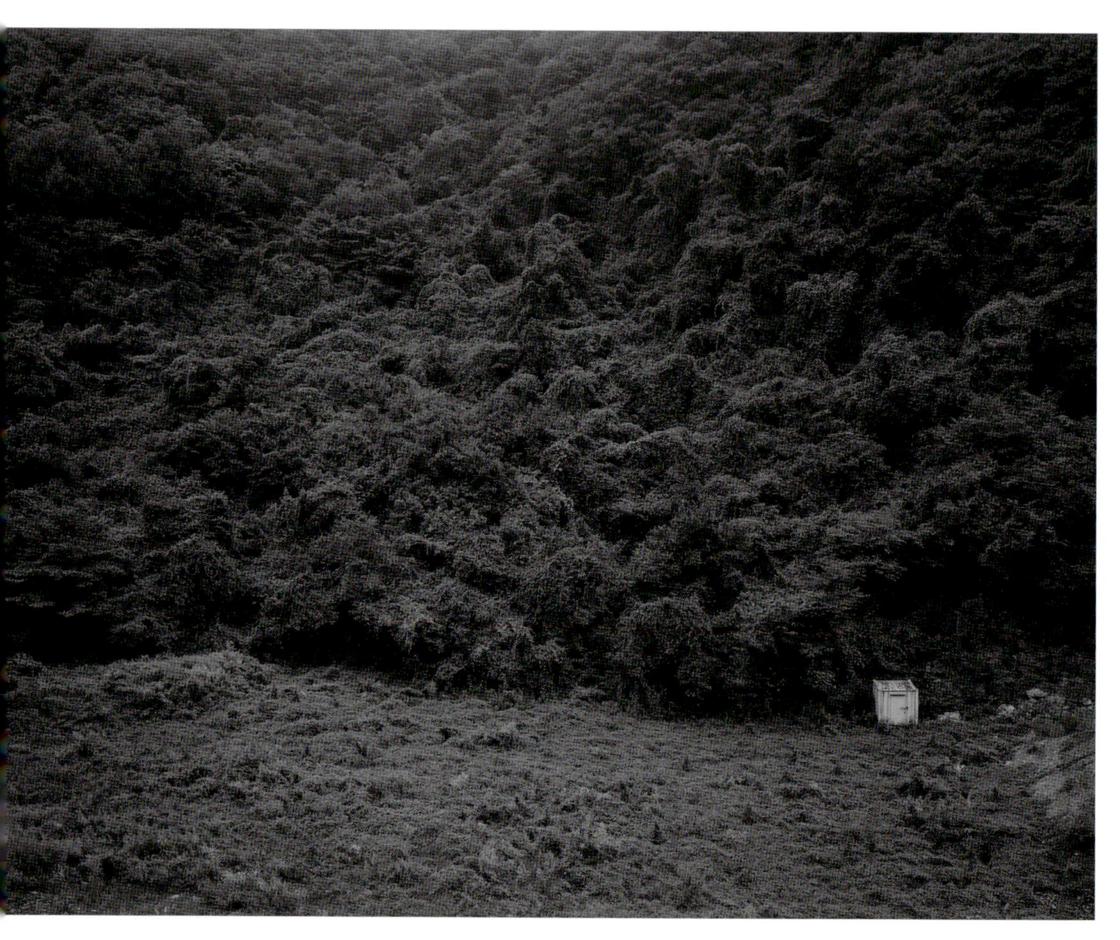

Gun Young Lee
The white shaded backyard Yeongwol, 2008
MUG

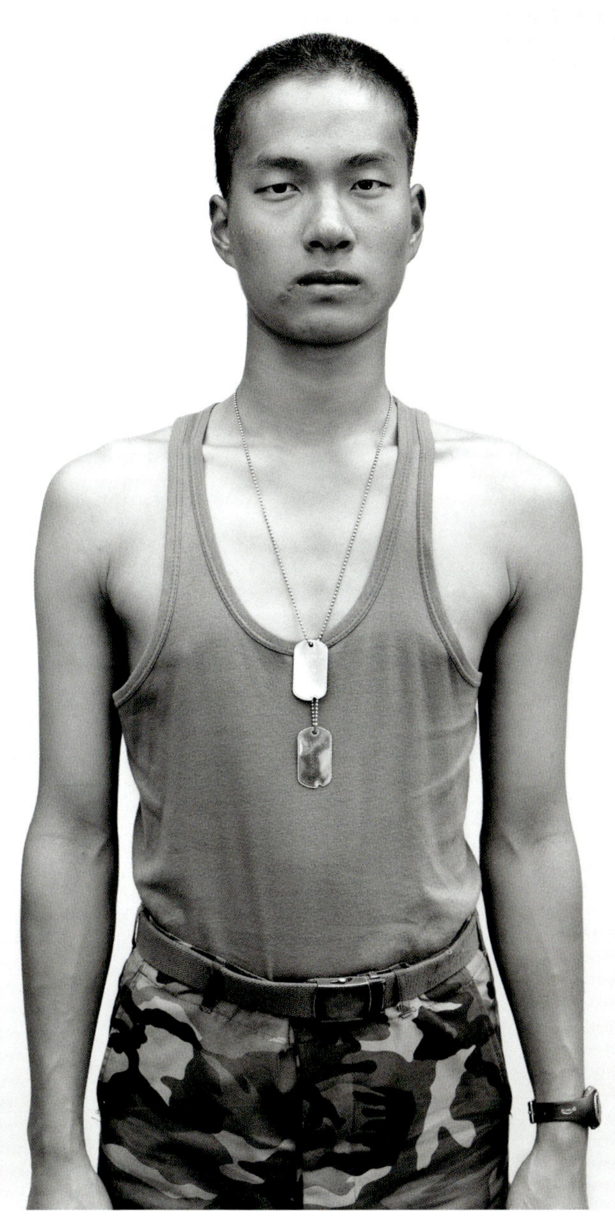

Jaegu Kang
Private #1, 2003
MUG

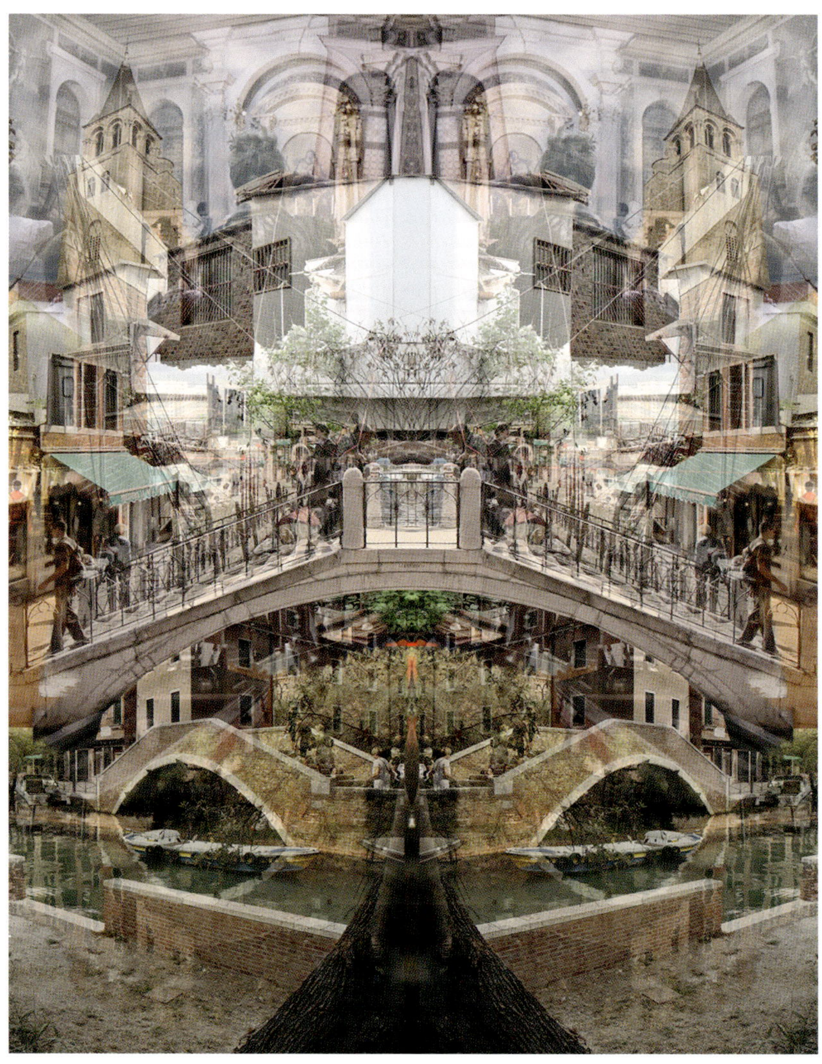

Jung Hoon Lee
Bridge of mind, 2015
MUG

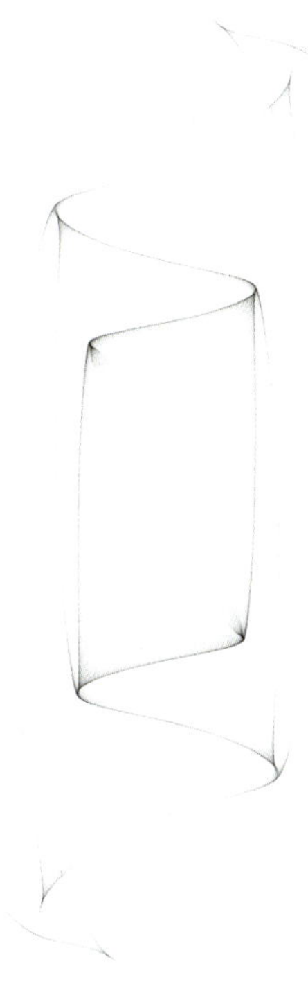

Gyoosik Kim
Pendulum movement #16003-09, 2016
MUG

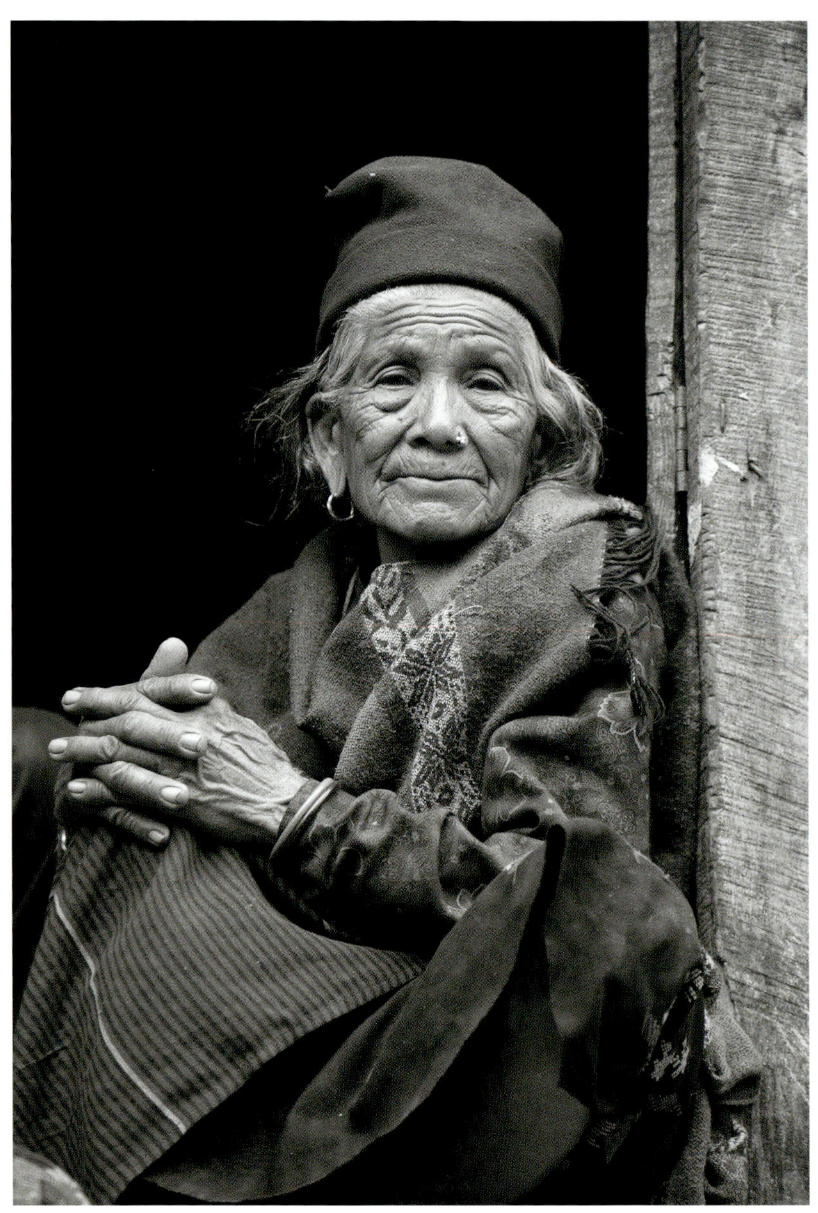

Vincent Chové
Dialogue avec la maturité, 2014
MODERN'ART

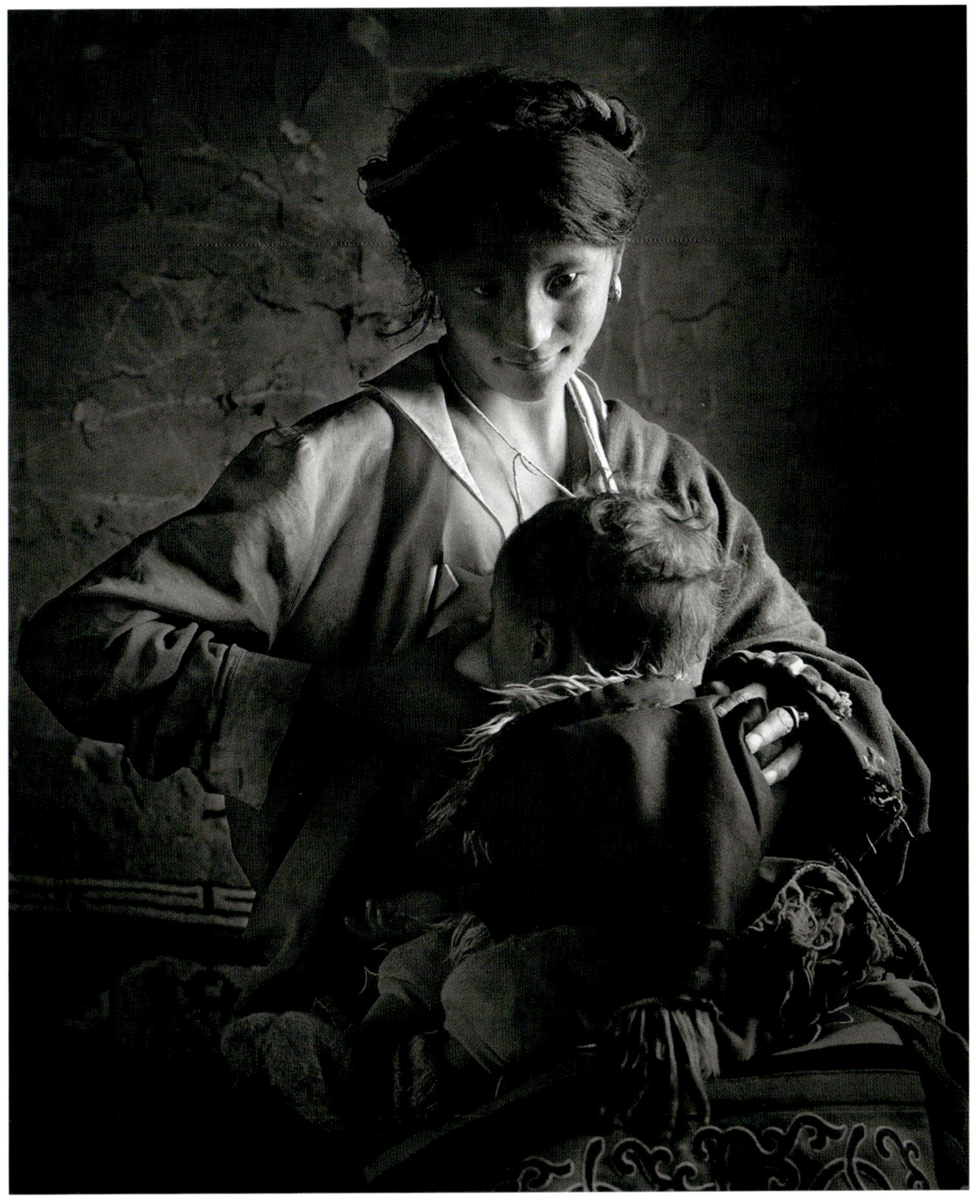

Huake Xue
La beauté de la jeune mère, 1999
NEO CONTEMPORAIN

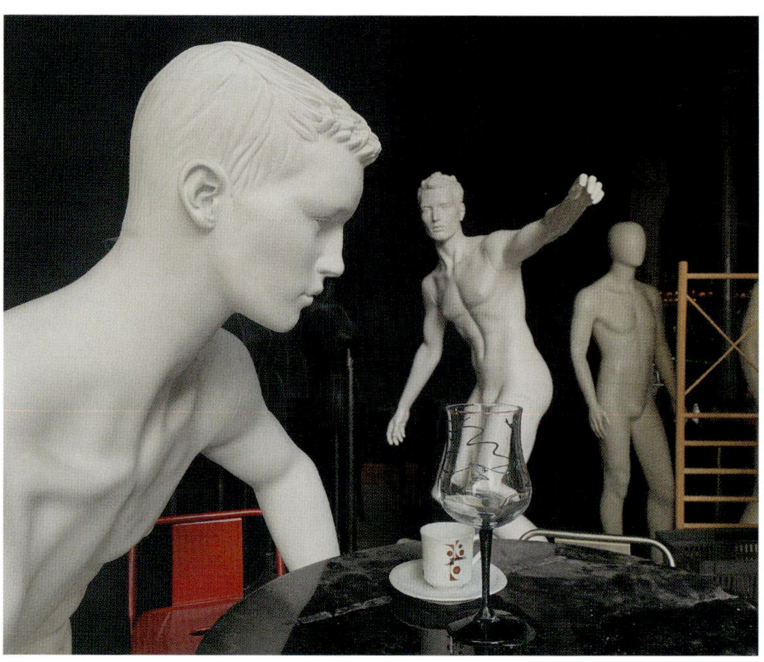

Yizhuo Wang
Emotion, 2018
NEO CONTEMPORAIN

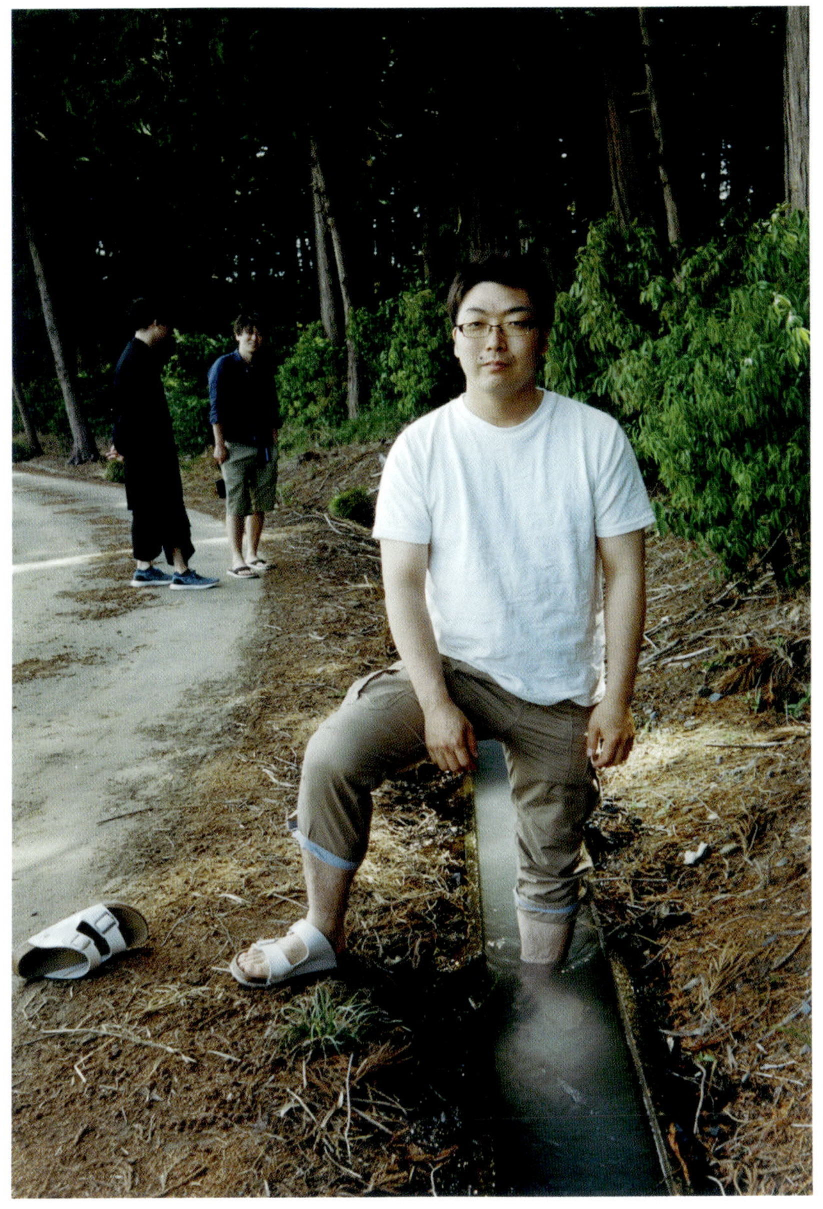

Takuya Yamahata
THE CANAL, 2019
ONTAMA PROJECT

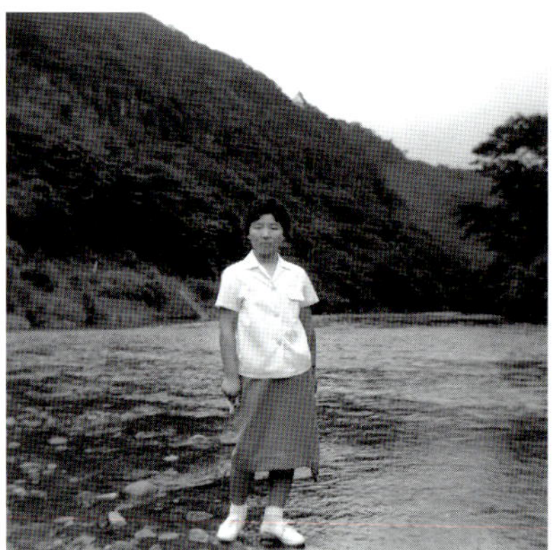

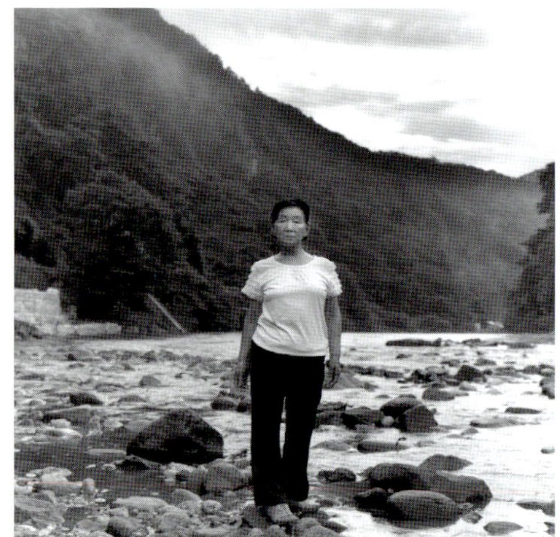

Kuniaki Konno
Between the Times, 2018
ONTAMA PROJECT

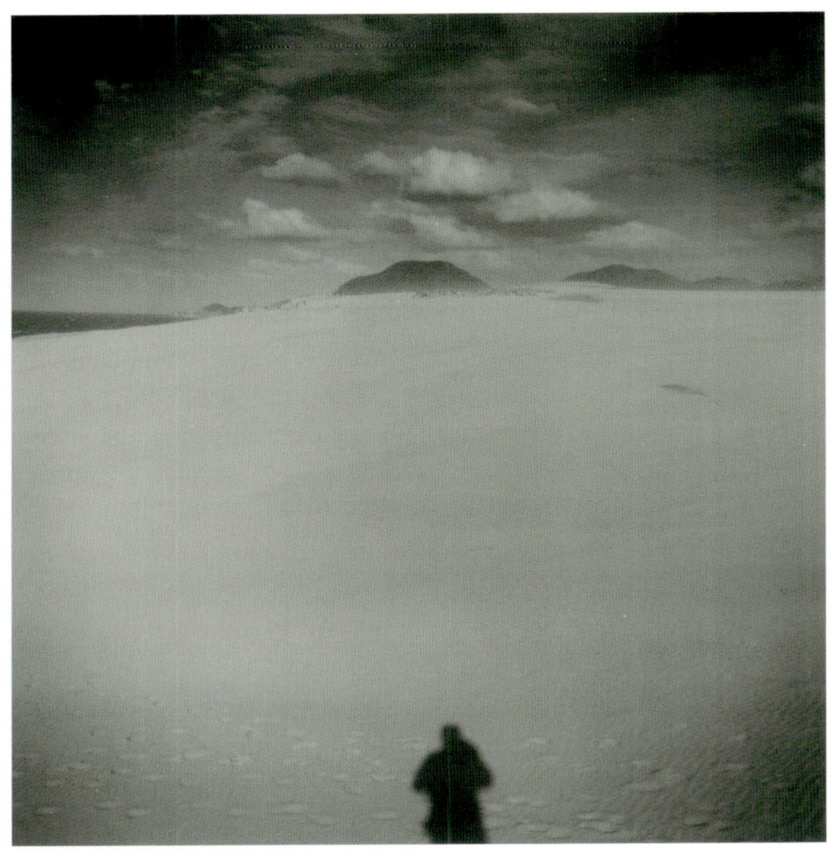

Yutaka Masutani
Dune, Alone, 2015
ONTAMA PROJECT

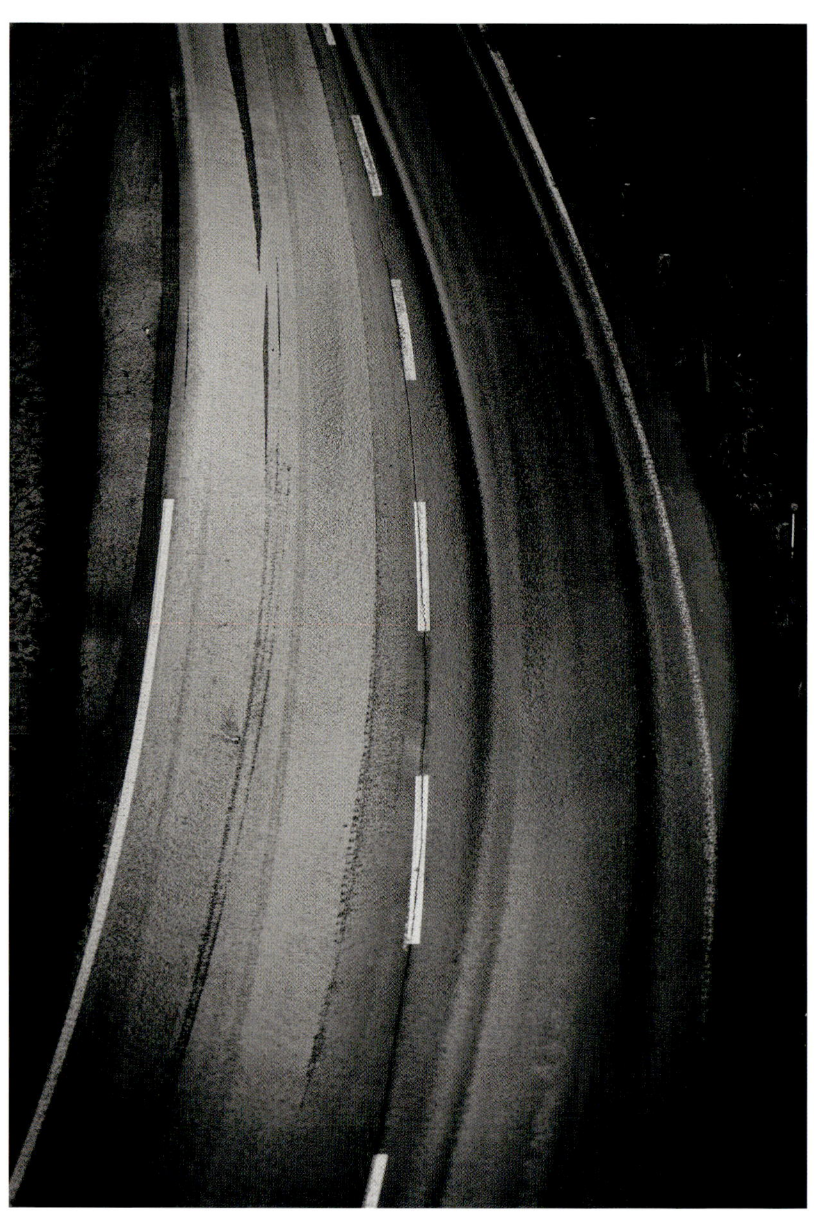

Yamadaya Chokko
Untitled, 2018
ONTAMA PROJECT

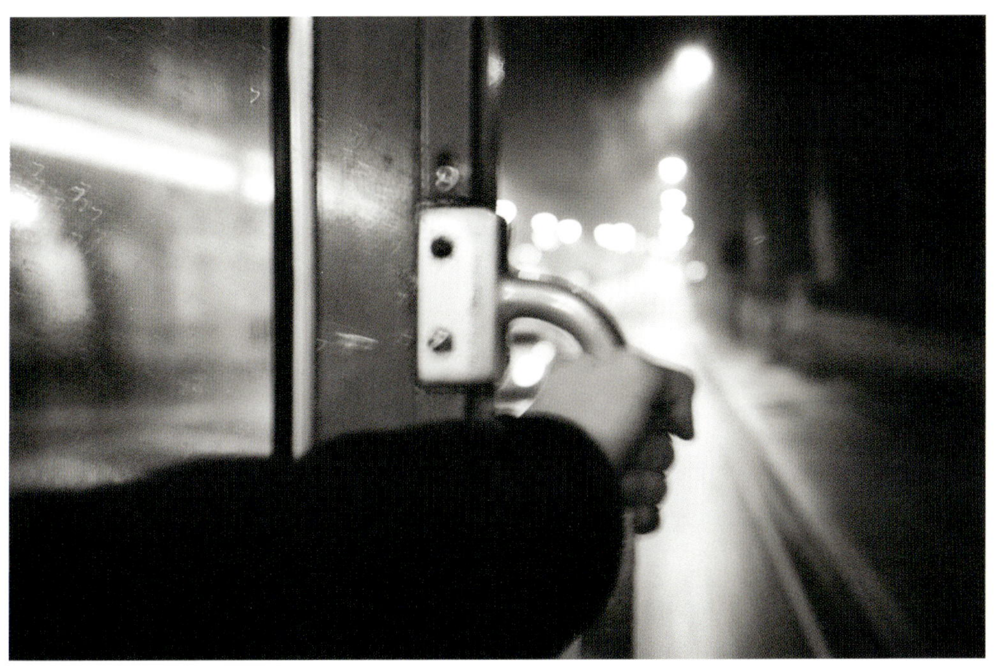

Guy Russell
Going Places, 2002
QGALLERY

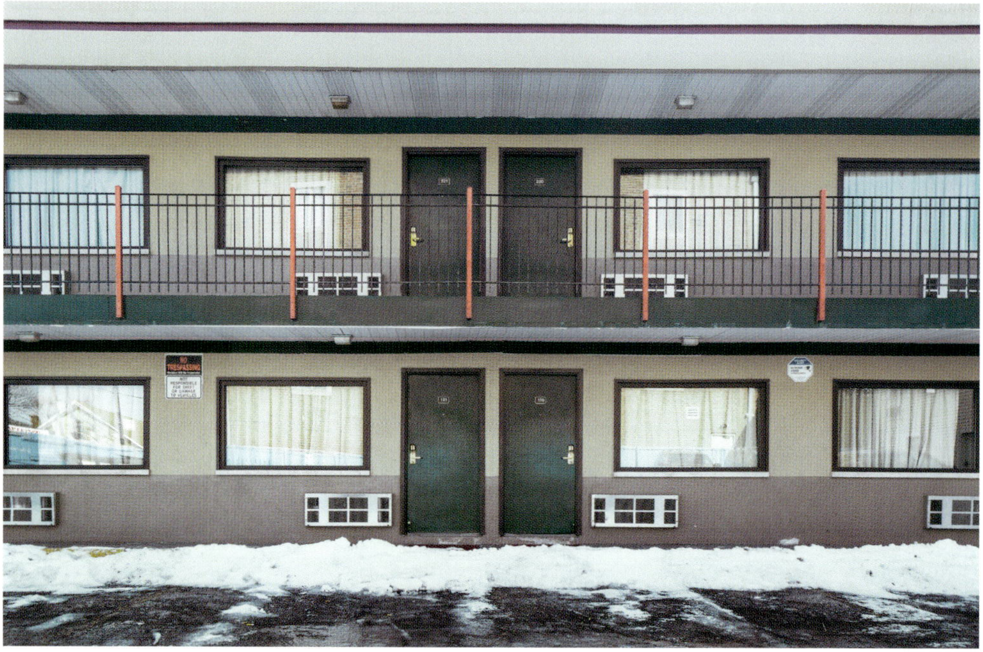

Liza Moura
Chicago love rooms, 2018
PHOTO SHOPPING

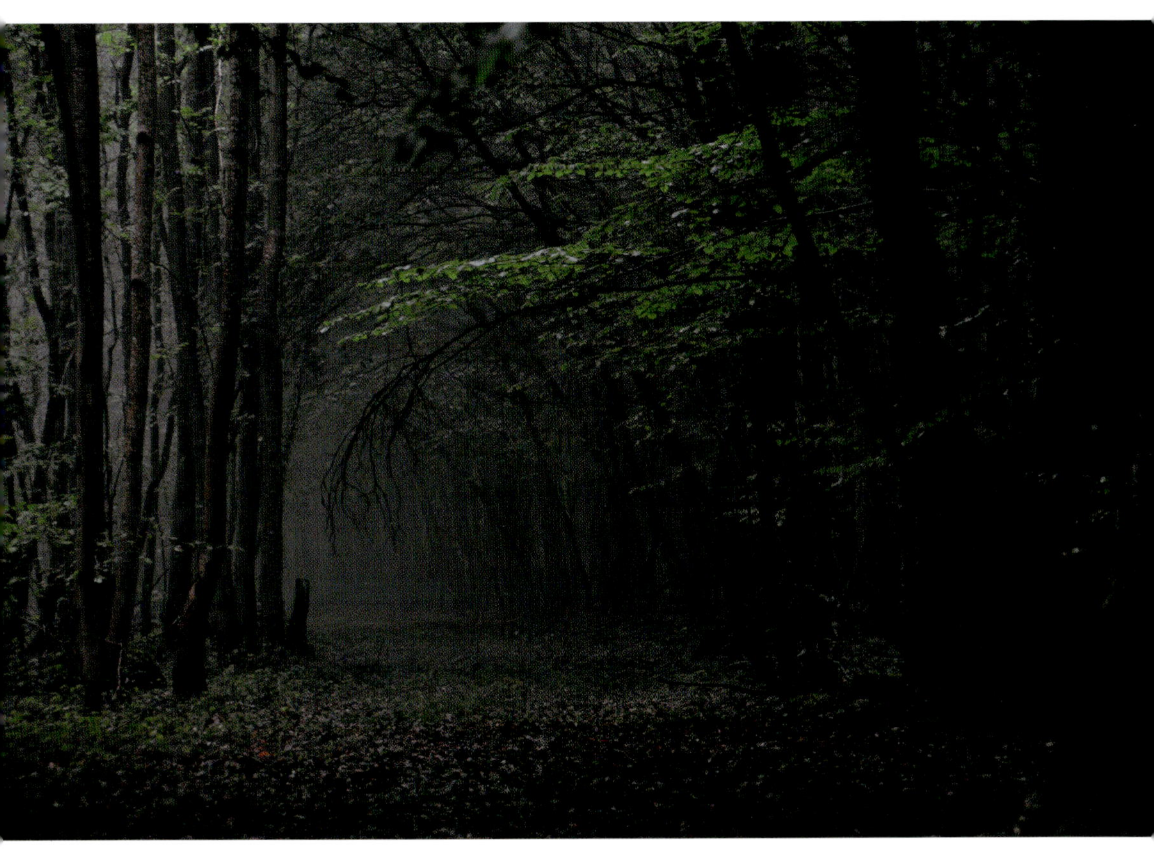

Carol Descordes
La voie, 2018
PHOTO SHOPPING

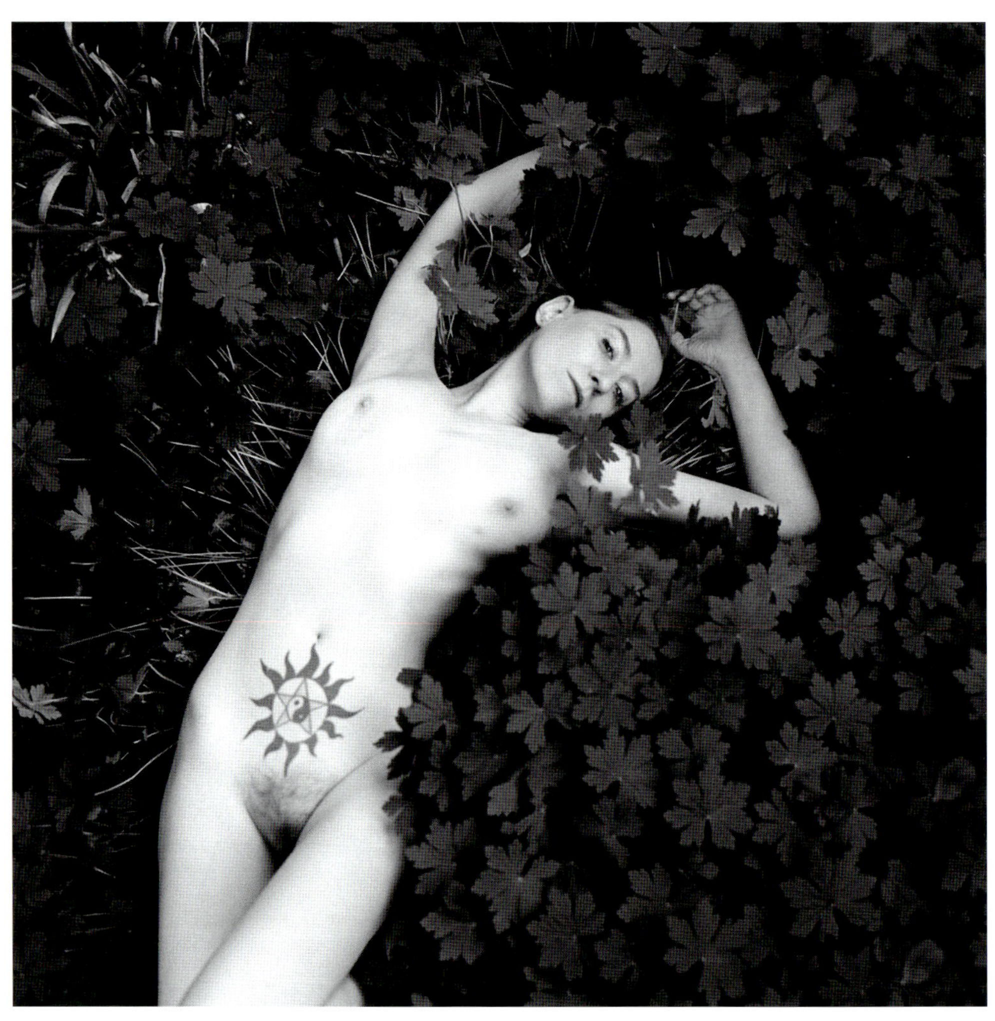

Philippe Blache
Caya allongée dans la trèfle, 2016
PODBIELSKI CONTEMPORARY

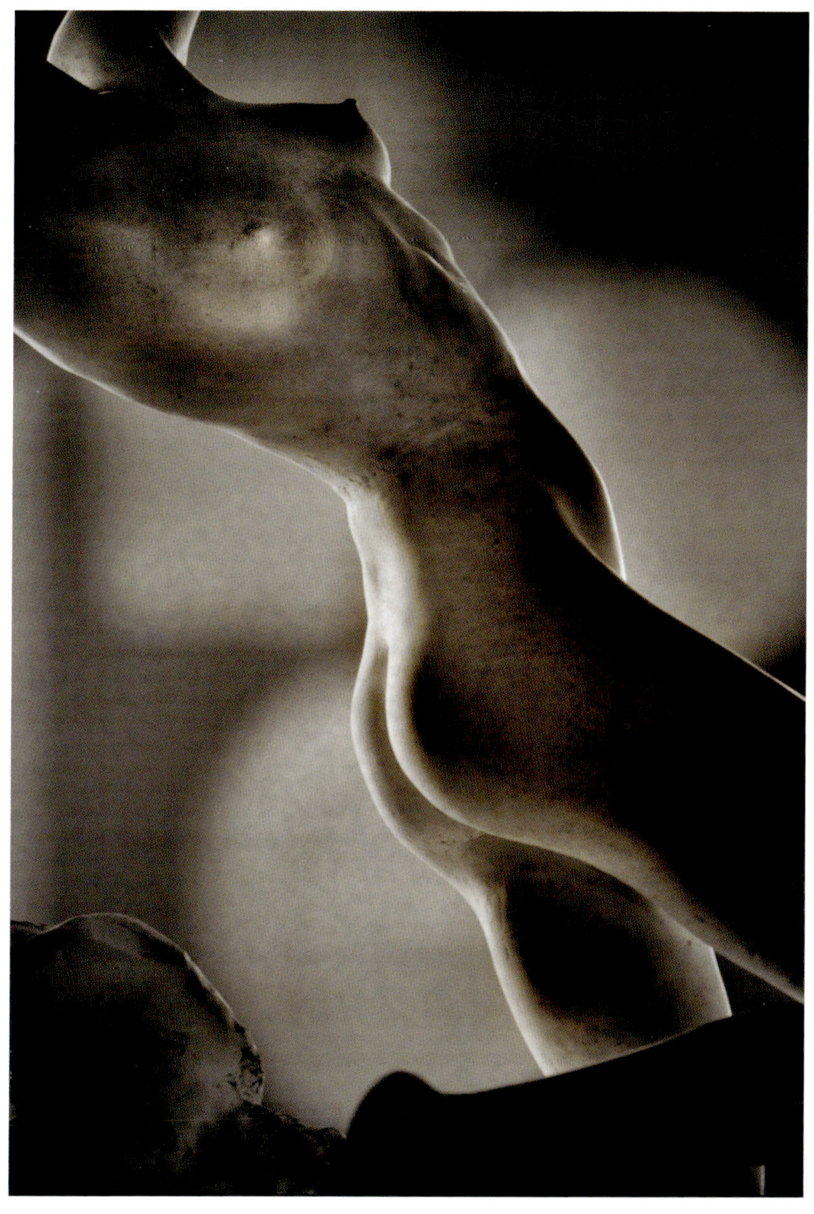

Bruno Cattani
Eros #17, 2009-2019
PODBIELSKI CONTEMPORARY

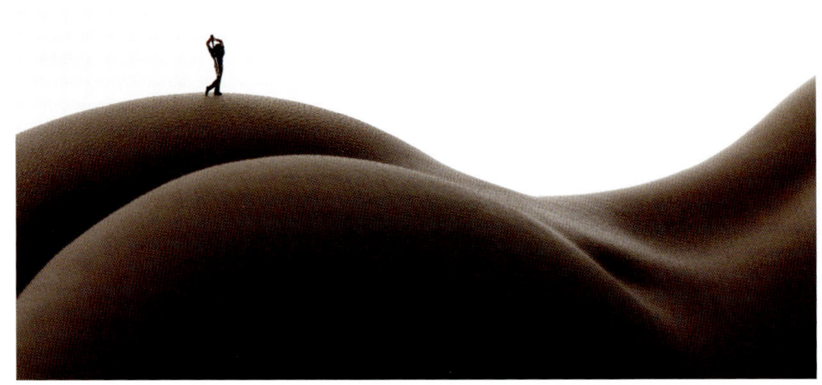

Jean-Léonard Polo
Most beautiful links golf course of the world, 2019
POLO ARTS

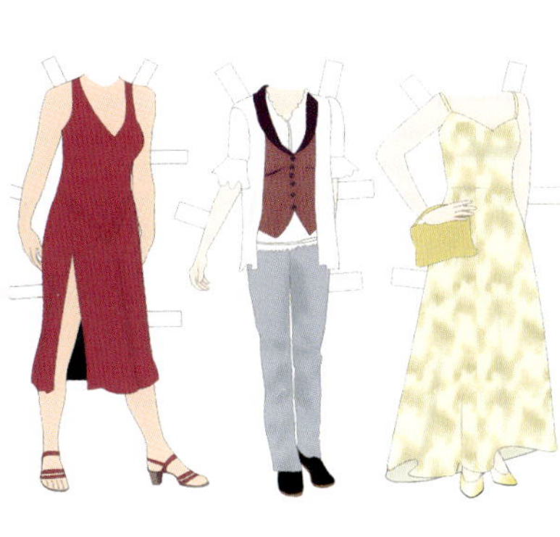
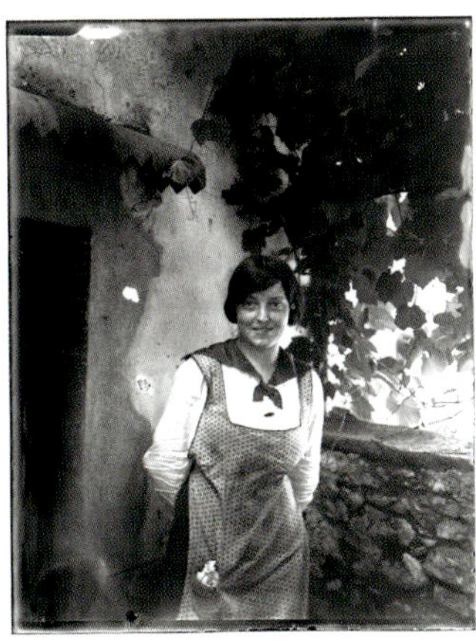
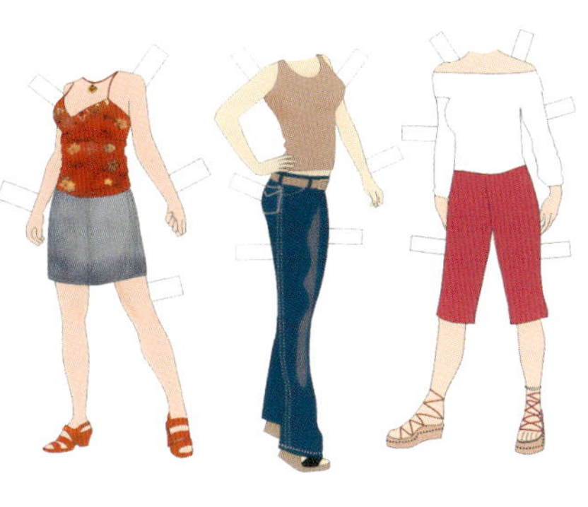

Giulio Cerocchi
Nuove identità 1, 2011-2019
SGALLERY

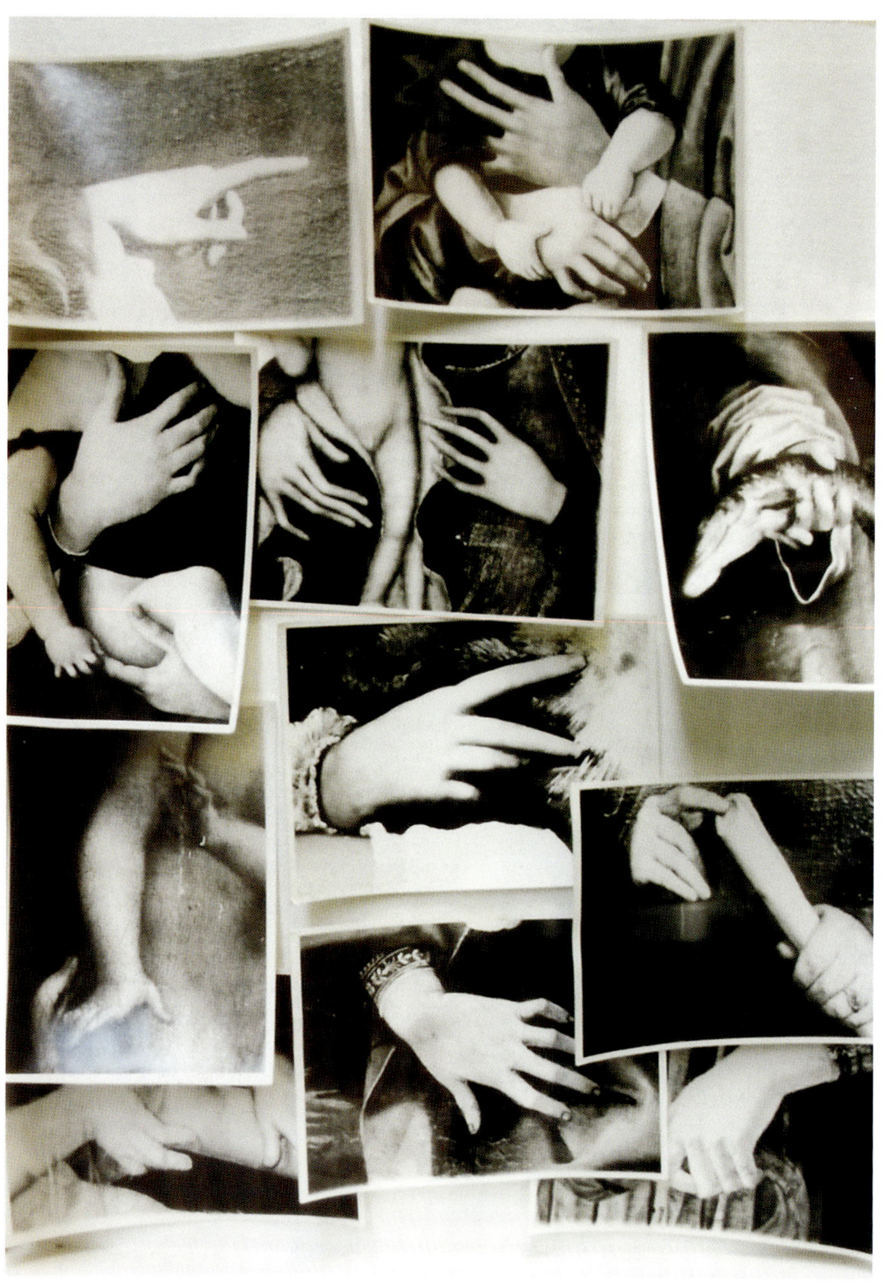

Nataly Hocke
Handabzug, 2012
SEMJON CONTEMPORARY

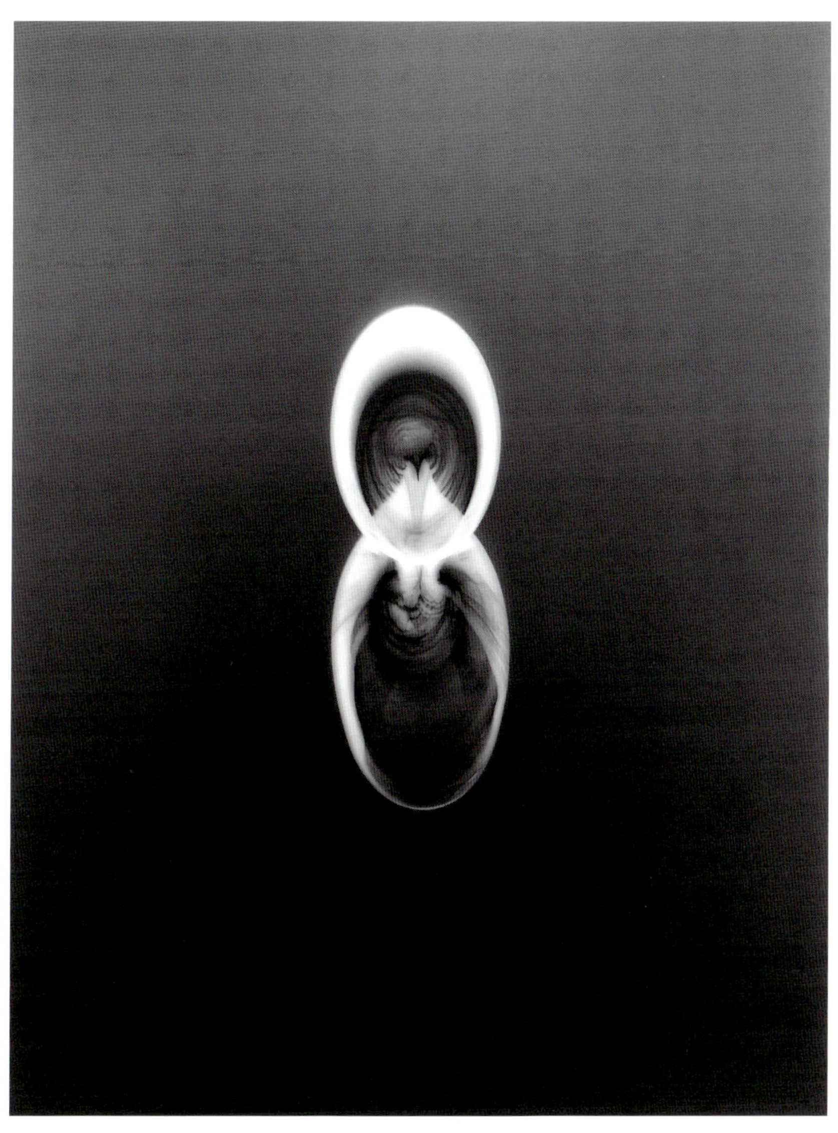

Gerda Schütte
Souvenirs d'Afrique N° D3, 2017
SEMJON CONTEMPORARY

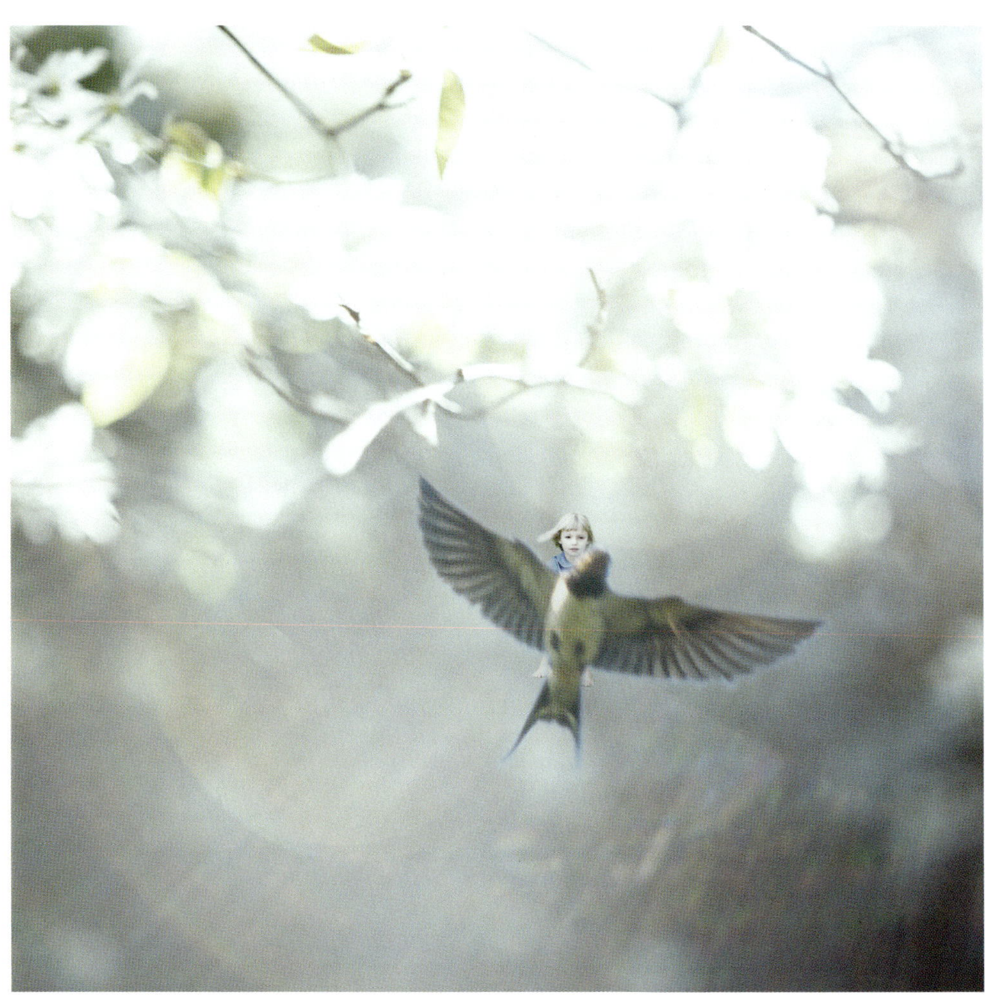

Marie Liesse
La petite Poucette, 2008
SIGNATURES

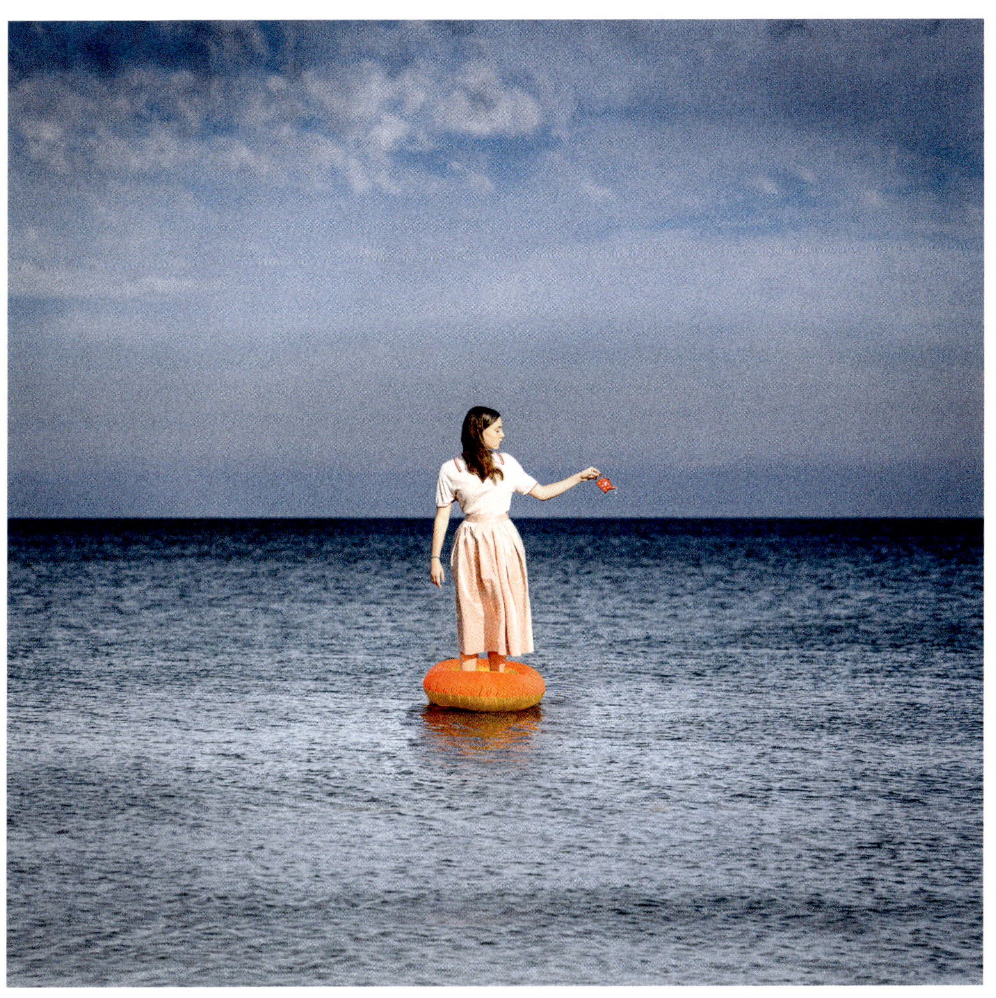

Florence Levillain
Une goute d'eau dans l'océan, 2019
SIGNATURES

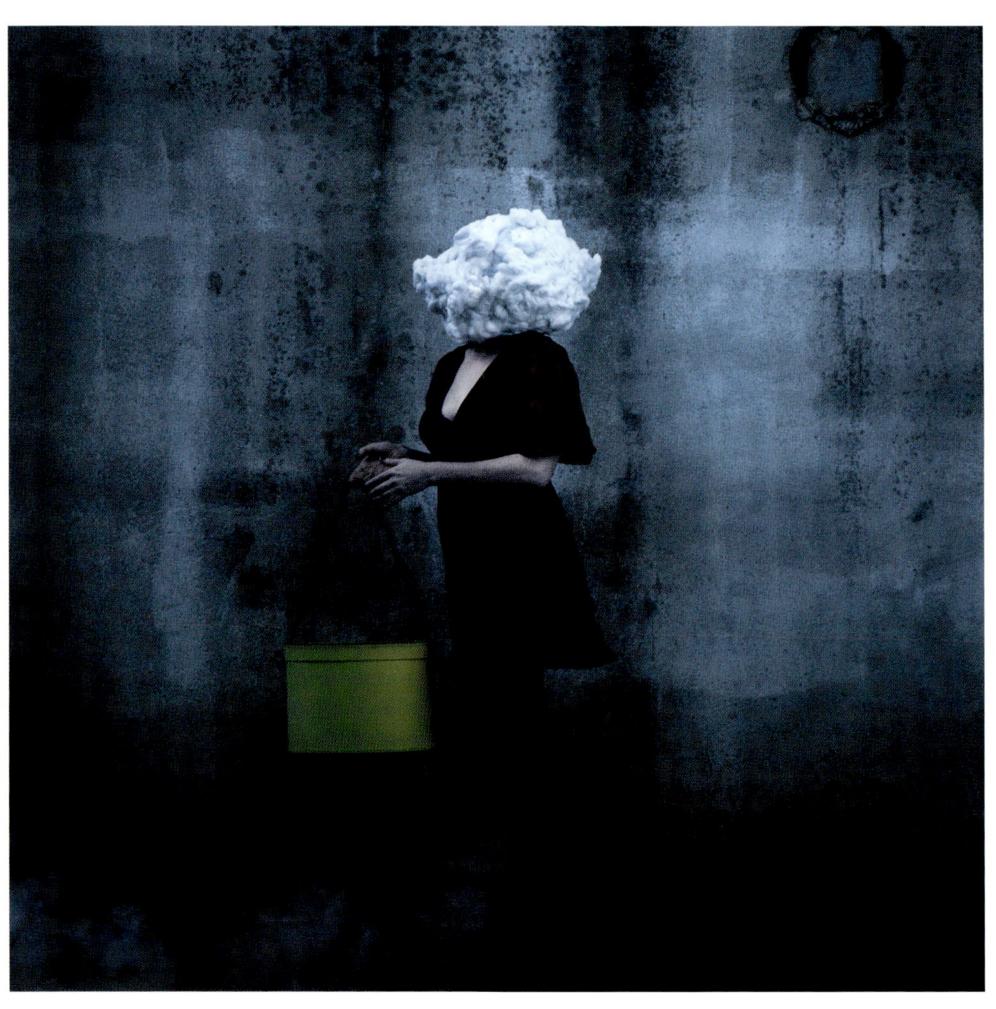

Joanna Tarlet-Gauteur
Nuages #7, 2018
SIGNATURES

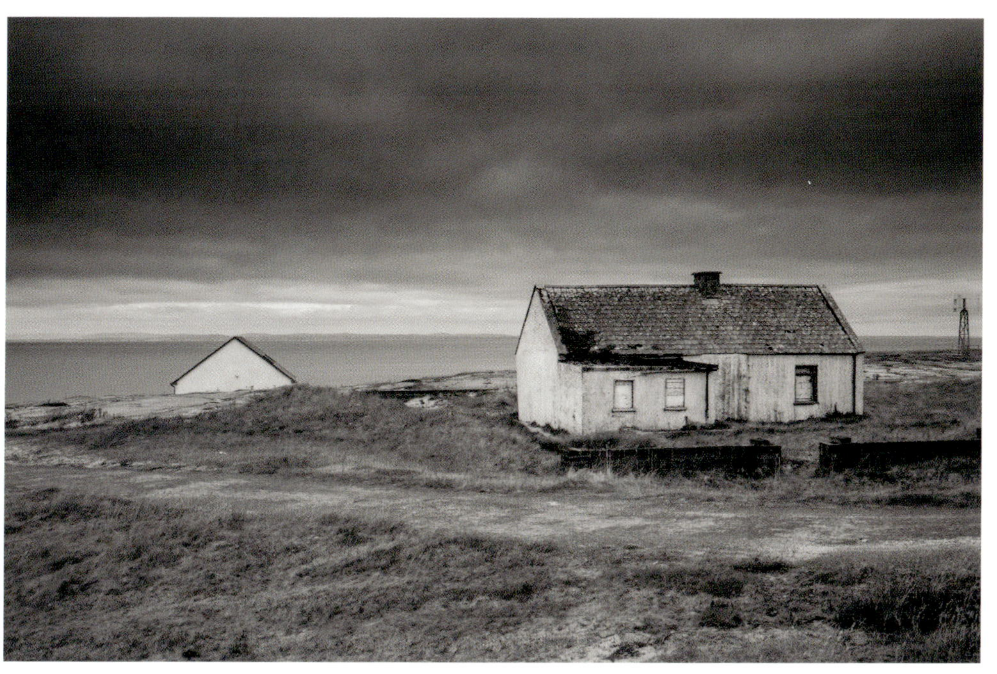

Gabriele Pierini
House of silence, 2018
SPAZIO FARINI6

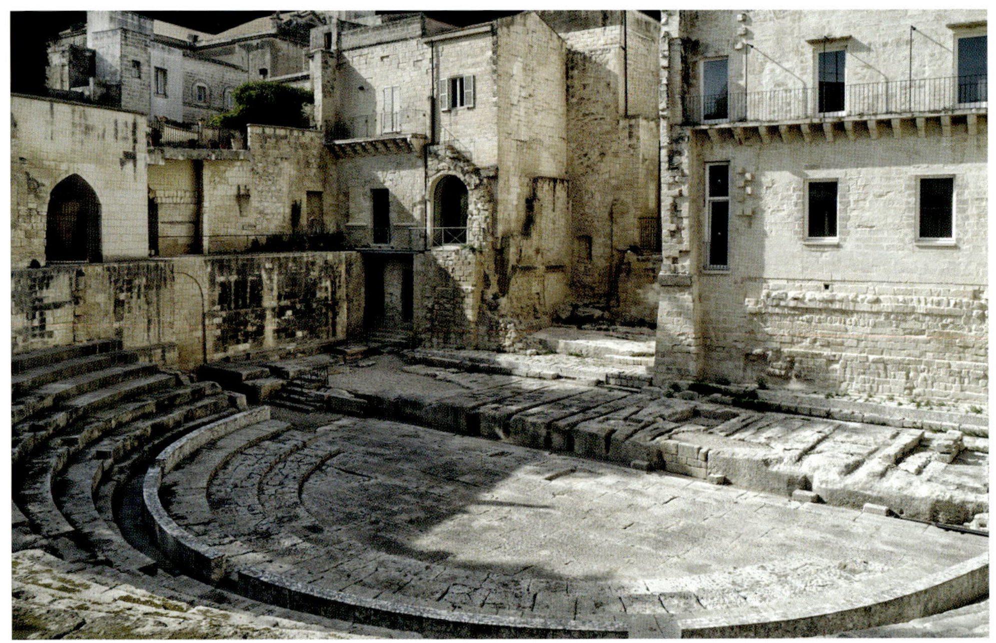

Gianna Spirito
Lo spazio teatrale #2, 2017
SPAZIO FARINI6

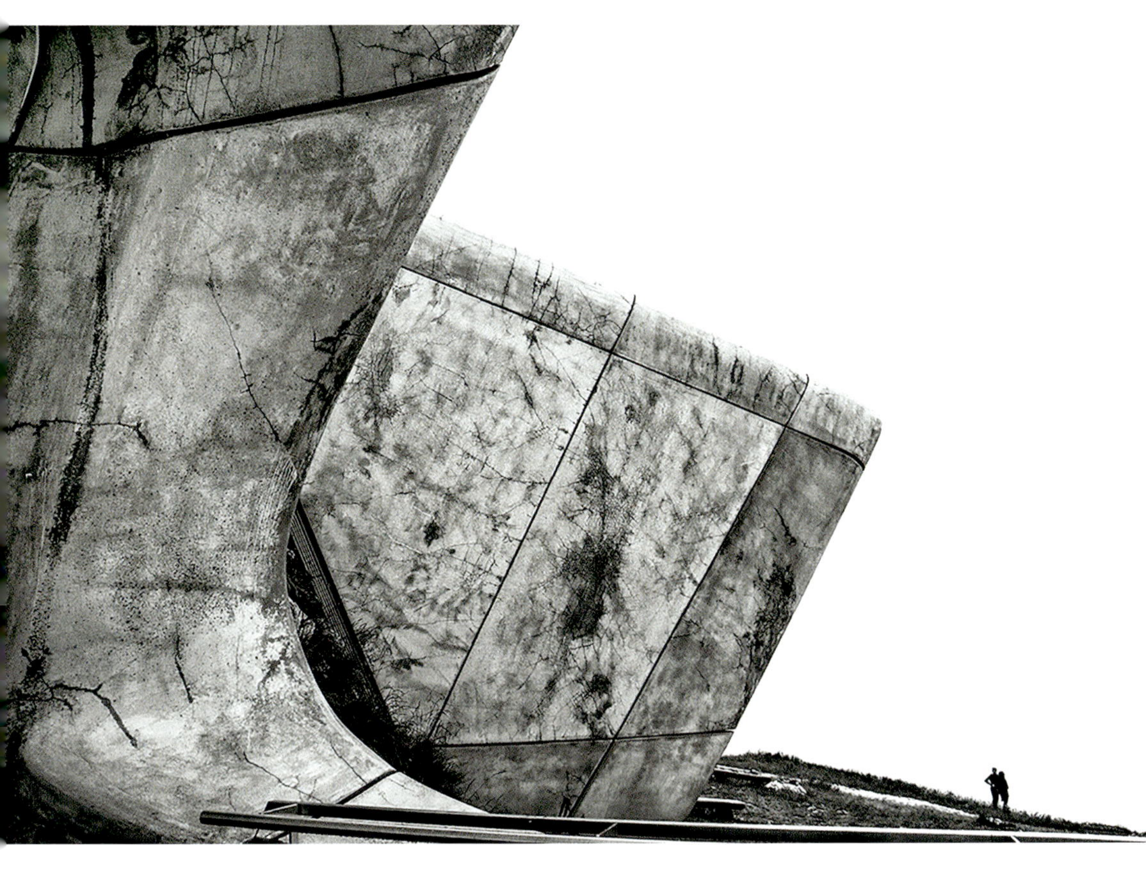

Antonella Sacconi
Infinito, 2018
SPAZIO FARINI6

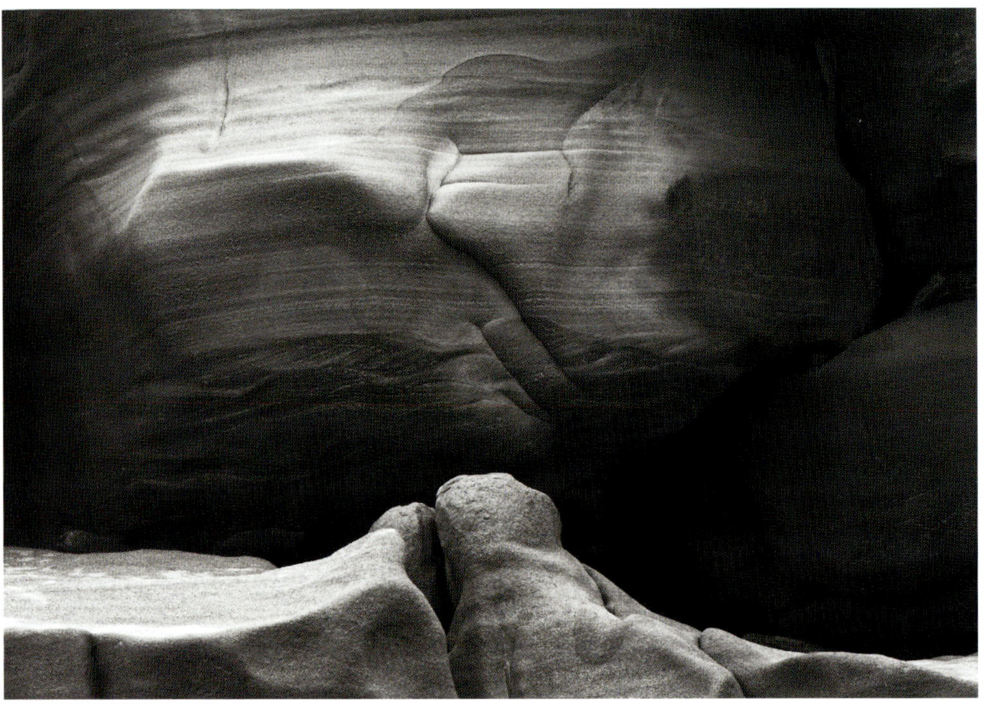

Wei-Ming Yuan
Waiting, 2013
STAR GALLERY

ChunChun Liu →
Reynisfjara Beach, 2018
V&E ART

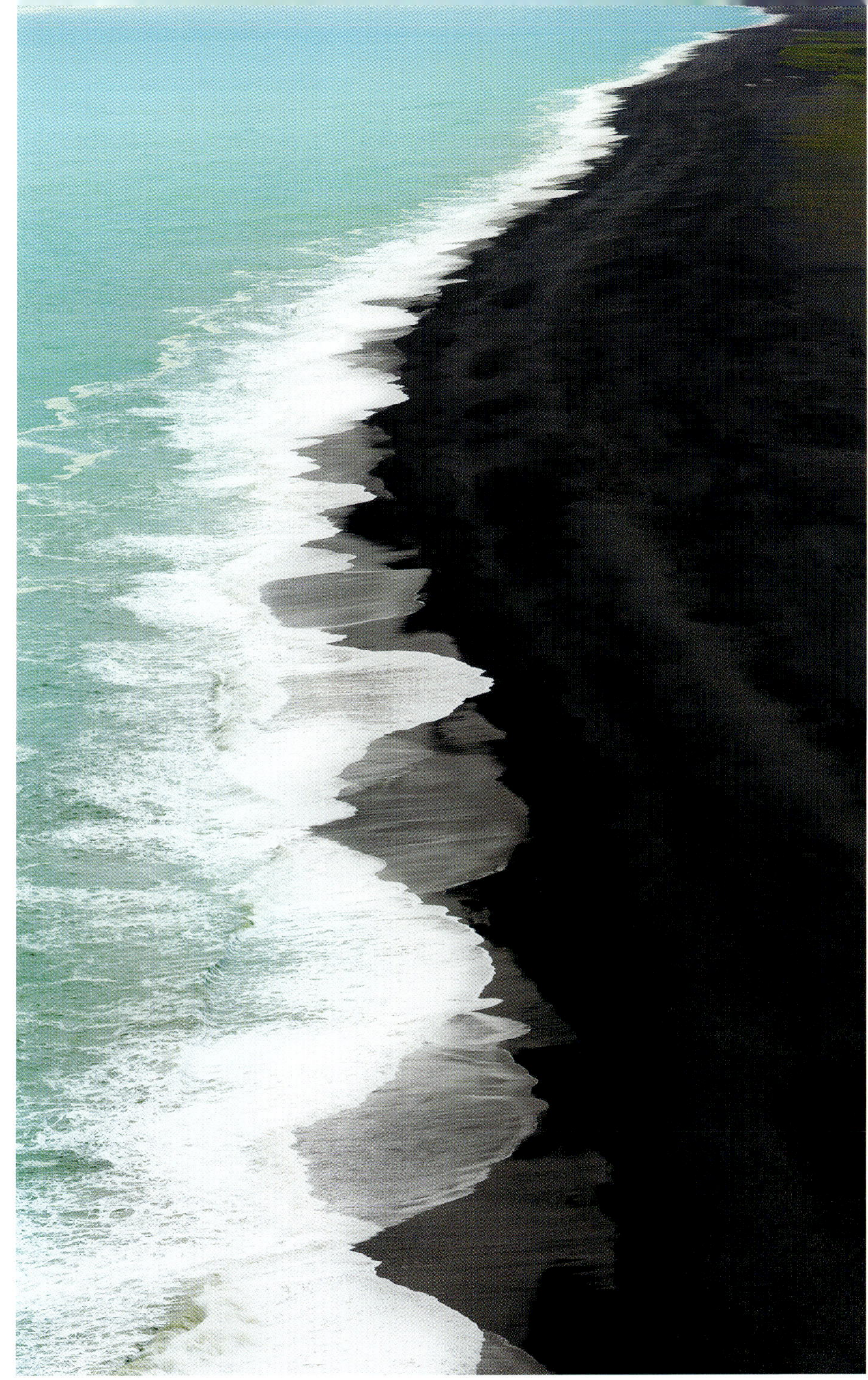

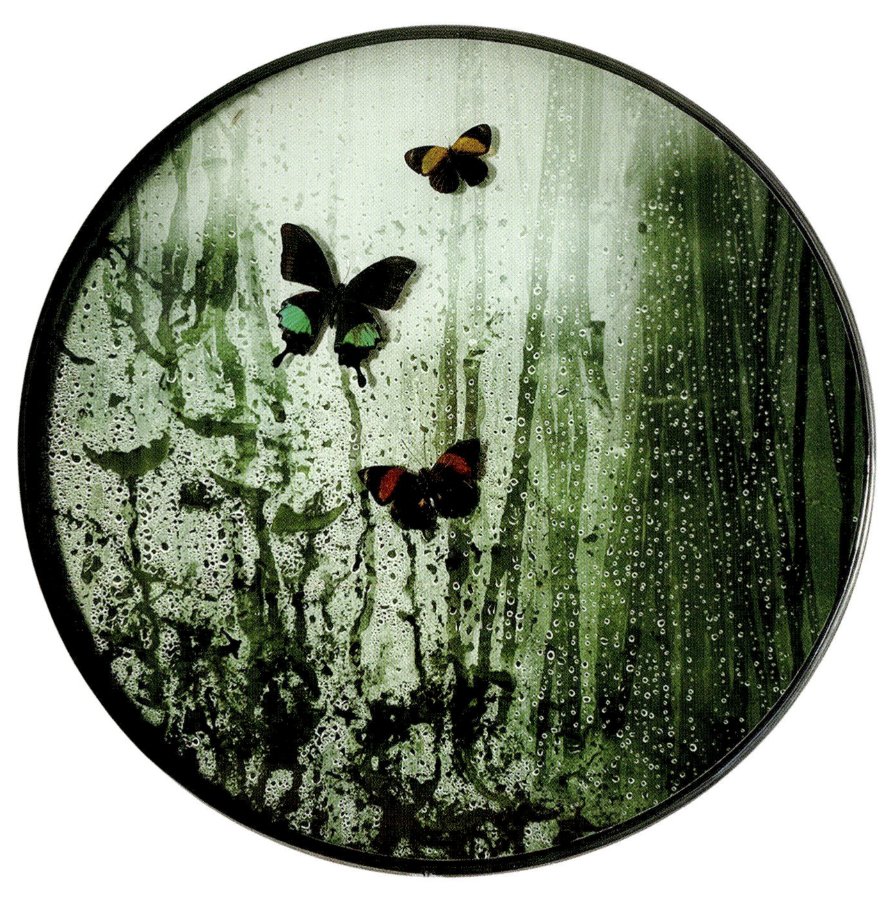

Caroline Gavazzi
Arias Trypon & Papilio Karma, 2018
THE LANTERNS

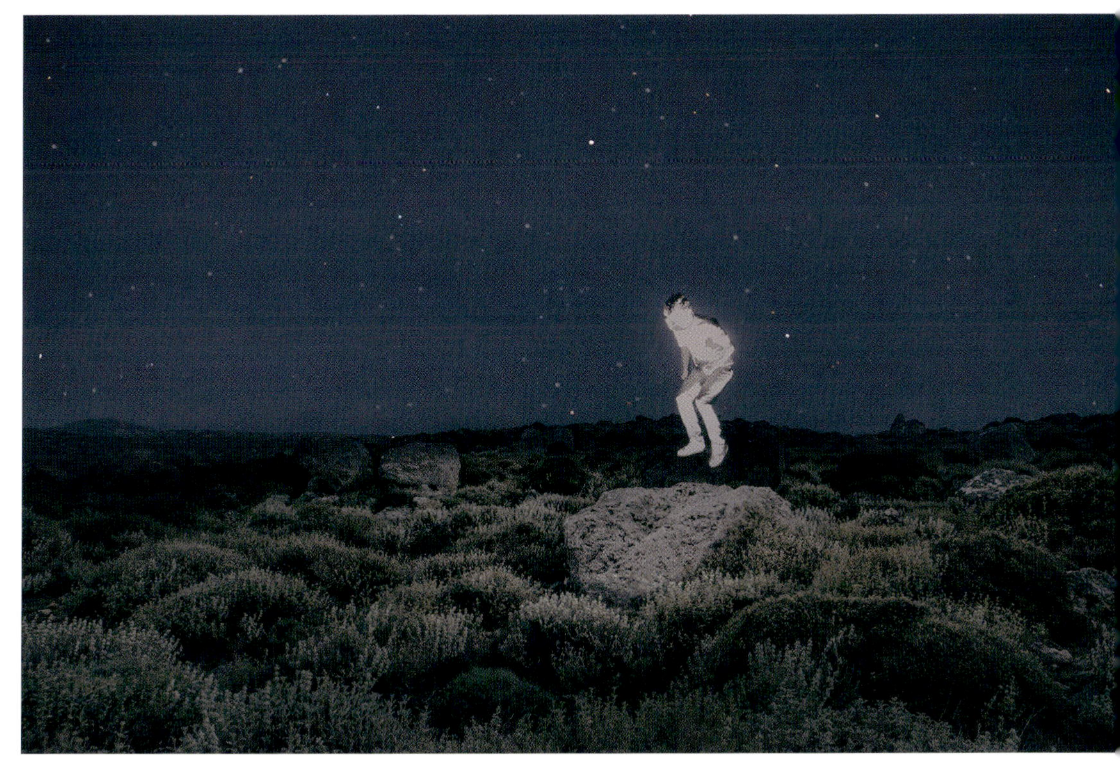

Yorgos Yatromanolakis
The Splitting of the chrysalis & the slow unfolding of the wings, 2018
ZETO ART

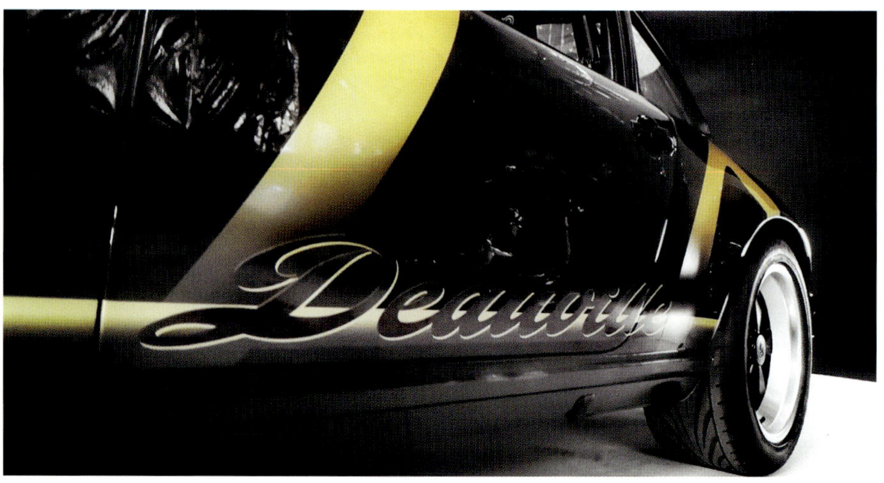

Stéphane Padu
Deauville touch, 2019
SWANY PRESSE

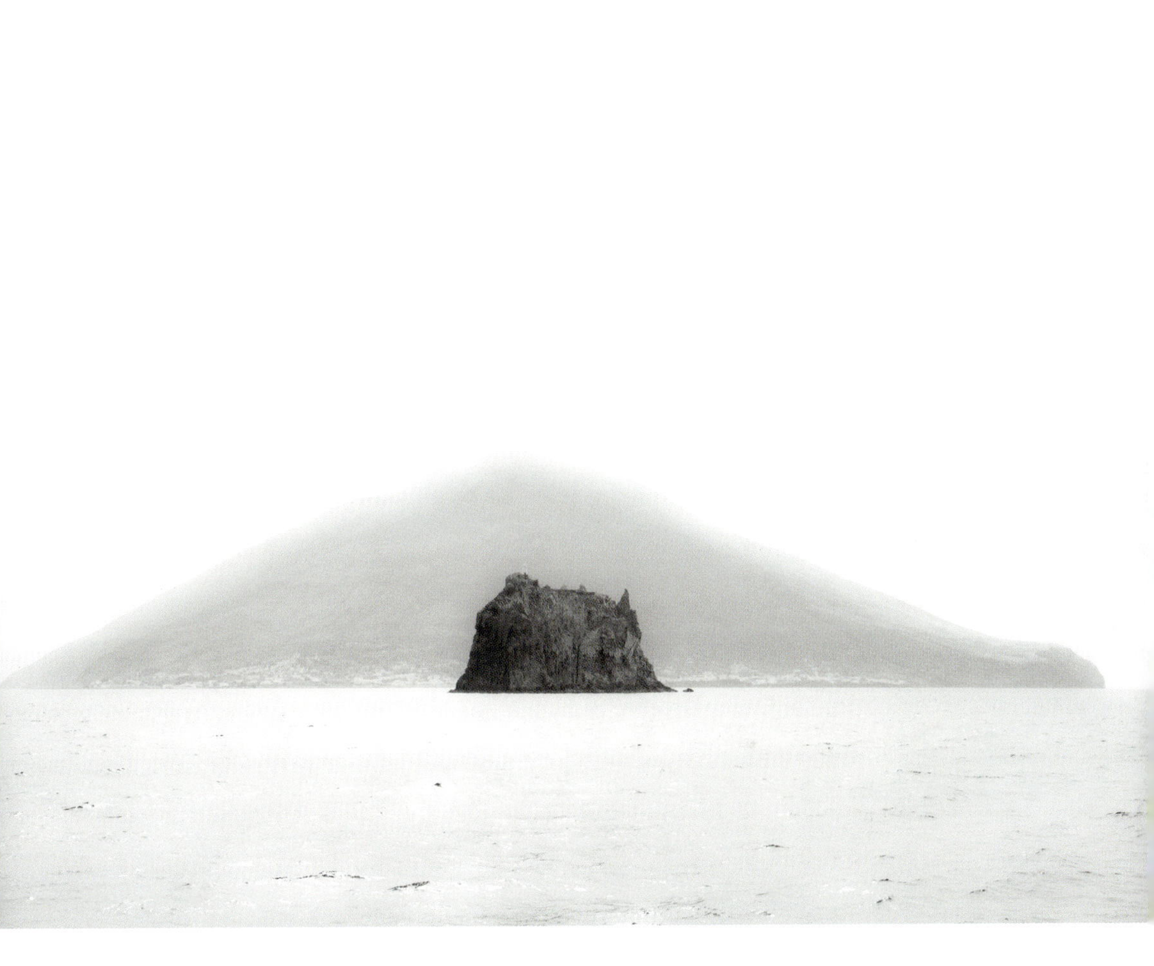

Maurizio Godot Villani
Strombolicchio, 2014
STUDIO GODOT

index
des exposants
exhibitors index

193 GALLERY
7 rue des Filles du Calvaire
75003 Paris, France
+336037078 26
cesar@193gallery.com
193gallery.com

---

60 Samuel Cueto

24P STUDIO
Shuangjing Fuhuaqi No. 796, 2nd Floor,
Building 2, Courtyard No. 39, Guangqu Rd,
Chaoyang District
100000 Beijing, China
+33678613576
studio24p@outlook.com
studio24p.com

---

54 Mingxi Fan
55 Nanjing Tang

6x7 GALLERY
Mysia, 3
00-496 Warsaw, Poland
+48226238240
ania@leica-gallery.pl
leica-gallery.pl

---

58 Łódź Kaliska Art Group
59 Sonia Szóstak

55BELLECHASSE
55 rue de Bellechasse
75007 Paris, France
+33175573939
info@55bellechasse.com
55bellechasse.com

---

56 Maxime Touratier
57 Niloufar Banisadr

AFFICHE (L')
Via dell'Unione 6 / via Nirone, 11
20123 Milan, Italy
+39286450124
gallerialaffiche@gmail.com
affiche.it

---

21 Lucretia Moroni
151 Alfred Drago Rens

ANGLE (L')
6 rue des Citronniers
64700 Hendaye, France
+33680062857
contact@langlephotos.fr
langlephotos.fr

---

39 David Tatin
156 Abel Bourgeois
157 Francesca Di Bonito
158 Fabrice Domenet

AJTNER FINE ART GALLERY
Vlieghuis Europaweg, 38
7742PR Coevorden, The Netherlands
+31623809932
ajtnerfineart@gmail.com
ajtnerfineart.com

---

13 Anna Ajtner
61 Beata Kilichowska

ALB (GALERIE)
47 rue Chapon
75003 Paris, France
+33981350080
anouk@galeriealb.com
galeriealb.com

---

30 Anaëlle Cathala

ALBANE (GALERIE)
1 rue Suffren
44000 Nantes, France
+33240740518
info@galerie-albane.com

---

18 Marie Rameau
33 Emmanuel Ligner

ALL YOU CAN ART
c/o thinknewgroup, Lindwurmstrasse 71
80337 Munich, Germany
+491729640824
hi@allyoucanart.de

---

66 Ewa-Mari Johansson

AN INC.

2F, 161-13, Seongmisan-ro, Mapo-gu
03980 Seoul, South Korea
+821027731350
arako.an@gmail.com
aninc.kr

---

62 Haejung Park
63 Seunghan Kim
64 Heesang Lee
65 Suna Yu
67 Anna Lim

ARCHIVIO FOTOGRAFICO ITALIANO

Via Don Luigi Testori, 14
21053 Castellanza, Italy
+393475902640
afi.foto.it@gmail.com
archiviofotografico.org

---

68 Claudio Argentiero
69 Mario Vidor
70 Roberto Bosio
71 Stefania Ricci

ARGENTIC (GALERIE)

43 rue Daubenton
75005 Paris, France
+33608905133
argentic@argentic.fr
argentic.fr

---

32 Roger Schall

ART D2

Via Aristide de Togni, 23
20123 Milan, Italy
+39239440381
info@artd2.com
artd2.com

---

72 Claudio Montecucco
73 Mimmo Dabbrescia

ARTE GLOBALE

71 - 75 Shelton Street Covent Garden
WCH2 9JQ London, United Kingdom
+442037576391
mariateresa.sacchi@arteglobale.com
arteglobale.com

---

74 Georgia Clemson
75 Eriko Kaniwa
76 Yener Torun

ARTIFY GALLERY

Unit 7, 10/F, Block A. Ming Pao Industrial Centre,
18 Ka Yip Street
Chai Wan, Hong Kong
+85235431260
info@artifygallery.com

---

78 Veronica Lam
79 Yick Kan Cheung
80 Bence Bakonyi

ARTYARD GALLERY

Landgraf-Wilhelm Str., 13
60431 Frankfurt, Germany
+491783663005
art@artyardgallery.de
artyardgallery.de

---

77 Formento + Formento

BARRIOL (GALERIE OLIVIER)

10 rue de la République
13001 Marseille, France
+336875166 52
olivier.barriol@follow-your-dreams.fr
follow-your-dreams.fr

---

16 Julie Lagier

BARROU PLANQUART (GALERIE)

51 ter rue de Paris
95680 Montlignon, France
+33682030956
contact@galeriebarrouplanquart.com
galeriebarrouplanquart.com

---

112 Brno Del Zou
113 Double You
114 François Bel

CARLO MARI GALLERY

Via Roma, 92
20025 Legnano Mi, Italy
+393396605060
info@carlomaristudio.com
carlomarigallery.com

---

81 Carlo Mari

FIFTY DOTS GALLERY
Sant Hermenegild, 24
080006 Barcelona, Spain
+34607624445
contact@fiftydots.com
fiftydots.com

---

12 Alejandra Carles-Tolrá
106 Dani García Sarabia
107 Nicholas Hughes
108 Israel Ariño

FLUX ZONE
Amargura 5 Plaza Del Carmen
01000 CDMX San Angel, Mexico
+5215530544949
atelier_k18@yahoo.fr
flux-zone.art

---

110 Miguel Soler-Roig
111 Isabel Miquel Arqués

FOTOFEVER PRIZE WITH DAHINDEN
5 rue Charonne
75011 Paris, France
info@fotofever.com
fotofever.com

---

6 Rose Lecat
8 Alain Polo Nzuzi
10 Julia Amarger

GALERIE PARIS 1839 (LA)
G/F 74 Hollywood Road, Central
00000 Hong Kong
+85255277181
cyril.delettre@lagalerie.hk
lagalerie.hk

---

38 Vincent Fournier
159 Nian Zeng
160 Ching-hui Chou
161 Almond Chu

GLI EROICI FURORI
Via Melzo, 23
20129 Milan, Italy
+39237648381
silvia.agliotti@furori.it
furori.it

---

146 Lia Stein

GODOT (STUDIO)
Via Giordano Bruno, 7
Milan, Italy
+393488660057
info@godot.info

---

199 Maurizio Godot Villani

GRISART
Méndez Núñez, 14
08003 Barcelona, Spain
+34934579733
cfabro@grisart.com
grisart.com

---

23 Irene Royo
144 Simone Coitiño
145 David Molero Saura

HEILLANDI GALLERY
Via Canova, 7
6900 Lugano, Switzerland
+41919211100
info@heillandigallery.ch
heillandigallery.ch

---

22 Giulia Agostini
119 Andrea Tonellotto
147 Margot Errante

HERISSON (COLLECTIF DU)
21 rue Chaudron
75010 Paris, France
+33661060426
jm.sartel@gmail.com
collectifduherisson.fr

---

89 Jacopo Baboni Schilingi

HO'S ART
No.22-5, Ln. 166, Sec. 2, Anle Rd.
20448 Keelung, Taiwan
+88624331250
mjisaho@gmail.com
isaho.info

---

115 Isa Ho

MAGREEN GALLERY
Via Della Pineta, 5/12
16035 Rapallo, Italy
+393298744128
alberto@magrin.it
magreengallery.it

---

165 Alberto Magrin

MEETING ART POINT
10 rue de Joinville
75019 Paris, France
+33142852505
nelly@meetingartpoint.com
meetingartpoint.com

---

135 Yuna Yagi

MELTING ART GALLERY
34 rue de la Halle
59000 Lille, France
+33614099614
contact@meltingartgallery.com
meltingartgallery.com

---

166 Vincent Descotils
167 Laetitia Lesaffre

MODERN'ART
9 rue du vieux Versailles
78000 Versailles, France
+33613426620
deniguay@aol.com
galeriemodernart.fr

---

172 Vincent Chové

MUG
55 Yangjaecheon-ro Seocho-gu
06754 Seoul, South Korea/Republic of Korea
+821071806569
mugplay3@gmail.com
mug-pub.com

---

168 Gun Young Lee
169 Jaegu Kang
170 Jung Hoon Lee
171 Gyoosik Kim

NEO CONTEMPORAIN
4 villa des Gobelins
75013 Paris, France
+33755703792
neo.contemporain@gmail.com

---

173 Huake Xue
174 Yizhuo Wang

ONTAMA PROJECT
3-2-7-2F Higashi shibuya-ku
120 Tokyo, Japan
+819018002128
y.masutani1221@gmail.com

---

175 Takuya Yamahata
176 Kuniaki Konno
177 Yutaka Masutani
178 Yamadaya Chokko

PHOTO SHOPPING
15 rue de l'Abbé Grégoire
75006 Paris, France
+33144789937
mannonay@artshopping-expo.com
artshopping-expo.com

---

180 Liza Moura
181 Carol Descordes

PODBIELSKI CONTEMPORARY
Via Vincenzo Monti, 12
20123 Milan, Italy
+390236747219
pierreandre@podbielskicontemporary.com
podbielskicontemporary.com

---

26 Erica Campanella
182 Philippe Blache
183 Bruno Cattani

POLO ARTS
17 rue de Passy
75016 Paris, France
+33950293362
jleofoto@gmail.com

---

184 Jean-Léonard Polo

PRIX OBS LES FEMMES S'EXPOSENT
beatricetupin@gmail.com
lesfemmesexposent.com

---

24 Andrea Olga Mantovani

QGALLERY
Bredgade 47, kld, tv.
1260 Copenhagen, Danemark
+4526297231
info@qgallery.dk
qgallery.dk

---

179 Guy Russell

R/G (GALERIE)
19 rue des Quatre Vents
75006 Paris, France
+33670048778
vincent.richelet.gin@icloud.com
galerierg.fr

---

34 Christophe Jacrot

RASTOLL (GALERIE)
16 rue Sainte Anastase
75003 Paris, France
+33661721309
contact@galerierastoll.com
galerierastoll.com

---

19 Karen Du Vivier
35 Marjolaine Vuarnesson
120 Daniel Karila-Cohen
121 CarCam

S&H DE BUCK (GALERIE)
Zuidstationstraat, 25
9000 Gent, Belgium
+3292251081
sdebuck@skynet.be
galeriedebuck.be

---

122 Willy Vynck
123 Peter Bracke

SEKSIK (LIBRAIRIE MICHAEL)
16 rue du Cardinal Lemoine
75005 Paris, France
+33612473058
michael.seksik@gmail.com
librairieseksik.fr

---

40 Ludovic Bollo

SEMJON CONTEMPORARY
Schröderstraße, 1
10115 Berlin, Germany
+491752082339
office@semjoncontemporary.com
semjoncontemporary.com

---

186 Nataly Hocke
187 Gerda Schütte

SGALLERY
Via Luisa Sanfelice, 3
20137 Milan, Italy
+393388684605
pamela.campaner@yahoo.com
sgallery.it

---

185 Giulio Cerocchi

SIGNATURES
70 rue Jean-Pierre Timbaud
75011 Paris, France
ff@signatures-photographies.com

---

188 Marie Liesse
189 Florence Levillain
190 Joanna Tarlet-Gauteur

SINTITULO (GALERIE)
10 rue Commandeur
06250 Mougins, France
+33617327671
mougins@galeriesintitulo.com
galeriesintitulo.com

---

109 Sébastien Arrighi

SOEURS GRÉES (LES)
Mercier-Ferrier
23340 Faux-la-Montagne, France
+33555677558
communication@pierreredon.com

---

48 Pierre Redon
164 The Minotaur

SPAZIO FARINI6

Via Farini, 6
20154 Milan, Italy
+39262086626
info@spaziofarini6.com
spaziofarini6.com

---

191 Gabriele Pierini
192 Gianna Spirito
193 Antonella Sacconi

STAR GALLERY

8F., No.27, Ln. 383, Xingshan Rd., Neihu Dist.
114 Taipei City, Taiwan
+886227939209
huang.liang.yeh@gmail.com
stargallery.tw

---

194 Wei-Ming Yuan

STP (GALERIE)

Mühlenstraße, 20
17489 Greifswald, Germany
+491726100833
info@galerie-stp.de
galerie-stp.de

---

20 Ramona Czygan
36 Alain Cornu
128 François Delebecque
129 Peter Mathis
130 Uwe Ommer
131 Silverfineart
132 Anna Muller
133 Walter Schels

SWANY PRESSE

+33668860661
swanyattacheepresse@gmail.com
instagram.com/swanypresse/?hl=fr

---

198 Stéphane Padu

TENDANCE FLOUE

2 rue Marcelin Berthelot
93100 Montreuil, France
+33148589060
tf@tendancefloue.net
tendancefloue.net

---

43 Tendance Floue

V&E ART

3F,NO.6, Alley 6,Lane 615,Welin Rd.
111 Taipei, Taiwan
+33643524792
vermeer@veart.fr
veart.fr

---

194 ChunChun Liu

VM FOR ART

+33675958354
valeriemarechal@me.com
instagram.com/vmforart

---

42 Jérémy Garamond

WALLPEPPER (GALERIE)

15 rue Clapeyron
75008 Paris, France
+33640480008
contact@marcjosse.fr
wallpepper.fr

---

134 Marc Josse

WALL SPACE CREATIVE

PO Box 957
93102 Santa Barbara California, United States
+18052325428
crista@wallspacecreative.com
wallspacecreative.com

---

27 Bootsy Holler
82 J.K. Lavin
83 Eleonora Ronconi
84 Marian Crostic

XII (GALERIE)

14 rue des Jardins Saint Paul
75004 Paris, France
+33142782421
vagiscard@live.com
galerie-photo12.com

---

25 Tingting Wang
136 Nicolas Baghir
137 Charlotte Mano
138 Wenlong Ye

YI (GALERIE)
706 North 2nd Street, 797 Road, No. 4
Jiuxianqiao Road, 798 Art Zone, Chaoyang District
100016 Beijing, China
+33645269371
yaxingluo521@gmail.com
yigallery.com

---

139 A Yin

ZETO ART
253 rue Saint Honoré
75001 Paris, France
+33664839680
zeto.art@outlook.com
zetoart.com

---

197 Yorgos Yatromanolakis

index des artistes

artists index

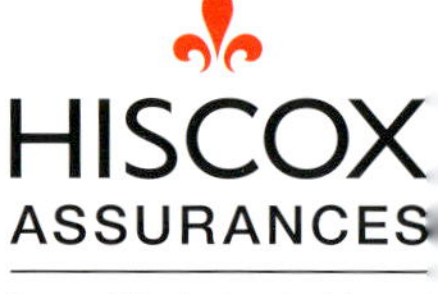
HISCOX
ASSURANCES
Penser à tout et surtout à vous

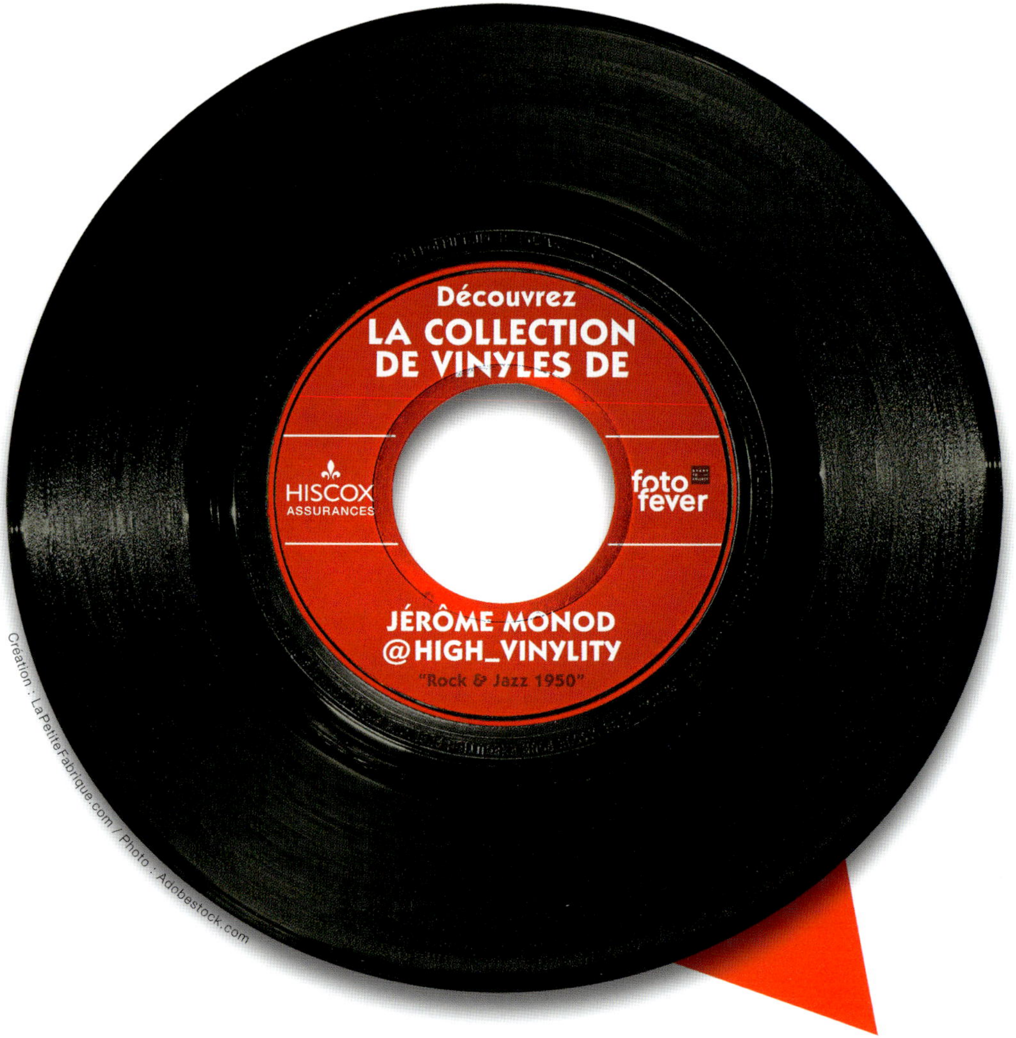

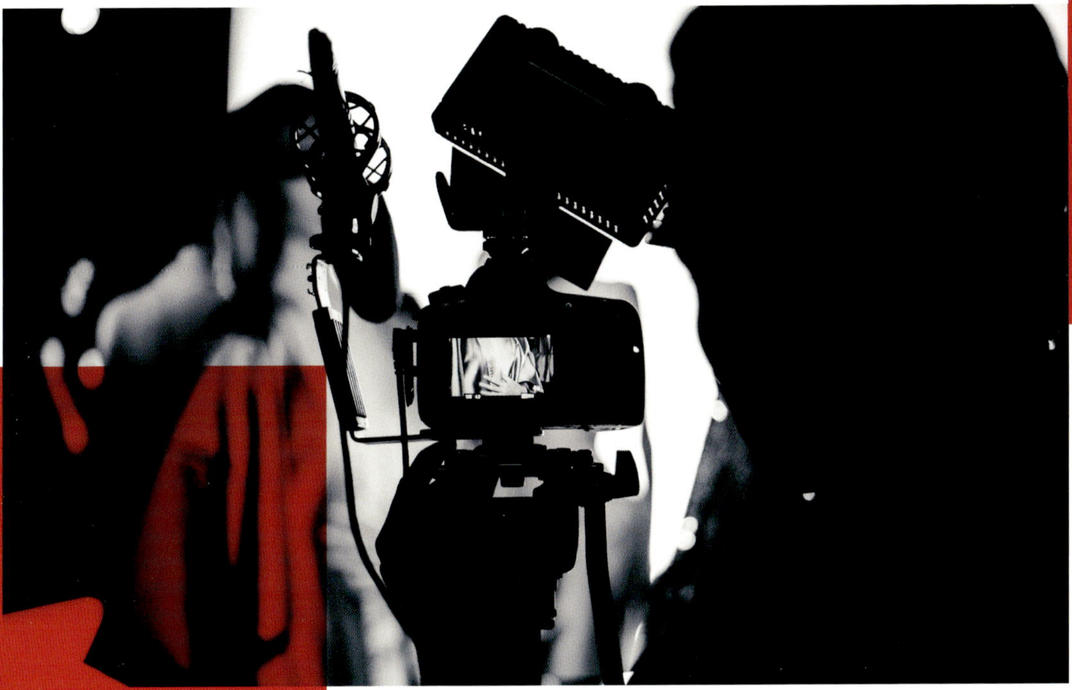

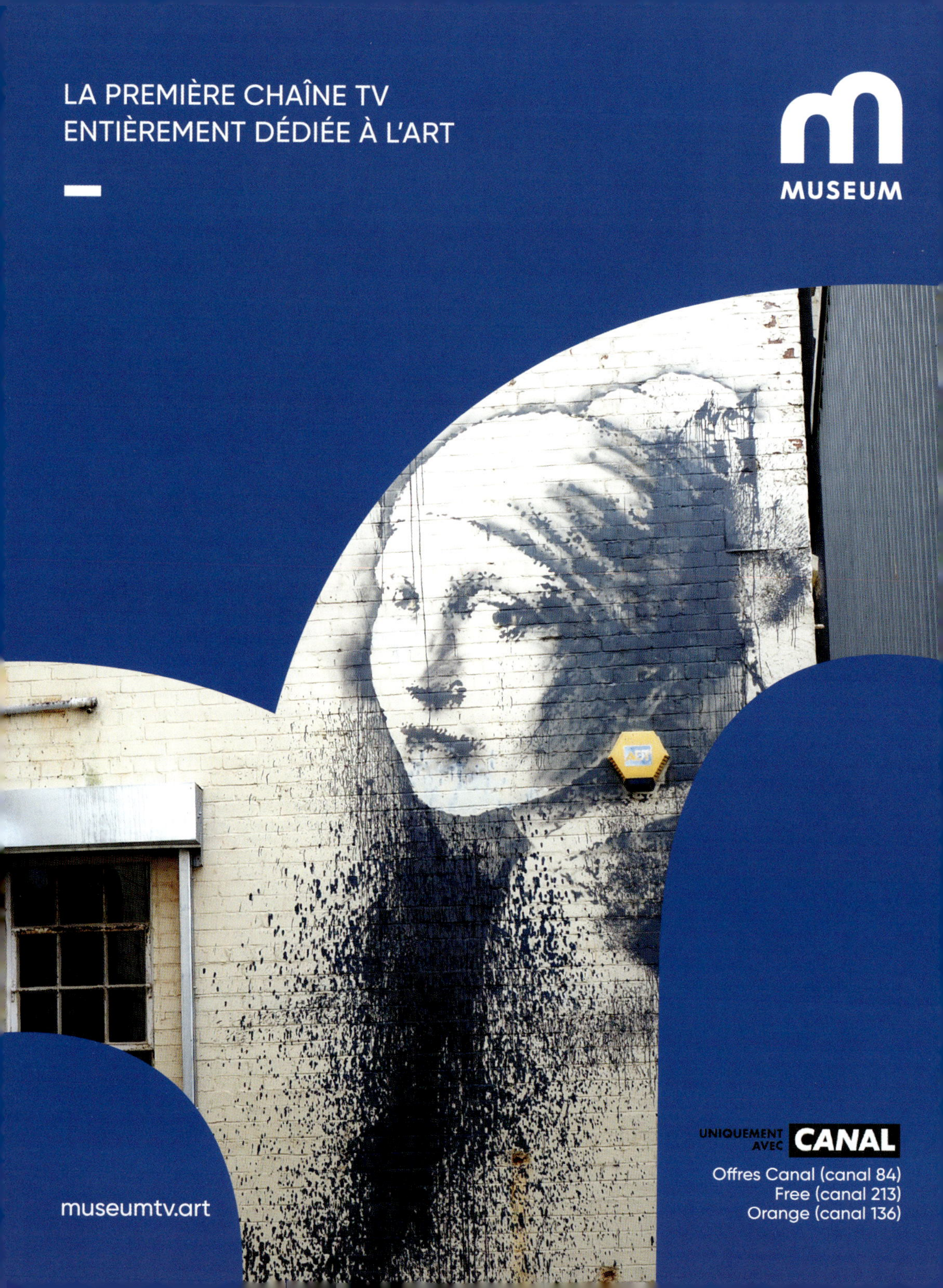

Merci à tous ceux qui sont à nos côtés pour cette 8e édition à Paris
Thank you to all our partners and suppliers in Paris

Antoine Munch – ART COLLECTOR INVEST
Clothilde Matta – ARTISTE
Clara Journo – ARTISTIK REZO
Stephen Blackman, Won Kim – ART GENIES
Alexandrya Delmau – ARTPRICE
Laurianne Simonin, Antoine Dumont – BARNEBYS
Jean-Sylvain Bailly – BLUE INFORMATIQUE
Anne-Caroline Briand, Stéphanie Gago – BNP PARIBAS BANQUE PRIVÉE
Matthieu Le Stang-Heyn – CADOGAN TATE
Georges Baur, François Blanc, Anaïs Tridon – COMMUNIC'ART
Guy Boyer – CONNAISSANCE DES ARTS
Sarah Steiner – CULTURE SECRETS
Marie Ferrandiz, Fabienne Filliole, Emmanuelle Savoy, Bastien Speranza – DAHINDEN
Anaïs Fontaine, Rossella Rosano – EBERHARD & CO.
Christophe Gratadou - GALERIE CHRISTOPHE GRATADOU
Julien Lagaye, Clotilde Rocher, Florian Rocher – HAHNEMÜHLE
Anita Baltagi, Nicolas Kaddeche, Lucile Parrilla – HISCOX
Paul Koslow – HORTICUS
Florence Houdouin – LATHAM & WATKINS LTD
Anne Degroux, Béatrice Tupin – LES FEMMES S'EXPOSENT
Patrick Nsingi – LIBÉRATION
Chantal Nedjib – L'IMAGE PAR L'IMAGE
Anaïs Montevecchi – LE DÉCODEUR D'ART
Simon Baker, Yannick Le Guillanton – MAISON EUROPÉENNE DE LA PHOTOGRAPHIE
Marion Hislen, Franck Riester – MINISTÈRE DE LA CULTURE
Marie Joly, Sébastien Meyssan – MUSEUM
Marine Bachelet, Elodie Levasseur, Elie Rebeiz – NO MORE PENGUINS
Jacques Folliot – OPTIMA
Pierre Evrard, Philippe Litzler – OPENEYE
Florence Bourgeois – PARIS PHOTO
Dimitri Beck – POLKA
Léa Lombardo – QUOTIDIEN DE L'ART
Tristan Recorbet – REVOLUGO
François Bruschi, Dorota Cwiklinska, Antonin Roche, Jessica Tassan – ROCHE BOBOIS
Zoé Finkelstein, Coralie Gauthier – SILENCIO
Philip Van Bost – SNOECK EDITIONS
Cordelia Noe – THE ART GORGEOUS
Grégoire De Rubiana, Thomas Griffoin, Julie Kieffer – THE FULL ROOM BY DECOD
Fiona Cigliano, Thomas Guerin – WEEZEVENT
Eva Lafferrere, Alexandre de Metz – YELLOW KORNER

Merci à tous les exposants qui ont accepté notre invitation
Thank you to all our exhibitors

Swany Abdallah
Silvia Agliotti
Anna Ajtner
Cristina Albertini
Myriam Annonay Castanet
Claudio Argentiero
Jinhee Bae
Olivier Barriol
Virginie Barrou Planquart
Bessie Baudin
Yves Bigot
Eric Boudry
Pamela Campaner
Marta Ceribelli
Vermeer Chen
Véronique Cochois
Paolo Dabbrescia
Chris Davies
Hermine De Groeve
Cyril Delettre
Crista Dix
Chiara Fabro
Frédérique Founes
Ryo Futamura
Caroline Gavazzi
Valérie-Anne Giscard d'Estaing
Maurizio Godot Villani
Denis Guay
Luo Haixiao
Marc Harrold
Cherry Ho
Isa Ho
Etsushi Kaminaga
Oliver Klink
Ara Ko
Peter Konschake
Nelly Lacoste
Giovanna Lalatta
Anouk Le Bourdiec
Eric Lebrun
César Levy
Tanguy Lieske
Rafał Lochowski
Albane Lucazeau
Yaxing Luo
Alberto Magrin
Didier Mandart
Vincent Marcilhacy
Valérie Maréchal
Carlo Mari
Yutaka Masutani
Adrian Mei Gentilucci
Meliza Pascual
Stéphanie Perris
Oliver & Stefanie Pietsch
Pierre André Podbielski
Jean-Léo Polo
François Rastoll
Vincent Richelet
Delmari Romero Keith
Isabelle Romic
Guy Russell
Maria Teresa Sacchi
Laura Salvadó
Bertrand Scholler
Claudia Scholz
Michael Seksik
Clémentine Semeria
Semjon Semjon
Sae Shimai

Un grand merci à toute la team fotofever
Thank you to the fotofever team

Yuki Baumgarten
Raphaëlle Boudry
Louise de Couliboeuf
Chloé Fournet
Juliette Jabet
Laura Kosmenzoff
Cécile Montigny
Olivier Remy
Christelle Roubaud
Aurora Scheftel

Merci à l'ICART et ses étudiants pour leur aide précieuse dans la préparation et l'organisation de cette 8e édition à Paris
Thank you to the students from ICART for their precious help in preparing and organising this 8th edition in Paris

Nicolas Laugero Lasserre – Directeur
Valérie Guibert – Directrice des études
Marie-Alice Foulquier – Responsable partenariats
Melody Malka – Assistante pédagogique et administrative

Marché International de l'Art, 4e année

Barbara Abate
Elisa Adamon
Marguerite Aussedat
Gaspard Becimol
Morgane Boffelli
Polina Butenko
Isabelle Capalbo
Romain Caruana
Valentine De Gobbi
Gabrielle De Soye
Charlotte De Torregrosa
Margaux Depaquit
Aymone Faivre
Jeanne Fenateau
Hortense Ferron
Chloé Fournet
Elena Frantcuzova
Charles Franzini
Axel Fried
Cécile Granier
Eunbi Ha
Coralie Halgand
Valérie Javel
Lise Kiner-Wolff
Océane Kinhouande
Anastasia Le Goff
Yvan Leducq
Clémence Lenoir Vain
Hadrien Pierrot
Paul Ribault
Marvin Saker
Agathe Scherperel
Yurong Shi
Maël Wolff
Peiqing Yu

Marché International de l'Art, 5e année

Viktoria Aleksa
Hannah Assouline
Marlène Braach
Léonore Cachat
Tifenn Chaminand Hoting
Chang In-Wen Chang
Eva Chappert-Gaujal
Eva Dalanson
Elise De Brye
Océane De Melo
Anouchka Derouault-Knapik
Laure El Almawie
Noa Fedida
Henry Genneson
Emma Grozier
Héloise Haberberg
Pauline Hodee
Victoria Izraylevich
Juliette Jabet
Laudine Jacobee
Eleftheria Kasoura
Barbara Legras
Pauline Leroy
Mengni Ling
Marie Magnet
Camille Marchand
Salomé Monpetit
Léa Pailler
Manon Pallo Leduc
Charlène Paris
Julia Pellerin
Mathilde Renouard
Philippine Salle
Marie Segard
Jane Sizun
Mélanie Lea Spitzer
Yuexuan Wang